About the Black Sash

The Black Sash began in 1955 as a non-violent campaign of white women to protest against the removal of 'Coloureds' from the voters' roll. Over decades of brutal apartheid rule this single-issue organisation evolved into a powerful advocate for human rights. The Black Sash opened its first advice office in 1958, and many more followed, staffed by volunteers who provided sustained support to those impacted by the pass laws, forced removals and influx control, amongst other laws.

While the new constitutional democracy in 1994 was greatly welcomed, socioeconomic rights and social justice issues, particularly for the poor and marginalised, required vigilance and action. The Black Sash changed from a membership organisation to a non-governmental organisation, with a board of Trustees, that focused on socio-economic rights.

The Black Sash is now one of South Africa's oldest human rights organisations. Its emphasis is on social security and social protection to reduce poverty and inequality as well as improve access to socio-economic rights. It is committed to open, transparent and accountable governance. It values its partnerships with community-based and non-governmental organisations in different parts of the country, particularly in rural areas, small towns and peri-urban areas where people are most vulnerable to exploitation and injustice.

HANDS OFF
OUR
GRANTS

DEFENDING THE CONSTITUTIONAL
RIGHT TO SOCIAL PROTECTION
IN SOUTH AFRICA

THE BLACK SASH

Published by BestRed, an imprint of HSRC Press
Private Bag X9182, Cape Town, 8000, South Africa
www.bestred.co.za

First published 2022

ISBN (soft cover) 978-1-928246-50-3

© Human Sciences Research Council

The views expressed in this publication are those of the author. They do not necessarily reflect the views or policies of the Human Sciences Research Council (the Council) or indicate that either the Council endorses the views of the author. In quoting from this publication, readers are advised to attribute the source of the information to the individual author concerned and not to either the Council or the Institute.

The publishers have no responsibility for the continued existence or accuracy of URLs for external or third-party Internet websites referred to in this book and do not guarantee that any content on such websites is, or will remain, accurate or appropriate.

Cover design by Marise Bauer
Typeset by Robin Yule, cheekychilli
Proofread by Alison Paulin
Printed by Shumani RSA, Parow, Cape Town

Distributed in Africa by Blue Weaver
Tel: +27 (021) 701 4477; Fax Local: (021) 701 7302; Fax International: 0927865242139
www.blueweaver.co.za

Distributed in Europe and the United Kingdom by Eurospan Distribution Services (EDS)
Tel: +44 (0) 17 6760 4972; Fax: +44 (0) 17 6760 1640
www.eurospanbookstore.com

Distributed in North America by Lynne Rienner Publishers, Inc.
Tel: +1 303-444-6684; Fax: 303-444-0824; Email: cservice@rienner.com
www.rienner.com

Suggested citation: The Black Sash (2022) *Hands Off Our Grants: Defending the Constitutional Right to Social Protection in South Africa*. Cape Town: BestRed

We dedicate this book to all social grant recipients who bravely stepped forward and set in motion a tsunami that would stop unauthorised, fraudulent and allegedly unlawful debit and USSD deductions from their grants and transform the social assistance landscape. We remember in particular:

- the mettle of Ma Grace when she shared her case with Minister Bathabele Dlamini and a cohort of government officials;
- the relentlessness of Mr Sipho Bani who would not stop until he found answers; and
- the courage of Mrs and Mr Juries who secured the first collective refunds for fraudulent funeral deductions.

Contents

Acknowledgements

A heartfelt thanks to all the social grant recipients who bravely stepped forward – both in the cases reflected in this book and the many more contained in our various submissions made to the Department of Social Development, Sassa, the Financial Services Board and the Panel of Experts. We also acknowledge those grant recipients who battled and resolved their own cases without support.

The Black Sash is indebted to the David and Elaine Potter Foundation for the seed grant that enabled us to write the manuscript of this book and for granting us numerous extensions, particularly during the Covid-19 pandemic. We are also grateful to the Frank Robb Charitable Trust for the financial contribution for copy editing. We acknowledge with great appreciation the respective financial contributions of the Raith Foundation, Brot für die Welt, Claude Leon Foundation and the Social Justice Initiative for the very successful Hoog campaign.

We acknowledge the efforts of our partnerships:

- The staff of the Centre for Applied Legal Studies (Cals): Associate Prof. Bonita Meyersfeld (former Director), Nomonde Nyembe (Attorney), Wandiswa Phama (Candidate Attorney), Khuraisha Patel (Candidate Attorney), Akhona Mehlo (Attorney), Lisa Chamberlain (acting Director), and more recently Ariella Scher (Attorney), and Prof. Tshepo Madlingozi (new Director);
- Legal Counsel: Geoff Budlender SC (Lead Counsel), Gina Snyman (Cals In-house Counsel) and Zinhle Ngwenya (Junior Council);
- The Legal Resources Centre, and in particular former attorney Sarah Sephton in the Grahamstown Office who initially represented the Black Sash in legal matters.

Our deep appreciation for the efforts of our community-based partners in what seems like a protracted campaign: Community Advice Offices of South Africa, Social Change Assistance Trust and the independent community advice offices who engage with grant recipients at their point of need.

A special thanks to our community partners who attended the first meeting with Minister Dlamini and those who served on the Ministerial Task Team: Kabelo Modisadife from the Lebaleng Community Advice Office, Albert Makwela and Seth Mnguni of the Community Advice Offices of South Africa, Ms Joyce Muller from the Katolieke Ontwikkeling Oranje Rivier in the Northern Cape, Patricia de Lange from the Adelaide Advice Office in the Eastern Cape and Thulani Ndlovu from the Qedusizi Advice Centre in Mpumalanga. Our gratitude to Mary Burton and to Father Peter-John Pearson of the Catholic Bishop Parliamentary Liaison Office for witnessing the delivery of the first MTT report at Minister Dlamini's office in Parliament. We want to express our gratitude to the Witzenberg Rural Development Centre for coordinating two big recourse events in Ceres, particularly Marieta Hartzenberg, Noami Betana, Emmerentia Goliath, Anna Johannes and Brumilda Kaptein.

Our gratitude to: *amaBhungane*, *Business Day* (Ann Crotty), *Daily Maverick*, *GroundUp* and *Mail & Guardian* who regularly kept the deductions and social assistance-related issues in the public domain.

We acknowledge the dedication, perseverance and activism of Black Sash staff throughout the multifaceted Hoog campaign:

- National Office: Ratula Beukman (former Advocacy Manager: Social Security), Elroy Paulus (former National Advocacy Manager), Lynette Maart (former National Director), Esley Philander (Communications and Media Manager) and Hoodah Abrahams-Fayker (National Advocacy Manager);
- Gauteng Regional Office (Gauteng, North West and Limpopo): Thandiwe Zulu (Regional Manager), Vincent Skhosana (Paralegal Fieldworker), Ntsoaki Moreroa (Paralegal Fieldworker), Kgothatso Sibanda (National Helpline Paralegal) and Maureen Shabangu (National Helpline Paralegal Assistant);
- Eastern Cape Regional Office: Alexa Lane (Regional Manager), Jonathan Walton (Senior Paralegal) and Chuma Ngabase (Paralegal Fieldworker);

- Kwa-Zulu Natal Regional Office (Mpumalanga and Kwa-Zulu Natal): Evashnee Naidu (Regional Manager), Jerome Bele (Paralegal Fieldworker) and Nelisiwe Xaba (Paralegal Fieldworker);
- Western Cape Regional Office (Western Cape and Northern Cape): Leonie Caroline (former Regional Manager), Colleen Ryan (former Regional Manager), Abigail Peters (Paralegal Fieldworker) and Zoleka Ntuli (Paralegal Fieldworker);
- Administration, Finance and Fundraising: Brigitte Borgches (Finance and Operations Manager), Sonya Ehrenreicht (former Donor Compliance Manager), Tania Paulse (Finance Administrator), Lindsy Bunsee (Project Administrator), Shanaaz Rayner (Data Administrator, also PA to National Director) and the administrative staff in our regional offices.
- Former and current Black Sash **trustees** for their stewardship and strategic guidance: Mary Burton (2017), Janeen de Klerk, Mieke Krynauw, Nolundi Luwaya, Margaret 'Dolly' Khumalo (2017), Sibongile 'Bongi' Mkhabela, Mary-Jane Morifi, Maleshini Naidoo, Di Oliver (2017), Matilda Smith, Hilary Southall (2017), Jenny de Tolly (2017) and the current chairperson, Yasmin 'Jessy' Turton.

The research and writing of this book were done by a collective, in alphabetical order by surname: Colleen Crawford Cousins, Robin Foley, Moira Levy, Lynette Maart (also book project manager), Angie Richardson, Esley Philander and Natasha Valley. The research and contributions by journalists, including Ann Crotty, Craig McKune (*amaBhungane*), Lubabalo Ngcukana (*City Press*) and Barbara October (née Maregele) (*GroundUp*) added another layer of depth. Our heartfelt thanks to the Cals team, in alphabetical order: Basetsana Koitsioe, Tumelo Matlwa, Akhona Mehlo, Sandile Ndelu, Abongile Nkamisa and Gina Snyman for the legal case summaries, the foundation for Chapter 3. We acknowledge the conversations with Elroy Paulus, former National Advocacy Manager, and the invaluable assistance from Gina Snyman that shaped our thinking in drafting the book. We are grateful to Moira Levy for the compilation and the editing of the manuscript and engaging with the publisher.

Our heartfelt thanks to the HSRC Press, especially Jeremy Wightman (Publishing Director), Mmakwena Chipu (Commissioning Editor), Samantha Michelle, Mthunzi Nxawe and Charlotte Imani. Thank you for the partnership, encouragement and support, which helped us turn a manuscript into a published work.

Most of the images and photographs contained in the book were sourced from *GroundUp*, the Black Sash archives and project photographers including Eric Miller, Thom Pierce, Leopold Podlashuc, Erna Curry and Esley Philander. Special thanks to Richard Smith (Redzone) for the graphic design support.

And last but not least, we want to express our appreciation for the contributions of senior government officials, Dianne Dunkerley (Sassa) and Brenton van Vrede (DSD), for not dismissing the legitimate queries and deputes of social grant recipients; for dogged follow-ups to resolve these cases that helped to understand the phenomenon; for the robust and challenging conversations that led towards workable short, medium and long term solutions to resolve unauthorised, fraudulent and allegedly unlawful deductions from social grants.

Acronyms and abbreviations

ANC	African National Congress
BAC	Bid Adjudication Committee
BBBEE	broad-based black economic empowerment
BEC	Bid Evaluation Committee
BEE	black economic empowerment
BPDRM	Beneficiary Payment Dispute Resolution Mechanism
Cals	Centre for Applied Legal Studies
CAOSA	Community Advice Offices of South Africa
CBO	community-based organisation
CEO	Chief Executive Officer
CMAP	Community Monitoring and Advocacy Project
Cope	Congress of the People
CPS	Cash Paymaster Services
CSIR	Council for Scientific and Industrial Research
CSOs	civil society organisations
DA	Democratic Alliance
DPME	Department of Planning, Monitoring and Evaluation
DSD	Department of Social Development
EFF	Economic Freedom Fighters
EFT	electronic fund transaction
EPE	EasyPay Everywhere
FIC	Financial Intelligence Centre
FSB	Financial Services Board
FSP	Financial Service Provider
Hanis	Home Affairs National Identification System
Hoog	Hands Off Our Grants
IFP	Inkatha Freedom Party
IGPS	Integrated Grant Payment System
ILDA	Interchurch Local Development Agency
IMC	Inter-Ministerial Committee
Koor	Katolieke Ontwikkeling Oranje Rivier
LRC	Legal Resources Centre
MAC	Ministerial Advisory Committee
MTT	Ministerial Task Team
NCA	National Credit Act
NCR	National Credit Regulator

NDA	National Development Agency
NGO	non-governmental organisation
NPS	National Payment System
Paja	Promotion of Administrative Justice Act
PanSALB	Pan South African Language Board
Pari	Public Affairs Research Institute
Pasa	Payments Association of South Africa
PFMA	Public Financial Management Act
PMG	Parliamentary Monitoring Group
Popia	Protection of Personal Information Act
RET	radical economic transformation
RFP	request for proposals
RHAP	Rural Health Advocacy Project
Sapo	South African Post Office
Sarb	South African Reserve Bank
Sassa	South African Social Security Agency
SCA	Supreme Court of Appeal
Scopa	Standing Committee on Public Accounts
SDA	Special Disbursement Account (Sapo)
SLA	service level agreement
SSA	State Security Agency
TOR	terms of reference
UDM	United Democratic Movement
UEPS	Universal Electronic Payment System
USSD	unstructured supplementary service data
WRDC	Witzenberg Rural Development Centre

Foreword

This is a valuable book because it enables us to understand how vulnerable people – poor, inadequately informed, even illiterate people – were able to defend themselves against exploitation and malpractice. This book tells the story of a long struggle to protect the rights of social grant recipients to confidentiality, service delivery and control over access to their grants. It shows how corruption and greed can steal from government provision of basic social protection, and it points to the need to protect and strengthen the country's institutions, such as the Constitutional Court.

This is the story of a victory, not only of a team of urban-based human rights movements, public interest lawyers, and community-based non-profit organisations, but also of the millions of South Africans who depend on the social security provided by the government. It is about their victory against powerful corporate interests hungry for profits and it demonstrates what can be achieved when civil society organisations work together with citizens to defend their constitutional rights.

The early years of the 21st century brought new legislation to implement the constitutional requirement for equal treatment for all South Africans in terms of comprehensive social security. The South African Social Security Agency Act (No. 9 of 2004) established the South African Social Security Agency (Sassa), as the body responsible for the administration of social assistance. A procurement process ensued through which Sassa would appoint a service provider to manage the distribution of social grant payments.

This story began in 2012 when Sassa entered into a contract with a company called Cash Paymaster Services (CPS), a subsidiary of Net1 Applied Technology Holdings Ltd. Over time, Net1 came to acquire further subsidiary companies that provided products such as airtime, electricity, funeral benefits and loans. It emerged that CPS was providing these subsidiaries with the personal information of social grant recipients. Soon thereafter, the Black Sash began to receive complaints from recipients who alleged that they were experiencing irregular deductions from their grants which they had not authorised.

The Black Sash, initially under the Community Monitoring and Advocacy Project (CMAP), brought these recipients together with organisations that could offer legal advice, advocacy experience, and access to educational materials explaining the intricacies of the payment system and the right to correct administration and personal confidentiality.

Then followed months and years of monitoring, recording case studies, lobbying the authorities and eventually legal action. In 2013–14, the Black Sash launched the Hands Off Our Grants (Hoog) campaign which in 2017 led to a ruling by the Constitutional Court that finally resulted in the transfer of the responsibility for the administration of social grants back to the government. There have been many difficulties in the course of restoring this function back to Sassa, supported by the South African Post Office (Sapo), where it belongs.

The chapter in the book that records the stories of individuals who suffered so greatly through this period exposes what this meant for them and countless others. I will not forget the remarkable presence of a large number of individual social grant recipients sitting in the highest court in South Africa, wearing their orange T-shirts bearing the demand Hands Off Our Grants, as they listened to the Court proceedings.

It is a privilege to read this meticulously detailed account of a very complex campaign, particularly from my viewpoint as a past Black Sash member. This is an organisation that began in 1955 as a single-issue protest movement against the infamous pass laws and that evolved into decades of opposition to other infringements of people's rights. The Black Sash learned from visitors to its advice offices of the daily struggles of disenfranchised citizens and took on the challenge of redress.

The advent of constitutional democracy was welcomed with great satisfaction, yet even after 1994, there were issues of social justice that required vigilance and action. In response, the Black Sash changed direction. It closed as a membership organisation but decided that the advice offices should continue to function. Recent history has demonstrated that this was a wise decision.

Inequality and poverty have continued to bedevil South Africa, and the Black Sash has deepened its focus on socioeconomic rights and strengthened its links with community-based organisations and non-governmental organisations in different parts of the country, particularly in rural areas and small towns, which are the most under-resourced places of all. These areas are precisely where people are most vulnerable to exploitation and unjust treatment.

Through its community partnerships, the Black Sash has come to respect more than ever the strength and resilience of individuals and small organisations, who often do not have access to external resources, but witnessed problems with the administration of social grants and were determined to overcome them.

This is an illustration of the way in which civil society organisations and their partners, by listening to one another and learning from that process, can work together to achieve results that make a real difference to the lives of those who are most affected, and to create a climate for the recognition of the rights of all people.

South Africa's people need a capable state, a responsible state that cares for the wellbeing of its poorest citizens. This book is a story of dedication and eventual success, but it also reminds the reader of the need for ongoing monitoring and advocacy around improved service delivery for those who need it most.

Mary Burton
Patron and former National President of the Black Sash,
and one of the founders of the Black Sash Trust

Authors' note

The book frequently uses the terms unauthorised, fraudulent, and allegedly unlawful. For legal clarity, however, it is useful to understand the distinctions between them. Unauthorised deductions occur where a beneficiary gave no authority for the deduction, either at all, or due to consent that was not informed. This is in any event arguably unlawful. The generality of the unlawfulness or illegality of unauthorised deductions has not been pronounced on by a court, although they have been found to be unlawful in certain cases specific to individual beneficiaries. Deductions are also alleged to be fraudulent where beneficiaries experienced misrepresentations by agents of Net1 or Cash Paymaster Services and their affiliates or others providing financial services, where beneficiaries were seemingly intentionally misled about the distinctions of the various Sassa and EPE cards, and what cards they were 'required' to have to access loans, for example. This conduct also runs afoul of the National Credit Act (No. 34 of 2005) and in that way is allegedly unlawful. Similarly, where personal data appear to have been shared amongst the Net1 group of companies without a beneficiary's express consent or contrary to the award of the payment contract, this too is alleged to be unlawful.

There is a further distinction to be drawn between deductions that occur before or at the time of payment of the grant, and those that are akin to debit orders which occur after the beneficiary has received the (full) value of their grant, even though they are seemingly made simultaneously.[1] Beneficiaries have raised serious complaints regarding both, which are described throughout this book.

Background to the Hoog campaign

In 1994, when the democratically elected African National Congress (ANC) government took power, it inherited a racially skewed social security system that mostly benefitted white pensioners and people with disabilities. Social grants had slowly increased during the apartheid years but remained racially disproportionate, with very little provided for the disenfranchised, particularly African women. Today, access to social security is one of the socioeconomic rights guaranteed in the Constitution of the Republic of South Africa of 1996. The result has been a significant increase in the number of social grants allocated to the poorest of the poor, with women experiencing the greatest impact as the main caregivers. However, a serious gap remains in that social assistance is not available to those aged 18 to 59 years who have little to no income. The Black Sash and other civil society organisations are leading a campaign for the government to introduce a Basic Income Grant.

In 2002, the Committee of Inquiry into a Comprehensive System of Social Security for South Africa (also referred to as the Taylor Committee) was tasked by Cabinet to establish a holistic overview of South Africa's social policy requirements and to put forward recommendations for a comprehensive social security system for the nation.[1] The outcomes of the committee of inquiry informed the legislation relating to social assistance, including social grants, that has been developed and administered over the past two decades.

Certain non-contributory aspects of the social security system were established in terms of the Social Assistance Act (No. 13 of 2004). Initially, social grants were distributed provincially, but this resulted in discrepancies between provinces' grant payments and in overall efficiency. In 2004 the South African Social Security Agency Act (No. 9 of 2004) established the South African Social Security Agency (Sassa) as the national legal entity responsible for the administration of social security and, when necessary, temporary social relief of distress. One of the arguments for the establishment of Sassa was to standardise the payment service, consolidate and maintain a registry of all social grant beneficiaries, and minimise losses to the state due to fraud and corruption. Biometric technology was to become a key part of the government's techno-political programme.

Sassa answers to the Department of Social Development (DSD), which is responsible for delivering social development, protection and welfare services to the public.

Today, South Africa has one of the largest social grant systems in the world. Its scope has increased significantly in the years since democracy was introduced. Since 2003, five social grants have been available, namely: the child support grant, introduced by an Act of Parliament in 1998;[2] the foster child grant; the old age pension; the disability grant; and the care dependency grant for the disabled. In 2003, the year before Sassa took over grant administration, 6.8 million people of a total population of 45 million received some form of social grant. By the end of 2017, more than 17 million people received social grants and by 2020 this had increased to just over 18 million. The growth in the number of grant recipients between 1997 and 2020 is shown in Figure 1. The expansion and application of social grants can be viewed as one of the greatest post-1994 redistributive achievements.

Social grants are non-contributory and means-tested. They contribute to beneficiaries' basic needs, such as food, healthcare, shelter and education. They have a direct impact on the lives of the poor, and any disruption to receiving social grants can pose a life-or-death threat to beneficiaries.

Figure 1 Growth in number of grant recipients, 1997 to 2020

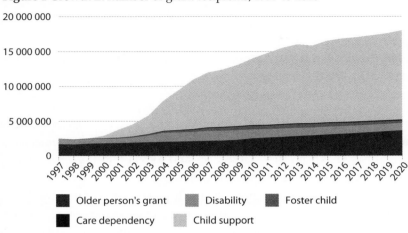

Source: Department of Social Development (Socpen), 2022

In November 2010, President Jacob Zuma appointed Ms Bathabile Dlamini, president of the ANC Women's League (ANCWL) and a strong Zuma ally, as Minister of Social Development. In 2011 a new tender process was initiated, and in January 2012 the contract for the national payment of social grants was awarded to Cash Payment Services (CPS), a subsidiary of Net1 Applied Technology Holdings Limited, through beneficiary bank accounts at Grindrod Bank. CPS was not new to social grants and had previously distributed grants in some provinces.

AllPay, which had been a service provider before 2011, launched a legal case to review the Sassa tender process and the lawfulness of the CPA contract, citing several challenges, including the late introduction of changes to the tender specifications with insufficient time to develop a response and the failure to vet the credentials of the black economic empowerment partners of CPS.

The Constitutional Court ruled that tender award invalid and Sassa was required to undertake a new procurement process to find a suitable service provider or to insource grant payments. To ensure that the payment of grants was not interrupted, however, the invalidity of the contract was suspended, allowing CPS to continue to provide payment services until a new service provider was appointed. Sassa was ordered to report to the Court on the progress of the new tender process.

THE BLACK SASH AND ITS HANDS OFF OUR GRANTS (HOOG) CAMPAIGN

With its long history of social justice activism in South Africa, dating back to the 1950s, the Black Sash has engaged in various forms of non-violent protest in pursuit of a more just and equitable society. Since the advent of democracy, its emphasis has been on social security and social protection for the most vulnerable, particularly women and children. In 1995, the Black Sash Trust was restructured and became a social justice non-profit organisation. Two of its long-term goals were the realisation of socioeconomic rights, particularly social security, and the protection and advancement of human rights through effective and efficient service delivery. Another long-term goal pursued by the Black Sash aimed at promoting greater discourse and shifts in practice to focus on reducing poverty and inequality. It also sought to strengthen and capacitate civil society, including community-based organisations (CBOs), non-governmental organisations (NGOs) and other movements for social justice.

Soon after the signing of the CPS contract, in 2012, the Black Sash, through its partnerships with advice offices and CBOs in its Community Monitoring and Advocacy Project (CMAP), became aware of increasing numbers of beneficiaries reporting irregular deductions from their social grants, deductions that appeared to be linked to Net1 subsidiaries.

That marked the start of years of protracted efforts by the Black Sash and its partners to get to the bottom of this injustice and bring it to an end. In 2012 and 2013, as part of the organisation's overarching objective of increasing the coverage and benefits of social security and social protection, the Black Sash initiated the Hands Off Our Grants (Hoog) campaign. The primary goal of the Hoog campaign was to stop these allegedly unlawful and unauthorised deductions. Another goal was to ensure that grant beneficiaries' personal and confidential data, entrusted to Sassa, was protected. The campaign called for the insourcing of administration and payment of grants, and for a Sassa-owned and controlled recourse system to be urgently put in place. It also demanded that CPS, Net1 and Grindrod Bank, the bank that held social grant accounts, along with Sassa, take full responsibility for disputed deductions and refund them, together with any related bank charges and interest, backdated to 2012.

A significant amount of the Black Sash's time and effort was spent on collecting and correlating the reports of various irregular deductions to gather sufficient documented evidence to present to relevant government authorities. Its Advocacy in Partnership programme deployed a set of strategies including direct advocacy of government entities; the creation of public awareness through media, communication and mobilisation; research; and where appropriate, litigation. The Black Sash worked in collaboration with Sassa, the DSD, the South African Reserve Bank (Sarb), National Treasury, the South African Post Office (Sapo), and relevant parliamentary portfolio committees and NGOs such as Corruption Watch and the Centre for Applied Legal Studies (Cals). It partnered with a network of community-based advice offices including those under the banner of the Community Advice Offices of South Africa (CAOSA), the Social Change Assistance Trust, and independent advice offices, and launched an education campaign, distributing flyers entitled 'You and Your Rights: Lawful Deductions from your Grants' and the 'Stop Sassa-CPS Debits Campaign'. It also engaged directly with CPS.

Through these initial and other direct advocacy initiatives, the Minister of Social Development was persuaded that the deductions from social grant beneficiaries' accounts had become a significant concern that warranted intervention.

By early 2017 it became evident that Sassa had no plan to insource the payment of grants when the invalid CPS contract expired, or indeed to outsource this critically important responsibility to a new service provider. This alarmed many civil society groups, including the Black Sash, who approached the Constitutional Court to intervene. The outcome of the litigation was that the invalid contract between CPS and Sassa was extended by a year and the Constitutional Court established a Panel of Experts to monitor and report on Sassa's progress in taking over as the grants paymaster. The Black Sash actively engaged with the Panel of Experts providing monitoring reports, testimonies, and case studies.

Meanwhile, Sassa's efforts to secure a new service provider had faltered, amid allegations that the process itself was engineered to fail. In terms of the Constitutional Court ruling, Sassa had undertaken to take over payments of social grants by 1 April 2017 when the CPS contract ended. Civil society monitored the process and was active in the efforts to place the social grant system in safe hands. It took many months, and a campaign of community mobilisation, ongoing litigation, media interventions and advocacy, and engagement with Parliament. The protracted process was subjected to all manner of twists and turns. In March 2018, faced with no practical alternatives, the Constitutional Court further extended the invalid contract for cash payments at pay points for an additional six months, when it was alleged that Sassa and the department appeared determined to retain the services of CPS.

This book focuses on the lived reality of social grant recipients in their struggle to raise their voices to demand recourse and government action. The media participated actively, and its contribution features throughout the book, as does the role of the judiciary and the legal system in protecting beneficiaries' rights to social security and dignity, as enshrined in the Constitution.

Chapter 1 gives voice to those beneficiaries, recounting their harrowing experience of the dissipation of their meagre social grants through unauthorised and irregular deductions. They listed deductions for electricity, airtime, funeral policies and loans that they had not authorised. They also described how in 2015, Net1 launched its EasyPay Everywhere (EPE) bank accounts, facilitating debit and unstructured supplementary service data (USSD)[3] deductions for financial products from Net1 subsidiaries, with dire consequences for grant recipients due to the depletion of their grants. The chapter presents the stories of some of those who turned to the Black Sash for help in stopping these unauthorised debit payments. It exposes glaringly the painfully difficult process beneficiaries experienced in trying to gain recourse, repeatedly being shunted from pillar to post, and paying for this with their time and their own money. Recipients faced massive obstacles in trying to withdraw from or find recourse for these irregular, unauthorised, and allegedly unlawful deductions.

The case studies and the stories they told made an impression on Minister Dlamini, and Chapter 2 tells how she recognised the systemic challenges faced by recipients and appointed a Ministerial Task Team (MTT) in early 2014 to explore options to stop the unauthorised and allegedly unlawful debit deductions. The Black Sash was represented on the MTT, along with CAOSA, various other civil society groups and senior officials from the DSD and Sassa.

The Black Sash initiated litigation as a last resort, and Chapter 3 records the legal battles in which the Black Sash engaged during this time, often as a friend of the court (*amicus curiae*). One of the Black Sash's most significant interventions was an urgent direct access application it brought to the Constitutional Court in 2017 when it became apparent that there was a risk of some 17 million grant beneficiaries not receiving from 1 April 2017 the grants on which they depended; an unthinkable eventuality which would have created a sociopolitical crisis of mammoth proportions.

Chapter 4 elaborates on Net1's business strategy and working model. It claimed to be introducing 'financial inclusivity' by providing previously inaccessible financial services to those excluded from the formal financial sector. However, the chapter reveals how the company, via the CPS contract, subverted this through its subsidiaries Manje Mobile, Smart Life and Moneyline, to 'offer' and sell their products to recipients in pursuit of profit. Net1's share price rocketed, as many people became very rich by amassing money intended for the poorest of the poor, enabled by inadequate oversight and due diligence by investors such as Allan Gray and the International Finance Corporation.

One of the central factors enabling Net1 to exploit recipients was the CPS contract with Sassa, its control of beneficiaries' biometric and personal data, and the sharing of that data among Net1's subsidiaries. Among various allegations levelled against Net1, the most serious is its disregard for grant beneficiaries' privacy, making personal information and data available to subsidiaries which allowed them to take advantage of recipients. The subsidiaries were able to access confidential information which was held by CPS in terms of the payment services contract with

Sassa. In this way they were able to trap unsuspecting recipients in a net of unintended and unaffordable debt. Chapter 5 situates this predatory conduct firmly in the context of state capture. This chapter refers to the 'Shadow State' that took control of aspects of the public service, including the social grant system. Key technical institutions and formal executive processes were intentionally weakened. Top officials were removed and replaced with people who would not be obstructionist. Officials were appointed in 'acting' positions, thus limiting the institutions' ability to take long-term strategic decisions that might have been in the interests of all the people of South Africa, rather than the few. In this way, the poorest of the poor paid the highest price for the capture of the social grant payment system, while the politically connected benefitted greatly.

This chapter tells the story of a shameful period that stretched over almost a decade. It reflects on the protracted manipulation by and of the state, through interference in tender processes, misgovernance and abuse of state power. It lays bare intergovernmental non-cooperation, contestation and delays in migrating to Sapo and its new model of social grant disbursement.

Chapter 6 provides a chronological overview of how the social grants payment crisis played out, and exposes the inadequacy of Parliament's oversight role in seeking to hold the minister accountable, where ministerial intervention and non-cooperation disabled the relevant committees.

Finally, Chapter 7 describes the mobilisation of civil society behind the Black Sash and its partners in the Hands Off Our Grants (Hoog) campaign. It describes how civil society activism defended those for whom South Africa's first-class social grant system provides dignity and some hope. It also illustrates how sustained media coverage and utilising the law and the fundamental institutions of democracy can unseat those in positions of power, making this book an unusual story of state capture in which the victims ultimately triumphed.

When the DSD, Sassa and CPS put a gun to the heads of millions of South Africans by threatening to stop grant payments without an alternative, the stark erosion of state capacity was revealed. The significant role civil society groups played, by approaching the Constitutional Court, needs to be acknowledged. Together with officials who spoke out, this configuration has made it possible to keep the grant payment system more or less on track to the benefit of millions. Had there been no intervention, a likely possible scenario would have been that CPS was awarded a new contract, thus making possible massive profits for a company and its associated networks off the backs of South Africa's poorest. Thankfully, this did not happen.[4]

It is important to state that Net1 and its subsidiaries have denied all wrongdoing to the public, and in the various legal challenges described in Chapter 3, they placed limited information before the court and did not confirm the interoperability of the systems between their various affiliated companies. Net1 has consistently denied that it shared confidential information with its subsidiaries across its various platforms, and this has not been adjudicated or pronounced on by a court.

As discussed in Chapter 4, the Black Sash and its partners (as well as Parliament, the MTT and other public actors) have relied on the publicly available reporting of investigative journalism, Net1's own reports to shareholders and its earnings calls, the bid documents in the initial social grant tender, the affidavits filed in the various AllPay matters and the subsequent limited explanations Net1 placed before the courts. In Chapter 6, much of the information was drawn from the website of the Parliamentary Monitoring Group, which provides reliable and comprehensive reports of parliamentary committee meetings and hearings.

Finally, the experiences of social grant beneficiaries, and the whistleblowing of various CPS and Net1 employees (and agents of affiliated companies), helped unravel the modus operandi of the Net1 business model, as described in Chapter 4. In this way the attack on South Africa's social grants system, on which many citizens depend for their livelihood and dignity, was exposed and ultimately stopped.

1 *The experiences of grant beneficiaries*

The tender awarded to Cash Paymaster Services (CPS) by Sassa in 2012 – the first wave of the Net1 business model – resulted in the establishment of 10.5 million Sassa-branded Grindrod Bank accounts. The second wave began in 2013, when CPS launched the sale of airtime and electricity via its unstructured supplementary service data (USSD) platform, linked to the Sassa-branded Grindrod Bank accounts. Beneficiary complaints about unauthorised, fraudulent and allegedly unlawful deductions began almost immediately (see Chapter 4, Net 1's 'first wave/second wave' business model).

This chapter highlights some of the experiences of grant beneficiaries who came forward to ask for assistance from the Black Sash and its community partners around the country, and it serves to illustrate how Net1's subsidiaries and other firms are alleged to have deducted money illegally from their social grants.

The information was provided by grant beneficiaries, mostly from rural or peri-urban areas across the country, who contacted the Black Sash and advice offices run by its partners. These case studies were compiled by the Black Sash and its partners. Most of them were included in a report by the Black Sash to the Panel of Experts established by the Constitutional Court. It soon became apparent from beneficiary narratives that a pattern of alleged tampering with social grants was emerging country-wide. The Black Sash realised something was seriously wrong as similar stories were being reported from the network of advice offices by staff and paralegals who had interviewed grant beneficiaries. For the purposes of this book, pseudonyms have been used for those beneficiaries quoted or referred to who said they preferred to remain anonymous. Actual names have only been used with the express consent of the beneficiaries concerned who granted permission for their names and the information they shared to be published.

In June 2015, the EasyPay Everywhere (EPE) current account card (also known as the 'Green Card') was launched to facilitate the sale of Moneyline loans, Smart Life funeral policies and Manje Mobile airtime and electricity. The EPE was a product of Moneyline and Grindrod Bank (with Net1 operating as IT specialist). By June 2016 there were 1.1 million EPE cardholders. Vendors used the planned expiry of the Sassa-branded Grindrod Bank card in December 2017 to pressurise grant beneficiaries into opening EPE accounts. They were told that when the Sassa card expired, the EPE card would be the alternative Sassa payment method, and that the loans they were taking out were granted by Sassa. CPS agents working at pay points were salespersons of Net1 financial products such as Smart Life funeral policies. The agent signing up a grant beneficiary for an EPE bank account had automatic access, via a card chip, to the personal and biometric data of the grant beneficiary. A loan was available almost immediately after an EPE account was opened, but EPE cardholders were often obliged to take out a Smart Life funeral policy and buy airtime and electricity if they wanted a Moneyline loan. EPE card accounts were opened from the boots of cars, at private residences and in vehicles by agents who earned commission on each aggressively marketed EPE card. The terms and conditions of this bank account were not made available and were not explained to beneficiaries, and the paperwork, in small print, was in English only.

The terms and conditions of the EPE card referred to EPE branches where accounts could be closed. In reality, there were no walk-in EPE branches where a beneficiary could close an account. In desperation, some beneficiaries visited a Net1 office in an attempt to obtain a statement or close their bank account. This often involved travelling long distances, as there were only 120 Net1 offices in the country. For rural grant beneficiaries this was particularly onerous and costly. A grant recipient living in Ceres, for example, would have to make a round trip of 100 km to Worcester. This made it extremely difficult, if not almost impossible, to cancel an EPE card and bank account. This meant that one of the most pressing consequences was the challenge of withdrawing from the unauthorised, unsought or misleading contracts imposed using the EPE Grindrod Bank linked card.

Armed guards at the Net1 offices confronted beneficiaries and only allowed those with Sassa or EPE cards onto the premises. Black Sash personnel and beneficiaries' relatives and friends were prevented from assisting those who were seeking redress at these offices. This was particularly egregious where it was clearly the elderly and the illiterate who were being targeted. Here are three examples.

Example 1: Mrs Maolaotse Grace Bohokwane (Ma Grace), a pensioner living in Makwassie, a small grain-producing town 270 km south of Johannesburg, received an old age pension. In November 2013, she saw that R99 had been deducted from her bank account for airtime. Ma Grace did not own a cell phone. In December 2013, R50 was deducted, and R99 was deducted in January 2014. She was also informed of an advance request for airtime for February 2014.

She sought help from the Lebaleng Community Advice Office in her town. With family members, she went to the local Sassa office where a Sassa official blamed Ma Grace's relatives for requesting airtime and made no further attempt to resolve her query. The advice office then approached CPS via its helpline to find out who had bought the airtime without Ma Grace's consent. While CPS could furnish the cell phone number with Ma Grace's deductions, it claimed it could not trace the name associated with the number. The number did not belong to anyone in Mrs Grace's household.

The CPS employee insisted that Ma Grace had provided that number in her initial application form, which she denied. Ma Grace and the paralegal from the Lebaleng Community Advice Office then reported the matter to the Black Sash Gauteng regional office, who advised them to open a criminal case with the South Africa Police Services (SAPS) and complete an affidavit noting the facts. On 26 February, after reporting the alleged unlawful deduction to Sassa, Minister Bathabile

Dlamini instructed her staff to refund Ma Grace with immediate effect (see Chapter 2).[1]

Example 2: Ma Nobantu collected a disability grant on behalf of her adult daughter which she received through ABSA bank. She immediately noticed that there was a monthly deduction from the grant, which was then R1 260. When she queried this with Sassa officials she was told that the machines in Port Elizabeth were not functioning well. Ma Nobantu accepted that there was nothing to be done until she attended a community awareness meeting about unauthorised deductions and met an Adelaide Advice office paralegal who offered to assist her.

Example 3: The Adelaide Advice office also tried to assist Ms Gloria Mabindisa who had returned home to Adelaide after suffering a stroke in Cape Town in April 2012. After some difficulty, she succeeded in getting a permanent disability grant. In January 2014, she received a payment of R3 090.33, which was the total of three months' grant back pay. However, when she went to draw her next grant on 1 February at the First National Bank ATM in Adelaide, she was shocked to find only R270 in her account. She acknowledged that she had taken out a cash loan to cover the period between the suspension of her temporary disability grant and receiving her permanent disability grant, but insisted this loan had been settled. She had borrowed R600 from Importel (according to the bank statement), to be paid back over six months, at 60 per cent compound interest. She had also been charged R20 for a 'card replacement'.

A further R860 was withdrawn from her bank account the following month. In addition, R100 a month was deducted for 'funeral insurance' by people claiming to be working with Sassa. They turned out to be the same company that had deducted the money from her account as a 'loan repayment'. The manager at first denied that the firm had made the deductions, but when he realised that the Black Sash was involved, he agreed to reimburse Ms Mabindisa.[2]

Without the intervention of the Black Sash and its partners, vulnerable citizens such as Ma Grace, Ma Nobantu and Ms Mabindisa would have faced the might of the CPS, Sassa and the respective financial service providers on their own. Their stories are typical of the many cases that the Black Sash and its partners investigated and the many more reported by the media, in particular by the independent online news agency, *GroundUp*. The experiences described here serve as an introduction to the selection of more detailed case studies that follow, that illustrate the great suffering that unscrupulous businesses inflicted on the poorest and most vulnerable people in South Africa.

UNAUTHORISED DEDUCTIONS: MR LENNOX BANI

Elderly Mr Sipho Lennox Bani from Nyanga, Cape Town, received a state old age pension of R1 440 a month. He usually withdrew his grant money from his Sassa-branded Grindrod Bank account at Shoprite in Claremont, Cape Town. In September 2015, he received only half of his grant, an amount of R723.47. Mr Bani had taken a loan from microfinance lender, Kuyasa Fund, 'to build a wall, because the youngsters keep on jumping over my fence'. The loan deduction from Kuyasa was R394.09 a month and started on 2 November 2015. However, in May 2015 Mr Bani experienced a further monthly debit deduction of R307.24. By September that year, R1 843.44 had been deducted from his account.

Mr Bani tried to find reasons for these unexplained 'loan' deductions. He visited the Sassa office in Nyanga who sent him to Sassa in Gugulethu, who in turn referred him to the Gugulethu Paralegal Advice office, from which he was then sent to the CPS office in Lansdowne. There he was given a bank statement that showed that these deductions were being made by an entity named INFAJ FIN. CPS then sent Mr Bani to their office in Bellville, which identified the withdrawer as Finbank. Mr Bani set off to find a Finbank branch in central Cape Town, but Finbank had no record of his details.

The indefatigable Mr Bani refused to give up, and in November 2015 he decided to lay a charge of theft with the SAPS in Kuilsriver. His details were taken and the case was sent to Nyanga SAPS. When he received no response, he decided to take his complaint to the Sassa provincial office in Cape Town. There he was informed of purchases from his grant at a furniture shop in Pretoria that he had not heard of. On 26 November 2015, Mr Bani went back to Sassa in Cape Town where he was asked to complete a Sassa affidavit form. He was told to have it signed at the Caledon Square police station and return it to Sassa. Mr Bani finally sought assistance at the Black Sash regional office in Mowbray, Cape Town. By then he had spent between R400 and R500 on airtime, taxis and petrol trying to get to the bottom of the deductions. He said, 'it is bothering me a lot and I can't sleep wondering who is taking this money from me'.[3]

On 7 December 2015, the Black Sash presented Mr Bani's case at a Ministerial Task Team (MTT) meeting about the inadequacy of Sassa's recourse system. Sassa's Executive Director for Grants, Ms Dianne Dunkerley, agreed to help the Black Sash take Mr Bani's case forward. Yet even with intervention from the very top at Sassa, Mr Bani gained only a temporary respite. It is evident from subsequent events that he remained without effective recourse.

The R307.24 INFAJ FIN deduction was stopped later that month, and on 13 January 2016, Mr Bani's bank statement reflected six refunds of R307.24, amounting to R1 843.44. However, the process of full repayment had been protracted and had created expenses for Mr Bani. He had to make two further visits to the Sassa office in Gugulethu, where officials claimed that the money would be paid into his Standard Bank account because, Mr Bani was told, 'It was too much money to be paid at once. It can only be paid little by little into your Sassa account'. Mr Bani challenged that, asking, 'How do you know that I have a Standard Bank account and who gave you my banking details? I have drawn large amounts at Shoprite before. That reason cannot be true'.[4] The Sassa officials replied that they did not know how the banking details were obtained.

Shortly thereafter, on 21 January 2016, Mr Bani's troubles started again. When he went to draw his grant, he found there was only R614 in his account. Once again, he called Sassa and spoke to an official who promised him that he would be reimbursed at the end of January. Instead, more deductions were made from Mr Bani's Sassa bank account. On 4 February 2016, Ms Dunkerley wrote to Ms Colleen Ryan of the Black Sash who was supporting Mr Bani:

> I have requested Mr Bani's bank statements (attached).
> According to this, the EFT reversal was done on 13 January,

and Mr Bani still has a balance of R614.92 on his account as
at 1 February 2016. In the previous mail sent to you, you were
requested to contact Mercantile Bank to ensure that the EFT
debit was stopped at source. It would seem that this has not
been done, as the second EFT debit is back. I have arranged for
the reversal of the amount taken off for February (R323.90) and
will let you know when this has been done. In the meantime,
please urgently assist Mr Bani to cancel the EFT. The details
for this are as follows: Mercantile Bank (086 030 9250). Stop the
EFT debit with them as they are sending Net1 the EFT debit
instruction, which will be processed until stopped by the client.
On further investigation Net1 has been able to find details of
the company that has instructed Mercantile Bank to facilitate an
EFT debit on their behalf: Faj Financial Solutions, 3 Church St,
Uitenhage, Eastern Cape, South Africa. Mr Bani needs to contact
them in order to have the EFT debit cancelled on his grant. Until
he does this, his grant will continue to be debited.[5]

For the next three months the unauthorised deductions continued,
and every month they were reversed (except for one payment of
R394.09 which was never refunded). A representative from Mercantile
Bank told the Black Sash that the bank was unable to stop the deductions
and that a call to a company known as Kreevin Solutions CC was
necessary.[6] On 10 February 2016, in response to an enquiry from the
Black Sash, a spokesperson for Faj Financial Solutions claimed that a loan
was issued to a 'Petrus XX'. An incorrect digit in the account number
had resulted in Mr Bani's account being debited instead. The payment
file was reconciled and submitted to CPS by a company named Alp-I.

In May 2016, the MTT presented Mr Bani's case to the South African
Reserve Bank (Sarb) and the Payments Association of South Africa (Pasa).
Among the many questions raised were: Why were these unauthorised
loan deductions coming off Mr Bani's beneficiary account? Who in the
banking payment system had approved and authorised such deductions?
Why was the full refund not available in his bank account when Mr
Bani withdrew cash on 21 January 2016? Why was he told the funds

would only be in his account by the end of January 2016? How was it possible for a service provider in Uitenhage, Eastern Cape, to instruct Grindrod Bank to debit Mr Bani's account (he lived in Nyanga, Cape Town) without his authorisation? Furthermore, why was Mr Bani asked to stop an electronic fund transaction (EFT) deduction from his account by a Uitenhage financial service provider when he had never authorised such a deduction? How did the credit service provider in Uitenhage obtain Mr Bani's personal confidential data, including his ID number and bank details? What is Sarb's role, if any, in regulating such practices?

When financial service providers were asked where they had obtained access to Sassa grant beneficiaries' confidential information, their stock response was that they had obtained it from the Financial Intelligence Centre (FIC) when the beneficiary registered a bank account.

On 30 May 2016, Ms Lynette Maart, the National Director of the Black Sash, sent an email to Mr Pierre Coetzee at Pasa who agreed to follow up Mr Bani's case. On 7 June, Mr Coetzee wrote back to say that he had sent Mr Bani's ID to Grindrod Bank and was awaiting feedback.[7] The Black Sash received no further response. Meanwhile, on 30 May 2016, Mr Bani's case was presented to the Western Cape Legislature's Portfolio Committee on Social Security, and on 1 June 2016, an article about Mr Bani's situation appeared in *News24*. Soon after this, Ms Maart received a call from Ms Hope Malaza, Head of Marketing for Mercantile Bank. Ms Maart asked Ms Ryan of the Black Sash to follow up. Ms Malaza's reply, dated 11 July 2016, stated:

Good morning Colleen,

Thank you very much for all the information provided.

We have completed a thorough investigation that included all relevant parties from our regulators, alliance partners (client) and the bank that deals with the Sassa accounts.

Our client was able to provide the 'signed' mandates relating to these deductions, however the agreements related to a different pensioner, who is an existing client of Faj Financial Solutions. On 3/11/2014, the pensioner took out a new loan with Faj Financial Solutions and when the account number was completed on the mandate one digit was incorrect and this was not picked up by the pensioner or Faj Financial Solutions at the time. As such, the loan details were captured on the system with the incorrect details, resulting in the debit being unknowingly submitted by Faj Financial Solutions to the wrong account.

On 27/10/2015 Faj Financial Solutions received a call about the debits to Mr Bani's account. On investigation they picked up the error in the account number and stopped the debit to his account for the contract which had been queried. Unfortunately, however, they missed a new contract that had been signed on 3/9/2015 by the pensioner which also had the incorrect details and did not change the account details on this contract resulting in the incorrect debit being submitted on 2/1/2016 and 30/11/2016. As soon as they became aware of this error, they did a refund to Mr Bani's account. The other incorrect debits were received as disputes in December and were reversed in January.

As part of our investigation, we found that Mr Bani had already been refunded for all debits to his account submitted through MBL. The refund was R1 228.96.

Please kindly check with Mr Bani on these refunds and advise.

Thank you again for your patience and we look forward to your response.

Regards,

Hope[8]

TRANSAFRICA LIFE: ALLEGED FRAUDULENT SALE OF FUNERAL POLICIES

Between May and June 2016, a group of young people pretending to be from the government approached grant beneficiary recipients at their homes in Tweefontein, Kwa-Mhlanga in Mpumalanga. They told the beneficiaries that if they received either the old age pension or a disability grant they were entitled to food parcels for a period of six months. To receive the food parcels, beneficiaries had to provide their ID numbers, proof of address, contact details and the name of a dependent. At no time during any of these interactions was the company TransAfrica Life mentioned.

In August 2016, deductions for funeral policies of between R40 and R141 per month were made from these beneficiaries by a company called TransAfrica Life, even though the beneficiaries had given no authorisation to this company. Some already had funeral policies and were now experiencing double deductions. In addition, the beneficiaries received no food parcels.

The affected beneficiaries approached the Sassa Customer Care desk at their local grant pay point to lodge a complaint and were directed to the Sassa local office. When the beneficiaries received no help from Sassa, they contacted a Black Sash community partner working in the area. Mr Thulani Ndhlovu, from Qedusizi Advice Centre and Home-Based Care, approached the Sassa office in Kwa-Mhlanga to follow up. He was informed that Sassa had received many complaints from beneficiaries in villages throughout the area served by the Kwa-Mhlanga office with the same promises of food parcels.

Affected beneficiaries lodged complaints with Sassa Customer Care, filled in the complaints form, and were told to travel to the SAPS station about 10 km away to complete an affidavit that they then had to return to the Sassa local office. Some beneficiaries reported that they had filled in the necessary documents on multiple occasions but had received no response from Sassa.

Between March and May 2017, Qedusizi Advice Centre and Home-Based Care administered a survey that the Black Sash had designed to investigate the deductions in Tweefontein. On 20 July, a register of 28 beneficiaries was presented by the Black Sash to the Regional Manager of TransAfrica Life Funeral Policies, Mr Elias Matselele, at TransAfrica Life's offices in Waterkloofridge, Pretoria. Mr Matselele said these allegations were not new to him. Claims in other areas had been investigated and cancelled, with monies refunded to beneficiaries. He said he had never received any communication from Sassa in relation to any affected beneficiaries in Tweefontein, although all had told the Black Sash that they had lodged complaints with Sassa. Mr Matselele suggested that their subsidiary company, Golden Funerals, which had an office in Kwa-Mhlanga, 'may have employed unethical brokers'.[9]

By July 2017, only one beneficiary interviewed by the Black Sash had managed to stop the deductions, and no beneficiaries had received a refund. The beneficiary whose deductions had been stopped achieved this on his own at considerable personal cost.

The Black Sash KwaZulu-Natal regional office contacted Mr Matselele on Wednesday, 16 August, almost a month after the initial meeting. Mr Matselele responded that they were close to completing their investigations and would give the Black Sash a full report by Friday, 18 August. On Monday, 21 August, when no report had been received from TransAfrica Life, the Black Sash phoned Mr Matselele, who promised that he would provide the report on Tuesday, 22 August.[10]

The Black Sash and several community partners met with the Financial Services Board (FSB) on 25 August and presented at least 68 beneficiaries' alleged funeral deduction cases involving TransAfrica Life as well as 1Life/Emerald Wealth Management (discussed later in this chapter) which appeared to be unlawful or fraudulent. The FSB agreed to investigate the matter and requested a sample of affidavits from the affected beneficiaries to corroborate and verify the sequence of events. These affidavits were drafted and completed at a community meeting with beneficiaries on 11 October 2017 in Tweefontein, and submitted to the FSB, but nothing further was heard from them.

Meanwhile, during the meeting with the FSB, the Black Sash received correspondence from Mr Matselele stating that the investigation had been completed and that all policies had been cancelled as per the requests of the affected beneficiaries. He confirmed that there would be no deductions from September 2017.[11] TransAfrica Life asked to meet to discuss outstanding issues and to put a process in place to deal with any other cases that might come forward. The TransAfrica Life Chief Executive Officer (CEO), a Mr Smit, apologised and promised that TransAfrica Life would refund all affected beneficiaries with interest.[12] He subsequently contacted the Black Sash's KwaZulu-Natal regional office, which agreed to host a community meeting on 11 October 2017 in Tweefontein. At this meeting, the CEO of TransAfrica Life addressed the beneficiaries and apologised for the inconvenience and suffering caused. He assured them that the brokers who had taken advantage of them had been disciplined and had been asked to leave TransAfrica Life.[13] The 28 beneficiaries initially listed by the Black Sash were paid out a total of R34 088.30.

These cases are the tip of the iceberg. It is not known how widespread such practices are, or how many grant beneficiaries have been affected. However, this case study suggests that organisations selling financial products to beneficiaries exerted no or little control over their unscrupulous agents in the field. It asks questions about perverse incentives for agents acting on behalf of such businesses, and officials at Sassa's local branches who were not willing to help grant beneficiaries. Without the assistance and resources of the Black Sash and its community partners, it would have been impossible for grant beneficiaries to cancel unauthorised products or to access redress and repayment.

TRAPPED WITH NO ACCESS TO CANCELLATION OR RECOURSE: THE EPE CARD

Ms Eliza received a child support grant and was later granted a temporary disability grant for a six-month period between July and December 2015. She usually collected her grants at an ATM, but sometimes went to the Nyanga Community Hall pay point.

Ms Eliza had taken out a loan from Moneyline Financial Services, a Net1 subsidiary. The loan was for the period March 2014 to September 2014. The Moneyline salesperson had told her that because she received a child support grant, she qualified for a loan of R500.

She confirmed that the loan amount was R500 and, with the service fee, the total amount payable was R540. This denotes a service fee of 8 per cent of the loan amount. The loan repayment instalment per month, she understood, was R50.00 over a six-month period. However, repayments of R50 over a six-month period only amount to R300.00. Ms Eliza 'signed' a loan agreement, but she is unable to read.

The Moneyline salesperson who signed her up for the loan told Ms Eliza that to secure a Moneyline loan she had to sign up for an EPE current account, which was a product of Grindrod Bank and Moneyline, with Net1 operating as IT specialist. Ms Eliza agreed to this, but during the consultation she was never asked if she consented to any terms or conditions, such as 'transferring your monthly income to all debit orders from your bank account nominated during the enrolment of your EPE account, if you so elected during enrolment'.[14] The terms and conditions for the use of the EPE card and account were not explained to her. Furthermore, the affordability test required by the National Credit Act (No. 34 of 2005) was not carried out.

In February 2016, Ms Eliza found the full child support grant had been deducted from her EPE account. Her statement revealed deductions for the loan repayment, but also showed payments for airtime and electricity that she had never purchased or authorised. On 18 February 2016, when she had not received any grant money that month, she went to the Sassa office in Gugulethu. A Sassa official, Mr L Dyanti, helped her to transfer from the EPE card back to the Sassa card and assured her that she would receive her full grant in the Sassa-branded bank account at the beginning of March.[15] Ms Eliza could not say if she was charged a fee for the new Sassa card.

Before the next scheduled Sassa payment, Ms Eliza visited the Sassa offices in Cape Town to make certain that she would get her grant money at the next payout. She was assured by an official that her money would be in her new Sassa account since the payment to the EPE card had been cancelled. Yet in March 2016, and again in April, she received no grant payment.

On payment day in April, when there was still no money in her account, Ms Eliza went to Sassa at the Nyanga Community Hall pay point to enquire about her statement. It showed that money had been transferred from her Sassa card to the EPE card and that deductions for airtime and electricity from it had been made in February, March and April 2016.

She returned to the Sassa Cape Town office and the official who assisted her assured her that money would not be deducted again. She was not given a reference number. When Ms Eliza went to receive her next grant, once again there was no money on her card.

She returned to the Sassa office in Gugulethu where she was told that there was nothing that Sassa could do about it, that Sassa did not own Moneyline and could not control the banking system.[16] She was given the CPS's toll-free number and advised to go back to Moneyline, where she had taken out the loan.

On 4 April 2016, she went back to Moneyline in Philippi, Cape Town to enquire about the electricity and airtime deductions. The only answer she got from a Moneyline official was that the Philippi office could only issue cards, and if she wanted to cancel the card, she had to phone the office in Gauteng. Ms Eliza's husband tried to call this number but when the call was finally answered, he was kept on hold for so long that he ran out of airtime.

They turned to the Black Sash for help. Ms Ryan accompanied Ms Eliza and her husband to the nearest Moneyline office, in Athlone on the Cape Flats. However, a security guard at the entrance of the Moneyline office insisted that he would only allow people who had EPE cards to enter the building. After much vigorous persuasion, Ms Ryan was finally allowed to accompany Ms Eliza into the building. There a Moneyline employee informed Ms Ryan that they too dealt only with card applications and not cancellations. For cancellations, they had to go to Social Services. They returned to the Sassa office in Athlone, where a Sassa official told them they should go back to Moneyline, as there was nothing Sassa could do.

Ms Ryan pointed out that since the airtime and electricity deductions were unauthorised, Sassa should have a recourse mechanism to forward the case to CPS. The official replied that they had no such process in place. Ms Ryan then asked to speak to a more senior official and was referred to a Ms Page. After she explained the challenges experienced at Moneyline, Ms Page completed both a Dispute Form and an affidavit. She also called CPS and asked for a statement for Ms Eliza. The CPS employee said he would send a statement immediately, but he did not. After waiting in vain, Ms Page said that she would forward the completed forms by email, which she duly did.

On Friday 15 April, Ms Eliza's husband called the Black Sash office and told Ms Ryan that a Department of Social Development (DSD) official, a Mr Mtila, had come to his house that morning to say he would be investigating Ms Eliza's case and would follow up with the Black Sash. Mr Mtila also asked for a copy of Ms Eliza's ID. Ms Eliza's husband said that he had not mentioned to Mr Mtila that he and his wife had visited the Black Sash.[17]

The Black Sash tried calling Customer Care at the DSD to ask whether an official by the name of Mr Mtila worked for the Athlone Office. The person who answered said he did not have access to that information but would follow up and let the Black Sash know. The Black Sash did not hear from him.

Ms Ryan then called the DSD's Johannesburg number. Interestingly, when the call was picked up, Ms Ryan was told that she was through to Net1. Her call was then transferred and Ms Ryan once again explained Ms Eliza's case. She was put on hold. No one returned to the call. It appeared to be impossible to cancel the EPE card, and there was no recourse for alleged fraudulent and unauthorised withdrawals or deductions. Ms Eliza said in an interview on 12 April 2016:

> I have suffered psychological impact from this deduction and cannot relax because my ten-year-old child's school needs are not met. I am unemployed. It was for this reason that I applied for a social grant. My blood pressure is constantly high.
> When I go up and down for this case I always have to go with my husband because I can only express myself in isiXhosa. Therefore, transport fees are double the amount. I have five children in total that I must take care of. Not receiving the income and being unemployed at the same time is a living

nightmare. When will this ever end? Will I get my money back? These are the answers that play like a broken record.[18]

There are many stories of recipients being 'forced' to replace their Sassa card with the new EPE or Green Card and being threatened with the possible 'withdrawal' of their grants if they tried to cancel their EPE card. They also found themselves unable to revert to using their old Sassa cards.

When old age pensioner Ms Florah Tloubatla went to collect her grant in October 2015 at the Mabopane Sassa pay point, a person she assumed was a Sassa official told her that unless she registered for an EPE or Green Card she would not receive her grant in November. Many others were told the same. They were also told not to destroy their white Sassa cards, but to keep them safe. Ms Tloubatla was under the impression that the EPE card was the new Sassa card. She was given no information about the terms and conditions of the new Green Card, although her fingerprints were taken with a biometric machine.

On 4 May 2016, Ms Tloubatla went back to the Mabopane Sassa pay point to cancel her EPE card, but was told by an unidentified official to go to the police station to obtain an affidavit recording her reasons for cancelling the card. She was told that this was the procedure that had to be followed, and that cancellation would take three months. Because she feared that it would affect her grant, she did not go to the police station.

Ms Julia received an EPE card at the Sassa office in the Lifestyle Plaza in Mabopane. She and the other grant beneficiaries who were in the office at that time were told that the card would allow them to deposit savings into their accounts, which was not possible with the Sassa card. She said that they were all forced to change to the EPE card. Their fingerprints were taken and the new cards issued. She kept both the Sassa card and the EPE card. Ms Julia said that no information regarding the terms and conditions of the new card was shared with her. She was told that she would have to use the Green Card to access her grant in future, but when she found out that the EPE card carried a monthly cost she decided to cancel it and revert to the Sassa card.

Ms Julia returned to the CPS office in the Lifestyle Plaza on 4 May 2016, where Mr Wilson Shivhambo told her that cancellation of the card would take three months and that her grant would not be paid during this time. She asked to be given proof, in writing, that the cancellation process had been lodged but she said Mr Shivhambo refused to provide her with any documentation and told her that she had to wait for three months. He yelled at her, she told the Black Sash, saying that beneficiaries were 'irritating' because they had applied for the Green Card and later tried to cancel them after being misled by the Black Sash.[19] Ms Julia was afraid that her grant would not be paid for the next three months. While at the CPS office, she called the Black Sash for help. Mr Vincent Skhosana of the Black Sash tried to speak to Mr Shivhambo on Ms Julia's phone to ask why he refused to provide the beneficiary with written proof of cancellation and for more information on the CPS's card cancellation process. Mr Shivhambo responded that this was a matter between EPE and their client and hung up.[20] Further efforts to get hold of him on numerous occasions were unsuccessful. Mr Skhosana assured Ms Julia that her Sassa grant would not be cancelled as that would be a violation of her right to social assistance.

Ms Sonie received her EPE card at the Mabopane Sassa pay point in Zone 15, Ga-Rankuwa in Gauteng, after being told by an official that she needed to renew her card. She thought that Sassa was updating beneficiary cards, as it had done before, and she complied. She too was given no explanation of the card's terms and conditions. She said that she had no concerns at the time and the process went smoothly as it had previously when she had received her new Sassa card. She had no intention of taking out a loan.

On 9 March 2016, Ms Sonie went to the Sassa office to report that her Green Card was lost. She was told to provide an affidavit to Sassa, which she did. She returned later that month to the Sassa/CPS office to request the cancellation of her EPE card and was told the application would take 21 days. In the meantime, she should continue to use her EPE card. She was not told about a R50 cancellation fee.

On 28 April 2016, Makie Ngobeni from Sassa called Ms Sonie to confirm that the cancellation process had been completed and would be effective from 1 May 2016. She gave Ms Sonie a reference number.[21] On 4 May 2016, when Ms Sonie visited the Sassa pay point to use her Sassa card, she found there was no money in her account. Instead, the money was still in the EPE account – and had been decreased by R100. She said that she was frustrated and felt cheated by Sassa and went home without seeking help from any of the officials. She planned to lodge a dispute and follow up with Sassa using the reference number that she had been given.

Ms Louise received an EPE card in May 2015 at the Lifestyle Plaza shopping centre where the local CPS offices were based. A CPS staff member told her that the card was a Sassa card that would give her access to a saving facility and a funeral policy as well as her grant money. She was given no information about the terms and conditions attached to the new card and was under the impression that it was a Sassa card.

In June 2016, Ms Louise again visited the offices at the Lifestyle Plaza, and sought to cancel her EPE card. A CPS official told her that the Black Sash was misleading her and many other people and that Sassa was aware of the EPE card. He told her that they were authentic as they were registered and showed her a certificate. The Black Sash was not in the picture, he said. When Ms Louise insisted that she had a right to cancel the card if she wanted to the official threatened her by telling her that the cancellation would take three months and might affect her grant. Ms Louise decided not to proceed.

THE CONNECTION BETWEEN THE EPE CARD AND NET1 SUBSIDIARIES

The following case study demonstrates the connection between the EPE card and Net1 subsidiaries, and is one of numerous similar queries brought to the Black Sash and its partners.

Ms Hewu of KwaNobuthle, Port Elizabeth, lived with her mother, her uncle, her daughter (aged 29), her son (aged 20) and her grandson (aged 8) in her mother's house. She received a disability grant, her son received a child support grant, and her mother and uncle both received old age pensions. She started receiving the disability grant 'a very long time ago'. In December 2016, she and her sister needed loans to cover the costs of the initiation of her son and nephew over the Christmas period.

She went to Moneyline, a subsidiary of Net1. The Moneyline loan office in KwaNobuhle is a satellite site hosted by a family living in a house on Mama Street. Several times a month the Mama Street house hosted Net1 representatives who promoted EPE cards and sold loans and policies. Ms Hewu had heard about Mama Street or 'Mama' as it was known colloquially. Many people had told her that if she needed money she should go to Mama.

According to local knowledge, the owner of the Mama Street house was one of the first people from KwaNobuhle to visit the Net1 office in Green Acres, Gqeberha (formerly Port Elizabeth), to borrow money. Net1 was trying to establish satellite sales points in Uitenhage and KwaNobuhle, and the Net1 consultants asked their new client if she could gather neighbours wanting loans at her house every month in KwaNobuhle. She advertised through word of mouth, and very quickly built a reputation for being able to connect large groups of KwaNobuhle residents with Net1 consultants who would be at Mama at the beginning of every month.

A shack had been erected outside Mama's house to serve as the Moneyline office. Before anyone could enter the shack, Mama demanded R15 from each potential client. When loan-seekers protested about the payment, she replied that this was money she would use to clean her stoep.

Despite a report by accounting firm KPMG released by Net1 that sought to prove that clients were not forced to agree to have an EPE card in order to apply for a Moneyline loan, it was clear that people did not go to Mama's to sign up for the EPE card; they wanted a Moneyline loan. Ms Hewu described the scene inside the shack where three Net1 representatives sat in a row behind a big table. Two of the representatives operated various devices from long metal briefcases that contained the Net1 'kit', including a fingerprint reader, a card reader, a receipt printer and sometimes a computer.

Ms Hewu told the first Net1 consultant that she wanted a loan. She was told that she would be required to visit each of the three stations to apply for the loan. At the first station she was asked to sign paperwork.

At the second station her fingerprints and phone number were taken. Her Sassa card was put into a card reader, and she was issued with an EPE card. She was not told what this card was or that it was linked to a second bank account, nor was she told about the terms and conditions or the fee structure of the card. She was not given any paperwork for the EPE card. The only thing the consultant told her was that her Sassa money would now be accessible using this new card.

When Ms Hewu sat down with the third Net1 consultant, she was asked for her new EPE card, which was inserted into a card reader, and she was also asked for her thumbprint. She was not asked about her finances or household budget; the Net1 consultant did no verbal affordability test. She also did not have to provide additional paperwork, such as proof of address or a bank statement. Once Ms Hewu had put her finger on the touch pad, the Net1 consultants could access this information through their computer system.

The biometric system was paid for in part by Sassa, according to the terms of its contract with CPS. It was designed by Net1 for the registration of social grant beneficiaries. However, it is apparent that a suite of Net1 companies shared the technology that could read personal information from the EPE card. Unlike other card-granting agencies that only stored a person's PIN number on the chip, Net1 stored the data needed for the EPE card conversion process. Through their proprietary card reader, any Net1 company could access the client's bank statements. When clients gave their fingerprints, they were not aware, nor informed, of the amount and type of personal data they were also providing. It goes without saying that they did not provide informed consent to the sharing of their confidential information.

Based on the information gathered and stored by CPS on behalf of Sassa, Ms Hewu was denied a Moneyline loan. A long slip of paper was printed, but she was not allowed to take it with her. The consultant crumpled it up and threw it into the bin. Her questions about why her loan had been denied went unanswered, though she was still left with an EPE card to receive her grant.

For the following six months, Ms Hewu tried to cancel the EPE card. She returned on multiple occasions to the Mama Street house and told the consultants that she did not want the EPE card. 'You will be on the Green Card forever', she was told. 'Your money will always go there.'[22] The Net1 consultants gave her a phone number to send an SMS to. She was told that she would receive a call-back from that number, but although she tried many times, she never got a response. She went to the Sassa offices and was told by both Sassa and CPS staff that they could not help her. Sassa officials advised her to return to the place where she had attempted to get the loan. She returned several times to Mama Street to try to meet with the consultants, but was sent away. When she asked why she could not close the card at Mama Street, she was told this was for 'security reasons'.

She was eventually able to close her account when she had saved enough airtime to call the phone number on the back of the EPE card, a number that was different from the one she was given by the Net1 consultants at Mama Street. Her account was finally closed on 8 May 2017 over the phone, but she did not receive anything in writing or an SMS to confirm that it was closed.

Ms Hewu visited the Interchurch Local Development Agency (ILDA) offices where Ms Nobuzwe Mofokeng from ILDA and Ms Alexa Lane from the Black Sash took up her case. She wanted to make sure that her EPE card had, in fact, been closed. She believed her grant was still being paid into her EPE account and she also wanted assistance regarding the many deductions from her account.

Ms Hewu went to the Net1 Financial Services Office at the NU4 Motherwell shopping centre, Gqeberha, with her two helpers. An office manager asked what they wanted and Ms Hewu requested her account statement. After her ID document and EPE card were taken, she was called into the office manager's back office. Ms Lane and Ms Mofokeng tried to accompany her, but they were turned away. They were told that she had a 'right to privacy'. Ms Hewu asked to waive that right and have a personal representative accompany her at the consultation, but this was not permitted. Ms Mofokeng was told to phone Mr Ismail Cassim, the branch manager, to get permission to accompany Ms Hewu, but it seemed this was simply a delaying tactic. Mr Cassim in turn told Ms Mofokeng to call the regional office in East London.[23]

While sitting in the waiting area, Ms Hewu recognised the Net1 employees who sold EPE cards and Moneyline loans from the Mama Street house. It was apparent that these employees were not authorised to help clients cancel their EPE cards. Instead, beneficiaries were told to phone a (wrong) number or pay R66 to travel to the nearest Net1 office in Motherwell. A beneficiary could switch from the Sassa card to the EPE card in one easy step, but could not cancel the EPE card and automatically return to the Sassa card. It seemed the Net1 system only worked in one direction.

Ms Hewu was finally given her bank statement, which confirmed that her account had been closed on 8 May. She now had the paperwork showing that her account had been cancelled, but she was not yet receiving her grant in her Sassa account. Ms Hlobo and her helpers then went to the Sassa office to try to rectify this. They met the team leader at Sassa, a Mr Ngalo, who told them that once a client had been transferred to the EPE card, Sassa could no longer see their profile on their computers and therefore they could not provide any information about what had happened to Ms Hewu's money after the EPE account had been closed.[24]

According to the Social Assistance Regulations, for payments to be made into a different bank account, a beneficiary must submit a written request to Sassa. Mr Ngalo said that it was made difficult 'on purpose' as CPS and Net1 were 'all one company', and as one company they made some things very easy and others very difficult for both Sassa beneficiaries and Sassa itself. He said that if the transfer from the Sassa card to the EPE card was so easy, there was no technological or security reason for the transfer back to the Sassa card to be problematic.[25]

He called in a colleague who was responsible for helping beneficiaries who had cancelled their EPE cards in order to revert to the Sassa card. The colleague said she advised clients to call the toll-free number on the back of their new cards to ask for their money to be deposited into their Sassa account. However, CPS ran this call centre, and its computer system recorded EPE card cancellations and the opening of new Sassa accounts. She also said that loans on the EPE account might not be cancelled, particularly those granted by Moneyline. She said that it appeared that other loans might be cancelled, but then beneficiaries

would have to go to their creditors to have the debit orders transferred
to their new card. If they failed to so, she warned, those loan companies
might try to demand payment from beneficiaries. It seemed that the
Sassa officials wanted Ms Mofokeng and ILDA (who were well known
at this Sassa office) to test this process and alert them to any failures
or bottlenecks.[26]

Ms Hewu sat in the queue and waited to get her new Sassa card. The
CPS employee opening the new Sassa accounts 'scolded' beneficiaries
for switching cards.

FUNERAL POLICY DEDUCTIONS: 1LIFE/EMERALD WEALTH MANAGEMENT

The Social Assistance Act (No. 13 of 2004), Section 26A, makes provision
for one deduction from a social grant, of not more than 10 per cent of
the value of the social grant. The deduction is only allowed for a funeral
policy, and this is the only direct debit that can be deducted before
beneficiaries can withdraw their grants. Section 26A does not apply to
other types of debit orders.[27]

When the Black Sash's Ms Ryan visited the Paarl Advice Office in
November 2014, she found paralegal Ms Bukiwe Lakey surrounded
by Sassa beneficiaries from the Franschhoek area desperately trying to
stop 1Life funeral cover debit deductions from their Sassa bank accounts.
Together, Ms Ryan and Ms Lakey visited farms in the surrounding area
where beneficiaries told them about an agent, Mr Calvin Festus, from
Emerald Wealth Management[28] based in Bellville, who said that they
were instructed by Sassa or the Minister of Social Development to take
out 1Life funeral cover. (1Life was the underwriter of the policies sold
by Emerald Wealth Management.) Although many beneficiaries told
the broker they already had funeral policies, he nevertheless demanded
their identity documents and he and his agents proceeded to complete
application forms for them.

This agent was in a great rush. Nobody was given enough time and
opportunity to study the 1Life funeral policy and 'customers' were not
given information about the funeral cover they were about to purchase.

The agent also insisted on placing the beneficiaries' fingerprints on the completed application form, which some of the beneficiaries found undignified. Beneficiaries were told to pay their first funeral cover instalment over the counter at the post office and that subsequent deductions would come from their Sassa-branded Grindrod Bank accounts. However, the first instalment was in fact deducted from their bank accounts.

Mr and Ms Juries from Franschhoek exposed unauthorised 1Life funeral policy deductions in a television documentary series called *Grant Grabs.*[29] Soon after the screening, in March 2015, Emerald Wealth Management agents arrived at the Juries' home. They said they had come to investigate the conduct of Mr Festus, who was suspended after the exposé, subject to a disciplinary inquiry. According to the elderly couple, the agents, a white male and white female, were very intimidating and told the Juries that they were former police officers, and that while the Juries could cancel their funeral policies to stop the deductions, they were not entitled to a refund of instalments already paid. The Black Sash subsequently discovered that the refund was an integral item in the 1Life funeral policy offered to grant beneficiaries, which they were entitled to receive. This raises further questions about sales being commission based, which added to the difficulties beneficiaries faced when trying to cancel policies they did not want or were manipulated through misrepresentations into taking out, because agents did not want to forfeit their commission.

The Juries' contacted the Black Sash after their encounter with the Emerald Wealth Management agents. A Black Sash team spent hours with the group social grant beneficiaries in Franschhoek, to process the intimidation they received. Ms Juries, a frail, elderly woman, was visibly shaken by the encounter.

The Juries and their supporters in the community were acknowledged for their bravery in exposing the misrepresentation by Emerald Wealth Management of Sassa. Ms Maart and Ms Ryan from the Black Sash asked the Franschhoek group whether they were ready to fight for a refund of all the deductions, and all of the 18 beneficiaries gave the go-ahead. They wanted a full refund. It was agreed that calls from 1Life and

Emerald Wealth Management would be redirected to the Black Sash and the Paarl Advice Office to prevent intimidation.

Ms Ryan was assured by a 1Life official that all the deductions that had been made since they took out the policy would be paid back to the 18 policyholders.[30] On 13 April the beneficiaries, with representatives from the Black Sash and the Paarl Advice office, met two Johannesburg-based 1Life functionaries. At this meeting, Mr Kobus Wentzel from 1Life apologised to the Sassa beneficiaries and acknowledged that their treatment had lacked dignity.[31] All were handed cash refunds for one to four months' payments. Mr Wentzel said that 1Life had removed Mr Festus and were in the process of reporting Emerald Wealth Management (Bellville) to the Financial Services Board for unethical business practices.[32]

In April 2015, the Paarl Advice Office registered a further 25 cases with 1Life/Emerald Wealth Management, and on 11 May Ms Lakey reported that the 1Life policies for this second group of beneficiaries had been stopped. The Black Sash also registered alleged fraudulent funeral deductions in Mossel Bay, Riversdale, Beaufort West, Delft and Ceres.

Sassa was informed at an MTT meeting held on 11 May 2015 of the allegedly fraudulent 1Life funeral cover deductions.[33] The 1Life/Emerald Wealth Management agents targeted beneficiaries who already had their own, separate funeral policies. In a meeting on 19 February 2016 between Emerald Life management and the Black Sash, the Paarl Advice Office, Sassa and the DSD it was announced that Emerald Life management had parted ways with 1Life. Emerald was challenged on another 45 outstanding cases, and at the meeting the Emerald officials promised to refund policyholders.[34] It took more than a year for the second group of 45 beneficiaries to be refunded.

In addition to the misrepresentation and bullying on the part of Emerald Wealth Management, many nominees who did want to activate the death benefit did not know how to. Ms Koera, who had a child support grant, had bought a 1Life funeral policy from Emerald Wealth Management. She died in June 2017. Her husband travelled from the remote town of Saron in the Western Cape to the Paarl Advice Office at the cost of R1 200 to seek help. Although he was the nominated beneficiary, he was told that he did not qualify for the death benefit as the policy was less than six months old. Mr Koera was unaware that Ms Koera's funeral policy with 1Life had lapsed and that a new policy had been subsequently sold to her. When Ms Koera signed the policy, she thought that it was a continuation of her old 1Life funeral policy. The Paarl Advice Office and the Black Sash intervened and secured the death benefit of R12 500.

* * *

There are many more stories like those described in this chapter that the Black Sash has recorded. It partnered with the independent online news agency, *Ground-Up*, which enabled grant beneficiaries to tell their own stories and bring their plight into the public domain. Barbara October (née Maregele), Deputy Editor of *GroundUp*, said:

> By interviewing a beneficiary, we hoped to put a face to all the statistics and numbers that had been released by Sassa and other media at the time. We hoped that this would help readers understand that those affected by the problem were not 'just a small percentage of the total beneficiaries' as Sassa liked to say, but people who were among the most vulnerable in our communities. *GroundUp* has since published hundreds of reports on issues related to social grants in towns and major metros across the country. We have covered what has since become known as 'Sassa-Gate' through the multiple parliamentary hearings into the problems with social grant payment … the associated court cases; and the profits made by CPS and its parent company Net1 from the grant payment system. But mostly we have written articles from the ground, recording the snaking queues at pay points in rural areas and the plight of those … for whom the social grant was often the difference between survival and starvation.[35]

Many South Africans are unaware that most grant beneficiaries are the elderly and the young, who are the most vulnerable citizens in the country. Receiving a meagre social grant each month often makes the difference between starvation and being able to eat or put food on the table for the family.

2 The Ministerial Task Team

During 2012 and 2013 the Black Sash and its community partners, through its Community Monitoring and Advocacy Project (CMAP),[1] became aware of increasing and widespread unauthorised and allegedly unlawful debit deductions from the Sassa-branded Grindrod Bank accounts into which social grants were paid.

By the end of 2013, the Black Sash had engaged Sassa and the Department of Social Development (DSD) to find out how and why this was happening. However, the reports they received in response invariably blamed the grant beneficiaries themselves, and their relatives or members of their households, suggesting that family members or other dependents were setting up debit orders and purchasing airtime on the unstructured supplementary service data (USSD) platform, possibly unbeknown to the beneficiaries. The solutions proposed therefore focused on changing the behaviour of social grant beneficiaries and recipients. For example, Sassa placed adverts on national television – often during the breaks in popular soap operas – and on radio and in newspapers to educate grant recipients about protecting their cards and pins.

On 6 January 2014, as part of the Hands Off Our Grants (Hoog) campaign, the Black Sash and its partners sent an open letter[2] to the Minister of Social Development asking the minister to address five demands:

1. Stop all unauthorised and allegedly unlawful or fraudulent debit deductions from the Sassa bank accounts of grant beneficiaries.

2. Hold the DSD, Sassa, CPS and other third parties accountable for the allegedly unlawful, unauthorised deductions and put in place a proper system for recourse that poor people could access without having to use their limited resources.
3. Ensure that social grants are not used as collateral for credit and, where appropriate, change legislation and regulations to criminalise reckless lending by credit service providers.
4. Insource the administration of social grants by 2015, with the DSD and Sassa exercising proper control over their constitutional mandate to provide social security.
5. Immediately set up an Inspectorate to deal with violations.

The Black Sash received a reply from Ms Bathabile Dlamini, then Minister of Social Development, dated 21 January 2014.[3] Her letter indicated that she had led a team, comprising senior managers from the DSD and Sassa, to consult the South African Reserve Bank (Sarb), the Department of Trade and Industry, the National Credit Regulator (NCR) and commercial lawyers on how best to stop allegedly unlawful and fraudulent debit deductions.[4] The Black Sash requested a meeting with the minister. She was unavailable at the time but in her reply called for a meeting in February 2014, and added:

> In order to address speedily the challenges raised in your letter, I also need to indicate that I have instructed the Chief Executive Officer of Sassa, Ms Virginia Petersen, to stop all deductions; save for the allowed deductions made in terms of Regulation 26A (funeral policies) of the Social Assistance Regulations made prior to payment to beneficiaries by the Service Provider (reference to CPS).
>
> It should be noted that currently neither Sassa nor the Department of Social Development has control over the deductions that are effected post payment of social grant benefits into the accounts held by the beneficiaries, as those deductions or debits are effected within the National Payment System [NPS] to which both Sassa and my Department have no access.[5]

On 26 February 2014, Black Sash National Director Lynette Maart led a delegation to a meeting with the Minister of Social Development held at the Sassa Western Cape office. Civil society representatives comprised Ma Grace, a grant beneficiary from Makwassie in the North West Province; Mr Kabelo Modisadife from the Lebaleng Community Advice Office (who also acted as translator for Ma Grace); Mr Albert Makwela, Chairperson of the Community Advice Offices of South Africa (CAOSA); his colleague, Mr Seth Mnguni; Ms Joyce Muller from the Katolieke Ontwikkeling Oranje Rivier (Koor) in the Northern Cape; Ms Patricia de Lange from the Adelaide Advice Office in the Eastern Cape; Mr Thulani Ndlovu from the Qedusizi Advice Centre in Mpumalanga; Mr Elroy Paulus, the Black Sash National Advocacy Manager; and Father Peter-John Pearson of the Catholic Bishop Parliamentary Liaison Office. The government was represented by the Minister of Social Development, Ms Dlamini; the Deputy Director-General for Social Security, Mr Thokozani Magwaza; the Special Adviser to the Minister, Mr Zane Dangor; the Executive Manager for Grants Administration from Sassa, Ms Dianne Dunkerley and several others.

At this meeting, the minister established the Ministerial Task Team (MTT) to deal with the unauthorised debit deductions from Sassa bank accounts and to address the Black Sash's five demands.

This was the first time Ma Grace had left her province and travelled by aeroplane to Cape Town. Her account, delivered in her vernacular language, of how her monthly social grant was affected by unauthorised airtime deductions made such an impression on the minister that Ms Bathabile called in her own translator to replace the Black Sash's translator. Minister Dlamini instructed that Ma Grace be refunded immediately, although it took some months for this to be implemented, despite the minister's instructions.

Until then the minister, and many others in government, had accepted the rhetoric spun by CPS and those in the Net1 stable alleging that most deductions from Sassa bank accounts were due to misconduct by individuals and family members in the recipients' households. Sassa and the DSD were unable to verify the alleged unauthorised deductions as CPS controlled the grant payment system. CPS would not admit to having any role in these deductions, and insisted the problem was recipients' error. Ma Grace's story forced a rethink, and in a later media statement the minister cited Ma Grace's story to highlight the impact of the problem.

> Ma Grace lives in the small rural town, Makwassie, in the North West and receives an old age grant. She does not possess a cell phone yet was plagued for months with unauthorised advanced airtime deductions from her Sassa-branded Grindrod Bank account. When we learnt of her case, I instructed that she be refunded immediately and that these deductions must be stopped.[6]

In addition, the minister said that meetings must be convened with retailers to ensure that the grant beneficiaries were not forced to buy goods before they withdrew their cash. She also instructed that the Sassa office in Adelaide in the Eastern Cape, which had been closed a year earlier, without consultation, be re-opened.[7]

On 16 April 2014, the Black Sash and community partners travelled to Adelaide to join a community meeting hosted by the Adelaide Advice Office that was attended by 400 people. This was part of the Black Sash and its partners' 'Speak Out' initiative (see Chapter 7).[8] At this meeting, Mr Magwaza gave an undertaking to re-open the Adelaide Sassa office, which would improve service delivery to the community in Adelaide as well as in smaller adjacent towns and surrounding farms.[9]

At the Adelaide meeting, the Black Sash encountered a CPS official who alleged that PBel Pty (Ltd) – a company owned by Phillipe Belamant, the son of Net1 founder and CEO Serge Belamant – was implicated in unauthorised and even alleged abuse of the debit order facilities from thousands of Sassa-branded bank accounts in the Eastern Cape. The CPS official said that she had cancelled 'thousands' of airtime deductions, particularly from elderly grant beneficiaries, many of whom were illiterate and were often unaware of the transactions from their Sassa-branded Grindrod Bank accounts.[10]

The Sassa office in Adelaide was re-opened in May 2014 and served as an avenue for the local community to lodge complaints. The office experienced a steady flow of complaints about unauthorised and allegedly unlawful and fraudulent debit deduction cases, which started to reveal the magnitude of the problem. The re-opening of this office was an important victory for the local community and for the Adelaide Advice Office. Beneficiaries spoke for themselves and used their power and agency to get the attention of government. The bottom-up approach would become an important principle when taking up local cases and systemic issues with the MTT and engaging the banking sector and other stakeholders and regulators at a national level.

MTT TERMS OF REFERENCE

The broad mandate of the MTT was to work on the development of strategies to address these issues raised by the Black Sash. The terms of reference (TOR) stated that the MTT would deal with the following issues:[11]

- As a priority, stopping the unauthorised deductions (often debit orders or via USSD platforms) from the grant payments due to Sassa beneficiaries, as these deductions demonstrated unethical business practices on the part of the Sassa payment providers and other third party financial institutions which appeared to be unlawful or fraudulent.
- Developing appropriate recourse procedures for beneficiaries affected by these deductions.
- Implementing legislative, policy, regulatory and contractual remedies to cease these debit deductions from the accounts of grant beneficiaries.
- Monitoring the framework and process by which Sassa insources the payment of social assistance grants, based on a clear plan with key milestones, deadlines and resource allocations. Such monitoring would bear in mind that a separate Ministerial Task Team dealt with the technical aspects of this insourcing.
- Monitoring the process by which the Inspectorate would be established, based on a clear plan with key milestones, deadlines and resource allocations.

The MTT was co-chaired by Mr Magwaza and Ms Maart. Core members of the MTT representing government were Mr Magwaza, Mr Dangor, Mr Brenton van Vrede, Mr Buthelezi and Ms Dunkerley. Civil society was represented by Ms Maart, Mr Paulus and later Ms Ryan, all from the Black Sash, and Mr Makwela, Ms Muller and Ms Bukiwe Lakey from the Paarl Advice Office (Cape Town), and Mr Ndlovu.

There were two notable sticking points for the task team. Firstly, could the Black Sash serve on the MTT and continue with its advocacy work? The second sticking point was related to confidentiality versus transparency and accountability.

In response to the first, the following clause was included in the TOR: 'Participation by the Black Sash (and it's civil society partners) in the task team does not circumscribe its advocacy role with respect to issues of social security or the administration of social security'.[12] This enabled the Black Sash to work with government in solving challenges while at the same time enabling it to continue with advocacy, including, if necessary, being able to take the government to court on related matters.

With regard to the second issue, it was agreed that 'At each meeting of the task team, information of a sensitive, confidential or inappropriate nature will be identified. This will enable the task team members to identify the kinds of issues that can be reported on to stakeholders of parties not present at the task team meetings'.[13]

FIRST MTT REPORT AND RECOMMENDATIONS

In August 2014, the MTT presented its first report to Minister Dlamini at her offices in Parliament.[14] The Black Sash's partner from the Northern Cape, Ms Joyce Muller, summarised the issues in these terms:

The two sides of the same coin analogy

The big shark(s) in suits are now in the tank (with seemingly 'legal' access to Sassa bank accounts/cards and grant recipients' confidential data) and the little sharks are relegated

a distance away from pay points (with insecure repayments,
illegally detaining Sassa cards, often threatening recipients
with violence, and more likely to be prosecuted by SAPS [the
South African Police Service] and the NCR). In essence, the big
shark(s) have effectively eliminated the competition – but are
not being held criminally liable.[15]

In a later press statement Minister Dlamini agreed with all the
recommendations in the report and further committed the MTT to
address the following:[16]

- Short, medium and long-term interventions to stop the debit order
  deductions that were alleged to be unlawful and fraudulent from
  the Sassa accounts of social grant recipients.
- The re-run of the social grant payment tender ordered by the
  Constitutional Court, which offered an opportunity to change bid
  specifications, contracts and service level agreements (SLAs) for
  better alignment with legislation and regulations, including
  - better protection of the grant beneficiaries' confidential data
    obtained by CPS in the registration process; and
  - stricter limits on the Sassa-branded bank accounts to exclude all
    unauthorised or allegedly unlawful or fraudulent debit deductions.
- Sassa to insource the payment of social grants with protected bank
  accounts and protection of beneficiaries' personal data.
- Sarb to issue a directive, in the public interest, in terms of Section 12 of
  the National Payment Systems Act (No. 78 of 1998), to protect the
  Sassa-branded recipients' bank accounts and their confidential
  information. This was a direct request from the minister.
- The DSD to seek a declaratory order to interpret Section 20 of
  the Social Assistance Act (No. 13 of 2004) and the South African
  Social Security Agency Act (No. 9 of 2004) which is concerned with
  confidential information. The DSD and Sassa to seek an interdict to
  stop the unauthorised and allegedly unlawful or fraudulent debit
  deductions, subject to the outcome of a declaratory order.
- Legislative amendments: The social grant was not to be used as
  collateral for loans. Align legislation within other departments that

confuse, dilute or compete with the legislation relevant to the DSD and Sassa, and ensure that the Social Assistance Act and the Sassa Act take the lead as social security mandate carriers to ensure and affirm constitutional integrity.

- Implement a Sassa-owned and controlled recourse system to deal with unauthorised and allegedly unlawful and fraudulent deductions, backdated to 2012. Refunds to grant beneficiaries to include interest and bank charges.
- The minister to establish the Inspectorate as envisaged in the Social Assistance Act.

The minister further declared that 'The Ministerial Task Team will continue to monitor and ensure the implementation of the recommendations by the respective parties and to report periodically on progress against targets. As Government we have both a legislative and moral duty to take action against those who feed ruthlessly on the vulnerability of the poor'.[17]

SARB: ISSUING A DIRECTIVE

A challenge with the social grant payments was that Sassa was unable to access directly the payment system set up by CPS and Net1, which hampered its ability to investigate and stop the unauthorised and allegedly unlawful and fraudulent deductions from the Sassa-branded Grindrod Bank accounts, which initially did not even stipulate terms and conditions of use. There was no contractual relationship between Sassa and Grindrod Bank, despite the fact that more than 90 per cent of grant recipients held accounts with this bank, opened for them through the 2012 Sassa-CPS contract. Sassa held the contract with CPS for the payment of social grants, and Net1, the parent company of CPS, held the contract with Grindrod Bank (in which it also held shares) (see Chapter 4).

The Sassa-branded Grindrod Bank account only supplied terms and conditions approximately three years into the contract, and these were exactly the same as the terms and conditions of the EasyPay

Everywhere (EPE) bank accounts that came later, which were also held by Grindrod Bank.

One of the MTT's strategies was to approach Sarb to request a directive to exercise control of the grant payment system. Grindrod Bank operates within the regulated banking environment of the National Payment System (NPS)[18] and part of Sarb's mandate is to regulate and supervise the banking system, ensuring the effective functioning of the NPS. In terms of Section 12 of the National Payment System Act (No. 78 of 1998 as amended), the bank may from time to time, after consultation with the payment system management body, issue directives to any person (or entity) regarding a payment system or the applications of the provisions of the Act.

In April 2014, the MTT met with Sarb to explore further issuing a directive to provide a way of dealing with the unauthorised and allegedly unlawful and fraudulent debit order deductions. At the time, the MTT team believed that a directive would provide at least part of a solution by securing oversight of the Sassa-branded Grindrod Bank accounts. Mechanisms could also be put in place to stop the abuse of grant recipients' confidential data by third party creditors.

At the meeting, Sarb noted that the process of issuing a directive could take up to two years as it involved significant stakeholder engagement, including engagement with the Payment Association of South Africa (Pasa), which was comprised of commercial banks. Strong pressure by the DSD, Sassa, National Treasury and civil society collectively would also be required to secure such a directive. The South African banking community, with its narrow focus on the interests of the industry and its shareholders, was not likely to protect the interests of the poorest of South Africa's population, the approximately 16 million people[19] who received social grants. In follow-up correspondence Sarb stated:

> Whilst we note with concern that social grants paid to vulnerable persons are exploited by unscrupulous lending and other commercial practices, after careful consideration

the SARB decided against the issuance of such a Directive at this stage. The SARB is of the firm view that a Directive as requested could be challenged legally by other stakeholders in the NPS ... The SARB has engaged with SASSA, Black Sash and delegates of DSD and remains willing to continue meeting with the relevant stakeholders and providing input on possible actions that may be undertaken by all parties concerned, including the SARB, to resolve the matter both in the short and the long term.[20]

Sarb, however, did agree to support Sassa on scoping and implementing the banking requirements for the national social grant payment system. It also highlighted that the Sassa contract itself, involving the cohort of CPS/Net1/Grindrod Bank, presented considerable risk to the NPS.[21]

MANAGING THE CPS CONTRACT

In June 2014, Ms Virginia Petersen, CEO of Sassa, was invited to address the MTT on the efforts by Sassa to hold CPS/Net1 to account for the unauthorised and allegedly unlawful debit deductions. At the meeting she referenced correspondence between Sassa and the CEO of CPS and Net1 for the period between 16 October 2013 and 13 June 2014.[22] In summary, the substantive issues raised in the correspondence refer to:

- The contractual obligations of CPS as 'an independent legal entity' distinct from Net1 and its 44 entities globally.
- The (alleged) unlawful use of the Sassa brand or logo to market Manje Mobile by PBel (Pty) Ltd.
- CPS was to focus solely on the administration of grant payments while the declaration of the invalidity of the contract was suspended, and not supply airtime, loans and other financial services to grant beneficiaries. Assertions from Net1 and CPS (on 11 February and 13 June 2014) that their aim was 'to offer the best possible products to the less fortunate of society who are excluded from basic and responsible financial services' were noted.[23]

- CPS was not to supply confidential data of grant recipients to any third parties. This information was to be used strictly in accordance with the Sassa contract terms and conditions as well as the SLA.
- The marketing and sale of loans by Smart Life or any other Net1 subsidiary or financial service provider at or near Sassa pay points was a material breach of the SLA.
- Changes to the Sassa/CPS SLA in term of the USA Securities and Exchange Commission Regulations (applicable to Net1) have to be ratified by the CPS board.

It was evident from the correspondence that the roles and obligations of CPS had been conflated and merged with those of Net1 and its 44 subsidiaries. It was not in Net1's commercial interests for the allegedly unlawful and fraudulent debit deductions to stop. It was also apparent that Net1 was prepared to fight to maintain the status quo until the Sassa contract ended on 30 March 2017. It also appeared that Sassa was being held to ransom by CPS and that it seemed to struggle to enforce the contract and service level agreement (SLA). In addition to the R2 billion annual payment, CPS/Net1 also wanted access to the annual social grant budgets, which were R117.8 billion and R128.8 billion for the 2012/13 and 2013/14 financial years respectively.[24]

The AllPay Constitutional Court order in 2014 made it clear that a new tender process must be initiated. If a suitable service provider was not found, Sassa would have to insource the administration of social grants and it seemed highly likely that CPS may lose the Sassa contract and its revenue streams.

THE 'GREEN CARD'

In 2015 a new problem was brought to the attention of the MTT, namely the EPE card, also known as the 'Green Card'. The EPE card was linked to an account, which was a banking product of Moneyline Financial Services, a subsidiary of Net1, and of Grindrod Bank. It was a replica of the Sassa-branded bank card, also held with Grindrod Bank, as reflected in its applicable terms and conditions. Civil society organisations

(CSOs) collected evidence that showed that social grant beneficiaries, in particular those with loans from Moneyline, were being 'tricked' and coerced into opening an EPE bank account and being issued with a new EPE card (see Chapter 1).

A CPS employee who became a whistleblower described how this was done: 'There are three of us in a car, Moneyline car. There is this guy who's doing loans and the one that does EPE and the one that does Smart Life. So, the beneficiary will come to us for a loan, then the guy will issue the loan, but we must tell the beneficiary that we have to change his or her card (Sassa-branded Grindrod Bank account) to EasyPay. Then when he [is] finished with the EasyPay then he will come to Smart Life where he'll also [be issued with a] Smart Life policy.'[25]

When opening an EPE account, beneficiaries' funds were automatically transferred from the Sassa-branded account into their EPE account. Opening an EPE bank account was apparently viewed by Grindrod Bank, Moneyline and Net1 as an extension of the Sassa-branded Grindrod Bank account. The loophole created by CPS/Net1 was that because the EPE and Sassa-branded accounts were held at the same bank, Grindrod Bank, the accounts were linked as they would be in other commercial banks where the account holder had multiple accounts. However, unlike bank accounts at commercial banks, the switch from the Sassa to the EPE card made social grant money vulnerable to unscrupulous money lenders and could trap social grant beneficiaries in perpetual debt.

SASSA'S FUNERAL COVER CLEAN-UP PROJECT

In January 2015, Mr Frank Earl from Sassa made a presentation to the MTT about the Funeral Cover Clean-Up project (see also Chapter 3). This was followed by a second presentation in June. According to Section 26A of the regulations to the Social Assistance Act, the total deduction for a funeral policy cannot exceed 10 per cent of the value of a social grant.

It became a point of contention whether this cap on a 10 per cent deduction for a funeral policy applied to the deduction that occurred simultaneously with payment of the grant, or excluded 'debit order' deductions that occurred after a beneficiary has received the 'full' value of their grant, and made an election through informed consent to obtain additional funeral insurance policies where instalments would then be deducted by debit order.

The main aim of the project was to ensure that all funeral deductions complied with this legislation. Its broader objective included ensuring that funeral policies were accompanied by properly authorised and appropriate paperwork and offered beneficiaries value for money. The Funeral Cover Clean-Up project was in response to numerous irregularities noted in the deductions for funeral policies managed by CPS on behalf of Sassa.[26]

At the start of Sassa's Funeral Cover Clean-Up project in 2015, a total of 778 406 funeral policies were paid by direct deductions from the social grant through the CPS payment system. By the end of December, a total of 78 706 mandates had been collected by Sassa, including 3 000 new policies. Of these, a total of 164 222 were for child support grants and temporary disability grants.[27] The Black Sash and its partners presented a number of cases to the MTT to alert the government to changes needed in the system and the law.

In one such case, Sassa beneficiaries from the Franschhoek area in the Western Cape reported to the Black Sash that they were told by a representative of Emerald Wealth Management that Sassa or the Minister of Social Development expected them to take out 1Life funeral cover (1Life was the underwriter of the policies sold by Emerald Wealth Management). These company representatives ignored the many beneficiaries who said they already had funeral policies (see Chapter 1). After this was reported to Sassa through the MTT, the company reimbursed those it had signed up irregularly or apparently through misrepresentation. However, Emerald Wealth Management, which subsequently separated from 1Life, took months to comply.

The Black Sash and its partners raised other examples of blatant abuse and unethical behaviour by corporates in the insurance industry who were getting away with such practices. Together with DSD and Sassa officials, they held several meetings with the Financial Services Board (FSB).[28] However, the cases brought to the FSB's attention were not properly followed up (see Chapter 1). Two officials with whom the Black Sash had engaged left the employment of the FSB, and the FSB was also undergoing structural changes and revising its mandate at the time.

Abuse of funeral policies was highlighted in two different court applications in which the Black Sash intervened as *amicus curiae*, which played out concurrently. In one, Channel Life Limited and Sanlam Developing Markets approached the Pretoria High Court on an urgent basis to interdict Sassa from implementing certain aspects of the Funeral Cover Clean-Up project, such as requiring Channel Life and Sanlam to send notification letters to beneficiaries for the completion of mandates to expressly obtain beneficiaries' consent for their existing policies.[29] During the same period, Channel Life launched a similar application, but prior to the date of the hearing the DSD promulgated new regulations which made the Clean-Up policy requirement obligatory by law. Due to the changes in the regulations, the matter was postponed on 10 May 2016 without a future date.

In the other application, the High Court granted Lion of Africa[30] an interim interdict which temporarily halted Sassa from implementing a December 2015 moratorium on funeral insurance deductions from children's grants (see Chapter 3). The Black Sash intervened as *amicus curiae* when Sassa appealed this decision at the Constitutional Court and sought leave to have an independent actuarial report admitted into evidence.

The Black Sash was granted leave to intervene as *amicus curiae*, but the Constitutional Court declined to admit the new evidence the Black Sash sought to have admitted on appeal. The Black Sash had sought the assistance of an independent expert, Roseanna da Silva, an independent actuary and at the time head of the Actuarial Association of South Africa. Notwithstanding that her expert report was not admitted, the findings were significant. The report noted: 'I do not consider the provision of these funeral cover policies by for-profit companies to recipients of children's grants to be in the interest of the recipients of children's grants ... There is considerable market risk associated with allowing such premiums to be conducted prior to the payment of grants (intended for the cover of basic needs for children)'.[31] Ms Da Silva noted that these policies lapse

Table 2.1 Regulation 26A deductions from children's grants as at end December 2016

FSP	FCG	(FCG & CDG)	CDG	CSG	TOTAL
1Life	1 273	127	1 764	8 527	11 691
Affinity	878	27	837	29 385	31 127
Assupol	639	45	891	9 901	11 476
Channel	724	75	843	4 725	6 367
Emerald	983	60	871	26 036	27 950
Avbob	100	9	88	2 221	2 418
Guardrisk	0	1	0	3	4
Imbalenhle	45	2	26	237	310
Lifewise	0	0	0	3	3
Multisure	913	40	784	24 729	26 466
Prosperity	453	61	481	3 990	4 985
Regent	1	0	1	7	9
TransAfrica	1 369	72	1 033	38 433	40 907
Zuntal	43	2	64	400	509
TOTAL	7 421	521	7 683	148 597	164 222

Source: Third MTT Report to the Minister of Social Development, December 2016: 11
Note: FSP = financial service provider; FCG = foster care grant; CDG = child dependency grant; CSG = child support grant

when children reach 18 years of age, and that vendors stand to make large sums of money at almost pure profit, as the risk of children dying is low.

The statistics for Regulation 26A or funeral policy deductions from children's grants given in Table 2.1 show clearly how a lucrative market was created.

The financial service providers were afforded a six-month transition period to make alternative arrangements for the collection of the premiums for these policies, in line with the legislation. Deductions were due to be stopped from 31 December 2016, but due to administrative challenges, were finally halted by Sassa only in February 2017.

LOANS FROM CHILD SUPPORT GRANTS

In 2014 the National Credit Regulator (NCR) launched investigations into two Net1 subsidiaries, CPS and Moneyline. The NCR alleged that CPS and Moneyline had offered or marketed loans to social grant beneficiaries and recipients in breach of Section 68(1) of the National Credit Act (NCA) (No. 34 of 2005).[32] The National Consumer Tribunal held that as CPS was not a credit service provider, the Act did not apply, and that there were no reasonable grounds to suggest that CPS contravened Section 68(1) of the NCA.

In September 2014, the NCR announced that it had applied to the National Consumer Tribunal to cancel the registration of Moneyline for breach of the Act. The NCR pointed out that:

- Moneyline was providing credit to consumers receiving child support and foster child grants that were meant for the upkeep of children. Instead, these grants were being used as income for assessing consumers' ability to repay credit.
- Credit was granted without affordability tests being conducted or the prescribed forms and assessments being provided, and forms that were used did not contain crucial information about rights and obligations.

In a media release on 23 September 2014, the CEO of the NCR stated: 'The use of Child Support Grants and Foster Child Grants as income for purposes of conducting affordability assessments on credit applications is totally unacceptable. It deprives children of money meant to provide for their daily necessities.'[33]

Due to procedural and substantive defects, the case against CPS was unsuccessful. At the time of writing the NCR had yet to finalise the Moneyline case.

PROTECTION OF CONFIDENTIAL DATA

The re-registration of beneficiaries from 2012 using biometric capabilities to implement the Sassa/CPS contract placed confidential personal information of social grant beneficiaries and recipients (including caregivers and procurators) at the disposal of Net1 subsidiaries (see Chapter 4). The government paid for the collection and storage of information, including cell phone numbers, biometric data, and banking details, as well as the type and value of the social grant, on the proprietary database system of CPS/Net1, which Sassa was unable to access without assistance of the service provider. Access to this information together with the structure of the Sassa-branded Grindrod Bank accounts[34] enabled a plethora of unethical and unauthorised debit deductions, which may also have been fraudulent and unlawful, though this issue has not been determined by a court.

Throughout the Hoog campaign, the CPS and Net1 strongly denied using the confidential data obtained through the re-registration and ongoing registration of social grant beneficiaries. However, the grant beneficiary cases presented to the Black Sash and partners revealed that their confidential data were shared (see Chapter 1). A CPS employee, who became a whistleblower, confirmed this:

> We're using a biometric machine which is bio930 or biometric. We just put in their card and then all their information will be available for us to see who it is and then we process the policy that she or he is taking. The whole process is being done from that machine. You do all these things. You will put the card, it will tell you who the person is, how much is she getting [value of the recipient's social grant] and then it will go further [to] the steps about how much policies she or he is going to get.[35]

In correspondence to Sassa and the minister, CPS claimed it was using grant beneficiaries' confidential data obtained in terms of the Financial Intelligence Centre Act (No. 38 of 2001) registration process, and not the Sassa re-registration process. CPS (and Net1) also argued that Sassa had given it 'implicit' permission to market and sell various financial products as contained in its bid documentation and referenced in the contract.[36] This statement was disputed and denied by Sassa.

There are different laws that protect personal information (and therefore the privacy) of social grant beneficiaries and recipients. These include:

- The South African Social Security Agency (or Sassa) Act (No. 9 of 2004) allows the agency in concurrence with the Minister of Social Development to enter into contractual agreements with third parties to ensure the payment of social grants. Any agreement with such a third party must include certain terms to make sure that the partner service provider does not share any personal information of applicants or recipients of social grants without their consent or agreement. The agreement with the third party must also include fines if the terms of the agreement are not followed. The Sassa Act also protects information that is received when a person applies for a social grant application or a grant payment, benefit or assistance. Also, under the Sassa Act, a person may not disclose any information received as part of an application for a Sassa grant, payment, benefit or assistance, unless told to do so by a court or unless the person who made the application agrees in writing.

- The Social Assistance Act (No. 13 of 2004) specifically protects information about people who apply for social grants. This information is collected by Sassa and includes an applicant's name, age, nationality (or origin), physical address, financial information (including bank account details), medical information, identity number, and marital status. In terms of the Social Assistance Act, the personal information of an applicant may only be shared when instructed by a court, or when the applicant has agreed to this.

- The Protection of Personal Information Act (Popia) (No. 4 of 2013), and the regulations published under it, comprehensively protect the personal information of people (also called 'data subjects') by limiting when and how that information may be 'processed', including the collection, holding, use, sharing or transferring of information by the person in control of it (called a 'responsible party'). In other words, the Popia sets out what personal information is, how it can be used, and what can be done to protect people whose personal information is being used to exploit them by stealing or unlawfully using their information, particularly where they have not given consent.[37]

The Popia only became law in 2013, and therefore was not in full effect at the start of the Sassa/CPS contract. Only certain provisions were in force. Final regulations were published under the Popia in December 2018.[38]

The Social Assistance and Sassa Acts were further strengthened by two court judgments confirming Sassa's duty to protect the personal information of social grant beneficiaries:

- The judgment in *AllPay 1*[39] in 2014 is clear about the protection of confidential data: personal data obtained in the payment process remains private and may not be used in any manner for any purpose other than payment of the grants or any other purpose sanctioned by the minister in terms of Section 20(3) and (4) of the Social Assistance Act (see Chapter 3).
- In the 2017 Black Sash judgment the Constitutional Court ordered Sassa to protect the confidential data of grant beneficiaries: 'It is declared that SASSA is under a duty to ensure that the payment method it determines: 10.1 contains adequate safeguards to ensure that personal data obtained in the payment process remains private and may not be used for any purpose other than payment of the grants or any other purpose sanctioned by the minister in terms of section 20(3) and (4) of the Social Assistance Act'.[40]

The Constitutional Court judgment was an important victory for the Hoog campaign because the Information Regulator took the Black Sash court order as a mandate to intervene and ensure that Sassa and its service providers put in place measures to protect the confidential data of social grant beneficiaries.[41]

Subsequently, when the Sassa/CPS contract was granted a one-year extension in 2017, CPS as a third party also agreed to the provision protecting the confidential data of social grant beneficiaries. An addendum was signed between Sassa and CPS and between Net1 and Grindrod Bank to this effect.

The judgments and the Information Regulator's intervention had a significant impact on the provisions for the protection of confidential data in the contract with the new service paymaster, the South African Post Office (Sapo) in 2018. This included the creation of a ring-fenced Sassa Special Disbursement (bank) Account which does not permit debit or stop orders or USSD platform deductions.

Since 1 April 2018, CPS has not registered social grant beneficiaries or assisted them with the opening of bank accounts, which has effectively denied the Net1 cohort future access to the confidential data of grant beneficiaries. However, in November 2019, Moneyline, together with 14 EPE account holders, launched a legal case in the North Gauteng High Court[42] against Sassa requiring it to approve its biometric authorisation process, rather than the required Annexure C form that was submitted in respect of the EPE account.[43] The Panel of Experts appointed by the Constitutional Court in the Black Sash case only found 42 000 Annexure C forms, yet Sassa transferred social grant funds into more than a million EPE bank accounts each month from 2018. This was in violation of Section 21 of the Social Assistance Act regulations which requires a social grant beneficiary to submit an Annexure C form to Sassa giving Moneyline permission to pay their social grant into a private bank account. Moneyline and the beneficiaries subsequently withdrew their case.

To date, Net1 and Grindrod Bank have retained grant beneficiaries' confidential data collected during the period of the 2012 to 2017 Sassa contract, citing Banking Act 14 as justification. Although 80 per cent of the eligible 12 million social grant recipients have a Sassa/Sapo Special Disbursement Account, there are still those using the Grindrod Bank EPE account, and its subsidiaries and other companies in their network continue to profit from the beneficiaries' confidential information.

RECOURSE (BENEFICIARY PAYMENT DISPUTE RESOLUTION MECHANISM)

In a presentation to Minister Dlamini on 26 February 2014, the Black Sash and its partners noted: 'Seeking recourse for unlawful and unauthorised debit deductions is often difficult and with no success and has become the responsibility and onus of the grant beneficiary at considerable cost to themselves.'[44]

CPS's contract and SLA with Sassa had placed CPS almost fully in control of the social grant payment system. It had also allowed CPS (and Net1) to be both implementer and arbitrator, in that it both paid social grants *and* received and resolved complaints of allegedly unlawful and/or fraudulent debit and USSD deductions from the Sassa-branded Grindrod Bank accounts, usually done by companies affiliated to its parent company, Net1. Social grant beneficiaries, particularly in the rural areas, were obliged to self-fund their access to the recourse system, because they paid travelling costs to and from the Sassa office and telephone/airtime costs, which rendered recourse inaccessible for many. They had little success using the toll-free numbers allocated for queries and complaints (see Chapter 1).

In 2014, a first objective set by the MTT was to develop and finalise a Sassa-owned and controlled recourse system to deal effectively with allegedly unlawful and/or fraudulent debt deductions. The first MTT report to the Minister of Social Development also suggests that the system inventors and enablers (CPS, Net1, Grindrod Bank and Sassa) take responsibility for the risk exposure for social grant recipients and repay the deducted amounts in full, with interest and bank charges, that had occurred since the contract came into effect in 2012.[45]

By 2015 the MTT was no closer to a viable solution, even with the minister's public support for ensuring recourse and refunds for beneficiaries and recipients. The 2015 MTT report outlined how complex the issue of recourse was becoming. There were two views: Sassa argued that it was unable to stop debit orders from the Sassa-branded Grindrod Bank account by Net1 subsidiaries (that is, Moneyline, Smart Life and Manje Mobile) because the debit orders were authorised within the

National Payment System. Civil society organisations disputed this based on grassroots case studies which showed that often recipients did not know what the unexplained debit deduction was for or had not given consent for the deduction. Many grant recipients did not understand why their confidential and personal data, including biometric data, were in the hands of the Net1 subsidiaries. The CPS whistleblower confirmed this, saying:

> In some other areas, the guys that were reaching their targets it's because when a beneficiary comes to them for the loan, the loan guy (Moneyline) will issue the loan then pass the card to the one that is doing EasyPay cards and when he had finished he will then pass it to the one that is doing Smart Life policies without the client knowing it. He has been doing all these three things at one time.

> When he walks out [of] there he's got the EasyPay card and the [funeral] insurance policy without even knowing that … These machines that we are using are having (sic) the whole information. You just put in the card and then you will see his or her information. That's it.[46]

At least two MTT meetings, in February and June 2015, dealt with the conceptual framework of the Beneficiary Payment Dispute Resolution Mechanism (BPDRM), also referred to as recourse. The recourse document went through various iterations. During this process, civil society organisations (CSOs) continually provided feedback from beneficiaries' lived experiences of attempting to obtain recourse through grassroots monitoring and case studies.[47] Grant beneficiaries were sent from pillar to post between Sassa officials, CPS staff, the South African Police Services and other statutory bodies in their often fruitless attempts to secure recourse.

Advantages of the new BPDRM included, firstly, that Sassa officials could log disputes. It could also report on debit deduction complaints and hopefully would be able to provide figures and reports

Table 2.2 Disputes logged from January to December 2016

Type	Jan	Feb	Mar	Apr	May	Jun	Jul	Aug	Sep	Oct	Nov	Dec	Total
Funeral insurance	46	59	60	46	51	42	64	195	163	197	133	130	1 186
EFT (loans HP & others)	59	34	85	69	85	63	68	39	73	86	210	65	936
Electricity	1 850	1 728	1 679	2 041	2 106	250	89	204	382	54	85	10	10 478
Airtime	5 637	6 900	4 578	8 389	6 759	3 408	2 294	2 143	2 159	1 636	1 314	1 127	46 344
ATM	423	322	332	562	242	416	558	387	442	390	754	417	5 245
Airtime & Electricity	0	12 466	7 001	4 477	7 813	2 072	1 690	1 115	1 532	1 776	1 118	507	41 567
Total logged	8 015	21 509	13 735	15 584	17 056	6 251	4 763	4 083	4 751	4 139	3 614	2 256	105 756
Outstanding affidavits (Manje)	2 450	4 078	6 689	11 504	13 636	730	3 236	2 801	3 129	2 412	1 579	1 246	53 489
Refunds (Manje)	0	1 732	1 189	1 362	1 502	4 629	207	177	458	0	0	0	11 256
Non-refunds (Manje)	0	60	105	91	866	521	690	621	486	547	132	183	4 302
Pending investigation (Manje)	0	0	0	0	0	0	0	0	0	507	806	215	1 528
Pending investigation (Other)	5 565	15 639	5 752	2 627	1 052	371	630	484	678	673	1 097	612	35 180

Source: Second MTT Report to Minister, 2015

independently from CPS. However, at the time Sassa still relied heavily on CPS to provide the figures, and as Table 2.2 shows, CPS was able to delay matters by logging many complaints for further investigation or further documentation.

A total of 105 756 cases were logged from January to December 2016, but these were often disputed for various reasons: calls to register disputes were often dropped, information was lost and CPS/Net1 conducted their own investigations, all of which effectively frustrated recipients and prevented them from getting recourse. Of these logged disputes, the largest number relate to disputes over airtime (46 344) while the combination of prepaid electricity and airtime follows closely with 41 567 disputes.

The BPDRM was signed in August 2015 and a pilot training course for Sassa officials commenced in the Western Cape, with civil society organisations in attendance. However, the implementation of the new recourse system was still wanting, with ongoing and preventable hardship experienced by many beneficiaries.

For example, Sassa agreed to a toll-free number for both landlines and cell phones. However, the toll-free number was not actually free to beneficiaries using cell phones (the running of additional airtime costs would kick in once the recipients' airtime was depleted), and those without landlines continued to carry the financial burden of accessing the recourse system. There was also confusion about the respective roles of Sassa and CPS officials in the recourse system, with the latter still very dominant. This problem was compounded by the fact that Sassa officials were often not present and did not wear uniforms or name tags that distinguished them from CPS staff.

CSOs were of the view that while preliminary steps had been taken, the situation was far from the Sassa-owned and controlled recourse system envisaged, which was intended to be a 'one stop shop' where beneficiaries were treated with dignity and enjoyed administrative justice. For as long as the existing CPS contract was in place, unauthorised and allegedly unlawful deductions would continue. Most recipients found that deductions stopped when the Sassa/Sapo ring-fenced bank account was introduced from July 2018 and Sapo took over aspects of the social grant payment function. Drawing on the experience of the CPS contract, Sassa designed its own recourse system, with substantive input from the Black Sash and partners.

THE INSPECTORATE

The establishment of an Inspectorate was another key demand of the Black Sash and partners in a memorandum tabled at the first MTT meeting with Minister Dlamini in February 2014. The Social Assistance Act (No. 13 of 2004) defines the mandate of the Inspectorate as follows:

- Conduct investigations to ensure the maintenance of the integrity of the social assistance frameworks and systems.
- Execute internal financial audits and audits on compliance by the agency with regulatory and policy measures and instruments.
- Investigate fraud, corruption and other forms of financial and service management and criminal activity within the agency and in connection with its functions, duties and operations.
- Establish a complaints mechanism.
- In general, do everything necessary to combat abuse of social assistance.

While Sassa has a unit that investigates fraud, it cannot be both administrator and arbitrator, particularly regarding unauthorised, unethical and/or allegedly unlawful debit deductions. The Comprehensive Social Security branch of the DSD was tasked with developing a conceptual framework for the operations. A business plan with a budget and high-level strategies was developed. Preparations were undertaken, including the appointment of three chief directors who commenced duty on 1 October 2015. In several MTT meetings the DSD reported on progress in establishing the Inspectorate.

However, when the DSD attempted to operationalise the Inspectorate, it discovered that chapter 4 of the Social Assistance Act made provision for a fully-fledged government department, not a unit within the department. The Act would therefore require an amendment to accommodate a unit within the DSD. A legal opinion was sought from the State Law Advisor and an independent lawyer on whether the president could proclaim an amendment to chapter 4 without necessarily starting a new department, but both opinions suggested that this option may not be feasible.

At the time of writing this book, the Social Assistance Amendment Act (No. 16 of 2020) had been adopted by Parliament and proclaimed by the president, but the Inspectorate has still not been fully established. The legislation has been amended to allow the Inspectorate to be a government component within the DSD. The Black Sash and partners will continue to monitor developments and advocate for appropriate implementation.

LAW REFORM

The Declarator

By May 2015, discussions around the need for the DSD and Sassa to seek declaratory relief on legally permissible deductions had gained new momentum when it became increasingly apparent that Sassa was no closer to appointing a new service provider for the payment of social grants.

In correspondence with Sassa and Minister Dlamini, CPS asserted that the social grant is deemed paid when the money is transferred to the Sassa-branded Grindrod Bank account. It claimed that from this point, banking regulations supersede social security legislative frameworks. CPS asserted that neither Sassa nor CPS has any further obligation to grant recipients beyond the transfer of funds. In other words, what happens to the funds in the bank account is the responsibility of the account holder. This assertion was disputed by the DSD, Sassa and civil society organisations, who had additional concerns surrounding the manner and prevalence of seemingly unauthorised debit order deductions after payment of the grant.

Changes to the regulations to the Social Assistance Act

Another option to stop these contentious debit deductions from Sassa-branded Grindrod Bank accounts into which social grants were paid was to introduce changes to the regulations to the Social Assistance Act. Two sections were targeted, namely:

1. Stopping all other deductions made by debit order and unstructured supplementary service data (USSD) platforms off the Sassa grant payment system by amending Regulation 21 to limit deductions from the Sassa payment method.
2. Tightening the control of deductions made in terms of Regulation 26A for funeral insurance policies.

The following amendment was accepted and introduced: Deductions from child support and temporary grants are not permissible. This regulation seeks to limit funeral policy deductions, such as the old age pension and permanent disability grants, to adult grants only.

Clause 21 of the regulations to the Social Assistance Act deals with payment methods. It declares that the payment method provided by Sassa may not allow for any other deductions. An example of this is the Sassa/Sapo Special Disbursement Account. In May 2016, the minister promulgated an amendment to Regulations 21 and 26A seeking to limit permissible deductions.

The minister approved the amendments to the regulations to the Social Assistance Act on 28 April 2016 and the new regulations were published in the Government Gazette on 6 May 2016. Sassa wrote to CPS/Net1 to implement the new regulations, particularly Regulation 21. Subsequently the DSD and Sassa laid charges against CPS at the Sunnyside Police Station in Pretoria for non-compliance with the new regulations to the Social Assistance Act, which they later withdrew. This precipitated the launch of a suite of cases by Net1 and its subsidiaries.

Grant beneficiaries were given six months to make alternative arrangements for existing funeral policy deductions off children's and temporary grants. The new policy came into effect on 1 December 2016.

This would allow Sassa sufficient time to bring the amendments to the attention of caregivers and recipients of temporary grants, as well as giving them adequate time to make alternative arrangements. In June 2016, Net1 subsidiaries, including Moneyline, Manje Mobile and Smart Life and two other commercial companies, Information Technology and Finbond Mutual Bank, launched four court cases against the DSD, Sassa and others. The Applicants also cited Sarb, Pasa and Grindrod Bank as Respondents. In summary, the Net1 cohort argued that:

- The Sassa-branded Grindrod Bank account could not be viewed as a Sassa method of payment as envisaged in Regulation 21(1)(b) and must not be restricted.
- The Minister of Social Development had no jurisdiction over the electronic payment system (held by Sarb).
- The May 2016 Social Assistance Act regulations should be set aside as unconstitutional and invalid.

The minister and Sassa's consideration of seeking declaratory relief on the legality of deductions was overtaken by the funeral insurance policy court cases outlined in the description of the Sassa Clean-Up project, as well by this Net1 group of cases being heard in the North Gauteng High Court in October 2016 (see Chapter 3).

THE GAME OF INSOURCING AND OUTSOURCING

In the 2014 *AllPay* case, the Constitutional Court had declared that Sassa had to initiate a new tender process for the payment of social grants nationally or take over the payment of social grants, which the MTT believed would stop the allegedly unlawful debit deductions. In its first report to Minister Dlamini, the MTT noted that this was 'a small window of opportunity' for reviewing the tender specifications to include ring-fenced bank accounts that ensure that social grant beneficiary bank accounts are protected from fraudulent and immoral debit deductions and protecting the personal data of grant recipients obtained in the payment and re-registration processes by CPS.[48]

However, at the beginning of 2015, almost two years into the CPS contract, Sassa was no closer to appointing a new service provider. The Black Sash joined the *AllPay 2* case as *amicus curiae*, asking specifically for timeframes. In March 2015, the Constitutional Court ruled that the appointment of the new Sassa service provider must be made by the end of October 2015.

CPS used the development of the new tender specifications, supervised by the Constitutional Court, to register several objections, some of which were valid, while others were viewed as tactics to delay the tender process. The ring-fenced bank account and the protection of confidential data entrusted to third parties remained contentious for the CPS/Net1 cohort. In May 2015, the specifications were finalised and issued by Sassa. CPS/Net1 announced that it would not submit a bid for the new Sassa tender as the new contract was not commercially viable.[49]

In November 2015, Sassa's Acting Chief Executive Officer informed the Constitutional Court that the agency would not award the tender for the payment of social grants.[50] Sassa also presented the Constitutional Court with an eight-page document briefly outlining its intentions to insource the national payment of grants between March 2016 and March 2017. The CPS contract would therefore remain in place for the rest of the five-year contract period, which ended on 30 March 2017, and so these disputed debit order deductions continued.

With the tender process concluded, CSOs within the MTT shifted their focus to the insourcing of grant payments to Sassa. During this period, civil society struggled to obtain information from Sassa on the new social grant payment model. By September 2016, almost a year later, Sassa had failed to deliver an insourcing plan. The Black Sash and its civil society partners wrote a letter to the minister to intervene to ensure that:

- The outsourcing plan, with clear timeframes, was delivered by the next meeting of the MTT on 26 September 2016.
- Sassa developed and implemented a new payment system by the end of the CPS contract on 30 March 2017 that ensured that the full cash value of social grants was paid into the beneficiaries' Sassa bank accounts.

In response to the letter from the Black Sash, Sassa indicated that it was not ready to present the insourced grant payment model, and that it would consult with civil society as an important interest group when it was ready. The letter also stated that in June 2016 Sassa had appointed work streams to assist the organisation in implementing the Ministerial Advisory Committee's recommendations on the future grant payment system.

An article in the media published at that time reported that the contract with CPS may be extended for a further period of between 18 months and two years.[51] Not only was CPS keen to extend the existing contract but also to increase the pricing.[52]

On 30 November 2016, Sassa and the DSD made a presentation to the Parliamentary Portfolio Committee for Social Development on the insourcing of the national payment of social grants and the future payment model. Various questions were raised by members of the committee about Sassa's readiness to take over the payment of social grants when the CPS contract ended and whether Sassa envisaged an extension of the CPS contract beyond 31 March 2017 (see Chapter 6).

In February 2017, Sassa and the DSD advised Parliament that they intended to extend the CPS contract by another year, ending in March 2018. At the time it became apparent that Sassa and the DSD were nowhere near the conceptualisation or implementation of a new social grant payment model. The Black Sash (as co-chair of the MTT) sent a letter to the minister requesting that an update be given on Sassa's progress regard the taking over of grant payments – a request that was declined. The Black Sash was then compelled to approach the Constitutional Court on an urgent basis, seeking direct access, to ensure that beneficiaries would receive their social grants come 1 April 2017, and the Black Sash launched its litigation against Sassa and the DSD in February 2017. At that point, the MTT disbanded abruptly and did not meet again.

That marked the close of the work of the MTT. Three MTT reports were developed, of which two were tabled with the minister. The MTT had lasted for approximately three years and ended abruptly in February 2017 when the Black Sash instituted court proceedings against the Minister of Social Development and the CEO of Sassa.

In this phase, the Black Sash and its civil society partners worked in tandem with the minister, the DSD and Sassa, as well as with the MTT. An array of options was explored to halt the unauthorised, unethical, and allegedly unlawful and/or fraudulent deductions from beneficiaries' grants, with varying success.

3 The Hoog campaign's strategic litigation

The right to social security for vulnerable people in need is entrenched in the post-apartheid Constitution, and in recognition of South Africa's international law obligations. While the numbers of social grant beneficiaries have grown exponentially since democracy, these gains, such as they are, have been under attack. The award of a government tender to a private company to distribute social grants has demonstrated a lucrative market to target products to social grant beneficiaries. While social grants were being depleted on an astronomical scale, government was slow to wake up and respond to the crisis. The state's efforts were met by a series of legal challenges opposing its clean up attempts and resisting legislative amendments.

The Black Sash and civil society stepped in. This chapter covers the litigation the Black Sash was involved in between 2013 and 2019 to protect the meagre social security provided by the government to people in poverty, to seek to protect their right to social security under the Constitution, and to protect them from the nefarious practices of private businesses.

As we have seen in earlier chapters, the integrity of South Africa's social grant system came under fire, firstly, from government, due to the instability and uncertainty regarding the administration of the payment of social grants. Secondly, from the private sector exploiting grant beneficiaries by depleting their grants in order to make enormous profits. This chapter covers the litigation the Black Sash intervened in and initiated as part of its broader advocacy strategies in partnership with other civil society organisations and grant beneficiaries. The Black Sash did not enter into litigation lightly, given that it considers it a last resort, as it is for many social justice organisations, due to the limitations of litigation alone as an advocacy strategy, and because it can be extremely expensive. It comes with the risk of devastating and crippling costs orders. The long timeframes involved while matters work their way through the system are also challenging for maintaining the momentum of campaigns. However, over the years the Black Sash has deployed litigation as a strategy alongside popular mass mobilisation, advocacy at both local and national levels, and a focused media strategy.

When it has engaged in litigation, the Black Sash has assumed the roles of applicant, respondent, *amicus curiae* (a friend of the court) or an intervening party in different cases at different times in pursuit of defending the right to social security. In the Hoog campaign, the Black Sash both opposed the Minister of Social Development when necessary and acted in support of government against companies that exploited grant beneficiaries. In contrast to the typical client and attorney roles, the Black Sash worked closely with the Centre for Applied Legal Studies (Cals) at the University of the Witwatersrand as its legal representatives and partner in pursuit of the Black Sash's objectives and those of Cals' Rule of Law and Business and Human Rights programmes. Some of the legal cases are outlined in this chapter.

The starting point must be the *AllPay 1* case, which challenged the way the government sought to consolidate differing provincial payouts into one national private service provider, and the challenges that have ensued. Sassa, as the organ of state responsible for the payment of grants, concluded a five-year contract with a private entity, CPS, in 2012 to provide services for the payment of grants. This contract was mired in controversy since its inception and was ultimately declared constitutionally invalid by the Constitutional Court, although the declaration of invalidity was suspended, requiring Sassa to award a new contract following a proper procurement process, or take over the payment of grants itself from 1 April 2017 when the suspended contract would expire.

The litigation described below is divided into two themes: the uncertainty of payment and the profitability of exploiting the poor.

AllPay Consolidated Investment Holdings (Pty) Ltd and Others v Chief Executive Officer of the South African Social Security Agency and Others (CCT 48/13) [2013] ZACC 42 (Date of Hearing: 10 September 2013; Date of Judgment: 29 November 2013)

Litigation started soon after Sassa signed its controversial contract with CPS in 2012. The *AllPay 1* case dealt with whether the awarded tender by Sassa to CPS for the countrywide payment of social grants was constitutionally valid. The case was brought by AllPay Consolidated Investment Holdings (Pty) Ltd (AllPay), an unsuccessful bidder, who argued that there were several irregularities in the procurement process and therefore the tender was constitutionally invalid. It called for a judicial review of the decision to award CPS the tender. The review application was initially heard in the North Gauteng High Court in Pretoria. The high court declared the tender process invalid, but declined to set the award aside because of the upheaval that would have resulted if the distribution of social grants to millions of beneficiaries was suddenly disrupted.

The matter then went to the Supreme Court of Appeal (SCA) which subsequently dismissed the appeal and found that there were no unlawful irregularities in the procurement process that were fatal to the contract entered into by Sassa and CPS.

AllPay then took the matter on appeal to the Constitutional Court asking it to determine:

- The proper legal approach that ought to be followed in determining whether a procurement process ought to be nullified.
- How the alleged irregularities in the procurement process fared against the above-mentioned proper legal process.

The Constitutional Court granted AllPay leave to appeal as the matter was of public interest and national importance. Regarding the proper legal approach that ought to have been followed by the SCA in adjudicating the matter, the Constitutional Court ruled that the fairness and lawfulness of a procurement process must be assessed in terms of the Promotion of Administrative Justice Act (No. 3 of 2000) (or Paja) and must be treated independently from the outcome of the tender process. Paja provided the constitutional and legislative procurement framework that determined which supply chain management prescripts are legally binding. If the application of Paja determines that the affected decision or conduct is unlawful, a just and equitable order must be made.

The Court held that there were two irregularities in the procurement process:

1. Sassa failed to ensure that the black economic empowerment credentials claimed by CPS were confirmed. The Court held that given the fundamental importance of redistributive policies to South Africa's constitutional democracy, Sassa's failure to ensure that CPS's claimed black economic empowerment credentials were objectively confirmed was fatally defective. Accordingly, the failure to make that objective determination fell afoul of Section 6(2)(b) of Paja (non-compliance with a mandatory and material condition) and Section 6(2)(c)(iii) of Paja (failure to consider a relevant consideration).

2. The second material irregularity was the Bidder's Notice 2 issued by Sassa, which failed to clearly specify what was required of bidders in relation to biometric verification. The consequence of this was that only CPS proceeded to the second stage of the procurement process. This rendered the process uncompetitive.

Moreover, the Bidder's Notice 2 also changed the weight given to bids that were able to provide biometric verification during the payment of social grants from a 'preferential requirement' to a 'mandatory requirement'. Thus, the requirements of Section 3(2)(b) of Paja (adequate notice of the nature and purpose of the proposed administrative action) were also not met. The purpose of a tender is not to reward bidders who are clever enough to decipher unclear directions. It is to elicit the best solution through a process that is fair and transparent. Because of the uncertainty caused by the wording of the request for proposals (RFP) and Bidders Notice 2, that purpose was not achieved.

For these reasons, the Court set aside the order of the SCA and declared the award of the tender to CPS constitutionally invalid. Despite this, the Court suspended the declaration of invalidity pending the parties' oral representations on 11 February 2014. In its judgment, the Constitutional Court made the important point that for many people in South Africa, the payment of social grants by the state provides the only hope of ensuring the constitutional values of dignity, freedom and equality. At the time, more than 16 million people depended on social grants.[1] These were the most vulnerable, living at the margins of society.

The outcome of this case was found to be a matter of national importance and public interest because procurement so palpably implicates socioeconomic rights that the public has an interest in it being conducted in a fair, equitable, transparent, competitive, and cost-effective manner.

AllPay Consolidated Investment Holdings (Pty) Ltd and Others v Chief Executive Officer of the South African Social Security Agency and Others (No. 2) (CCT 48/13) [2014] ZACC 12 (Date of Hearing: 11 February 2014; Date of Judgment: 17 April 2014)

This aspect dealt with the remedy for the Constitutional Court's decision to declare the tender awarded by Sassa to CPS for the payment of social grants constitutionally invalid. As we have seen above, the declaration of invalidity of the contract was based on two grounds. The first was that Sassa failed to ensure that the black economic empowerment credentials claimed by CPS were confirmed. The second was that the Bidder's Notice 2 issued by Sassa did not clearly specify what was required of the bidders in relation to biometric verification. This rendered the process uncompetitive and Sassa's decision was set aside because it failed to comply with various sections of Paja.

The Constitutional Court suspended the declaration of invalidity and ruled that a just and equitable remedy would be the correction and reversal of the invalid administrative action. In making this order, the Court relied on Section 172(1)(b)(ii) of the Constitution, which gives the Court the power to grant 'an order suspending the declaration of invalidity for any period and on any authority to correct the defect'.

Moreover, the Court reasoned that this remedy was just and equitable because it prohibited CPS from simply walking away from the contract.

As an organ of state, Sassa is required to administer social assistance in terms of the Social Assistance Act (No. 13 of 2004) and to respect, protect, promote, and fulfil the rights in the Bill of Rights. In terms of this contract the Court found that CPS exercised a public power and performed a public function in terms of the Act, enacted to give effect to the right to social security. The CPS therefore played a unique and central role as gatekeeper of the right to social security and effectively controlled beneficiaries' access to social assistance. Therefore, CPS had not only contractual obligations, but a constitutional duty to ensure that a workable payment system remained in place until a new one was operational. Therefore, despite the suspension, the contract remained operational and CPS remained bound to its contractual and constitutional obligations.

Similarly, the contract did not divest Sassa of its constitutional responsibility and public accountability for rendering public services. It remained accountable to the people of South Africa for the performance of those functions by the CPS. The Court exercised its wide remedial powers to ensure effective relief for a breach of a constitutional right by imposing a structural interdict requiring Sassa to report back to the Court at each of the crucial stages of the new tender process. Furthermore, the Court also ruled that although any invalidation of the existing contract as a result of the invalid tender should not result in any loss to CPS, the converse was also true. CPS had no right to benefit from an allegedly invalid contract, and any benefit that it may have derived should not be beyond public scrutiny. Considering its public power and functions in the execution of the contract, CPS ought to be publicly accountable for any gains or losses made under the now invalid contract. CPS was thus directed to provide financial information to show when the break-even point arrived, and at which point it started making a profit in terms of the allegedly invalid contract.

On 17 April 2014, the Court therefore made the following order:

1. The contract for the payment of social grants between Sassa and CPS dated 3 February 2012 is declared invalid.

2. This declaration is suspended pending the decision of Sassa to award a new tender after completion of the tender process ordered in paragraph 3 below.

3. Sassa must initiate a new tender process for the payment of social grants within 30 days of this order:

    3.1 The request for proposals for the new tender must, in addition to any other requirements that Sassa is entitled to prescribe, contain adequate safeguards to ensure that:

    (a) if any re-registration process is required, no loss of lawful existing social grants occurs;

    (b) the payment of lawful existing grants is not interrupted; and

    (c) personal data obtained in the payment process remains private and may not be used in any manner for any purpose other than payment of the grants or any other purpose sanctioned by the minister in terms of Section 20(3) and (4) of the Social Assistance Act.

    3.2 The new tender must be for a period of five years.

    3.3 A new and independent Bid Evaluation Committee and Bid Adjudication Committee must be appointed to evaluate and adjudicate the new tender process. Their evaluation and adjudication must be made public by filing with the Registrar of this Court a status report on the first Monday of every quarter of the year until completion of the process.

4. If the tender is not awarded, the declaration of invalidity of the contract will be further suspended until completion of the five-year period for which the contract was initially awarded:

4.1 Within 14 days of the decision not to award the tender, Sassa must lodge a report with the Registrar of this Court setting out all the relevant information on whether and when it will be ready to assume the duty to pay grants itself.

4.2 Within 60 days of the completion of the five-year period for which the contract was initially awarded, CPS must file with this Court an audited statement of the expenses it has incurred, the income received, and the net profit earned under the completed contract.

4.3 Sassa must within 60 days thereafter obtain an independent audited verification of the details provided by CPS and file the audited verification with the Constitutional Court.

Sassa initiated a new bidding process for the payment of social grants in 2014, but this process was slow-moving. CPS took issue with some of the specifications in the RFP which it considered would make the tender commercially unviable. The first was the price: Sassa had stipulated a maximum fee of R14.50 per recipient per month, an 11.8 per cent decrease in the fee charged by CPS at the time. The second was the biometric (proof of life) requirement, which CPS initially approached the courts to have Sassa revise. The third issue was that a ring-fenced bank account – without debit orders or USSD platform payments – would completely stop automatic payments to Net1 subsidiaries for financial services from social grants.

The Black Sash joined the *AllPay* case as *amicus curiae* when it became evident that there had been very little compliance with the Court's ruling and Sassa had not initiated a new tender process for the payment of social grants within 30 days, as stipulated by the Court. The Black Sash sought relief on three main issues relating to the bidding process: a declaration that the RFP (as it exists or with specified amendments) is valid; a declaration preventing parties from approaching the Constitutional Court for further relief unless it is necessary to protect the interests of beneficiaries; and a timeline for the finalisation of the new tender. The Black Sash hoped to ensure that the new bidding process was concluded as soon as possible and that the irregular deductions from grants be curtailed. The Constitutional Court addressed the various issues raised by the different parties and the RFP was revised and reissued on 24 March 2015.

On 5 November 2015, Sassa filed a progress report to the Constitutional Court informing it of the outcome of the tender process and outlining the steps that Sassa proposed to take over the payment function itself after 31 March 2017. Neither CPS nor AllPay submitted tender proposals. In the end the tender was not awarded to any of the other three submitting bidders. Two bidders were disqualified for not meeting the biometric requirement and the last bidder, Standard Bank, was excluded for providing a bid that was above the ceiling price. On 25 November, the Court issued an order indicating that it was satisfied with the proposal put forward by Sassa to take over the payment of grants and the Court discharged its supervisory jurisdiction over Sassa, as it was no longer viewed as necessary.

What ought to have followed was a payment system which would be operated in-house by Sassa and ready to get off the ground by April 2017, as Sassa had undertaken to the Constitutional Court when it discharged its supervisory role.

THE UNCERTAINTY OF PAYMENT

A new tender was not awarded during the period of the invalid contract, nor was Sassa in a position to take over the payment of social grants by 1 April 2017. By as late as February 2017, Sassa had no lawful plan to ensure the more than 16 million beneficiaries would receive their grants on 1 April 2017. This was widely reported in the media, acknowledged by Parliament, and later confirmed by the Court as a national crises, with the Court holding that 'it is difficult to conceive of a matter more urgent on a national scale'.[2]

Black Sash Trust (Freedom Under Law Intervening) v Minister of Social Development and Others CCT 48/17 – A (Date of Hearing: 15 March 2017; Date of Judgment: 17 March 2017)

In February 2017, the Black Sash urgently approached the Constitutional Court seeking direct access when it became apparent that Sassa had failed to put in place a mechanism to ensure social grants would be paid on 1 April 2017 when the contract with CPS expired, putting millions of beneficiaries at risk of not receiving their grants. The Black Sash requested the Court to make an order to ensure that Sassa complied with its constitutional obligation to provide social assistance to the beneficiaries of social grants.

On the same day that the Black Sash launched its application, Sassa eventually filed its own application in the Constitutional Court, seeking the Court's approval for an extension of the CPS contract, notwithstanding its undertakings to the Court two years before that it would be able to take over the payment of grants. Sassa subsequently withdrew its application two days later, ostensibly on the instructions of the minister, an indication of the internal conflict at the time between Sassa and the minister.

The Black Sash's application for direct access to the Constitutional Court was granted, and Freedom Under Law was permitted to intervene. Corruption Watch and the South African Post Office (Sapo) were admitted as *amici curiae*.

The Constitutional Court held that the threatened breach of the right to social security of the beneficiaries engaged the Court's remedial power to make a just and equitable order under Section 172(1)(b) of the Constitution. In exercising this power, and to avoid the impending crisis, on 17 March 2017 the Constitutional Court extended the suspension of the declaration of invalidity (in *AllPay*) of the contract between Sassa and CPS for an additional 12 months, ending on 31 March 2018, on the same commercial terms.[3]

In addition, the Court resumed its supervisory role, ordering Sassa to file, at first, quarterly, and later, monthly reports to a Panel of Experts to ensure that the payment of social grants would not be disrupted after the expiry of the suspension period. Sassa was also ordered to formulate a contingency plan to be implemented should it be unable to finalise a new regime for the payment of social grants before 1 April 2018.

The Constitutional Court had agreed to all of the demands made by the Black Sash and took the further extraordinary step of directing the establishment of a Panel of Experts under the auspices of the Auditor-General to receive reports from Sassa and provide oversight. The parties were called on to nominate and agree to the proposed experts. Not only was the Constitutional Court's oversight over CPS's extended contract with Sassa and the implementation of the grant payment system reinstated, but the Court also asserted that the confidential data of social grant beneficiaries must be protected. An addendum was added to the contract signed between Sassa and CPS/Net1 which purported to protected beneficiaries' confidential data, although Net1 subsidiaries continue to benefit from this data. The Black Sash remained committed to an in-house payment system, and the creation of a protected and ring-fenced Sassa bank account, free of deductions, including debit orders and USSD platforms by third parties.

Black Sash Trust v Minister of Social Development and Others (Freedom Under Law NPC Intervening) (CCT48/17 B) [2017] ZACC 20 (Date of Hearing: 10 May 2017; Date of Judgement: 15 June 2017)

In the matter above, the Court considered whether costs should be made against the erstwhile Minister of Social Development, Ms Bathabile Dlamini, in her personal capacity, for any role she might have played in the social grants saga. The minister was called upon to show cause in an affidavit why she should not be joined to the proceedings in her personal capacity and why she should not be ordered to pay the costs of the application out of her own pocket.

After considering all the further affidavits filed by former Minister Dlamini, the CEO of Sassa, Mr Thokozani Magwaza, and the Director-General of the Department of Social Development (DSD), Mr Zane Dangor, the Court had to decide on two issues, namely whether the minister ought to be joined in the proceedings and whether a costs order should be granted against the minister.

On the question of joinder, the Court held that there was a compelling reason for the minister to be joined in her personal capacity since there was a possibility of a personal costs order against her. The Court reasoned that joining her to the proceedings would give her an opportunity to advance reasons why a costs order should not be granted against her.

On the issue of the costs order, the Court clarified that personal costs orders against people acting in a representative capacity were based on conduct that was motivated by bad faith or gross negligence. The Court further reasoned that costs orders against state officials in their personal capacities were grounded in the values of accountability and responsiveness that founded our constitutional democracy. The basic values and principles governing public administration include: the promotion and maintenance of a high standard of professional ethics; the promotion of efficient, economic, and effective use of resources; public administration must be development-orientated; people's needs must be responded to; public administration must be accountable; and transparency must be fostered by providing the public with timely, accessible, and accurate information. Members of the executive are responsible for powers and functions delegated to them by the President and must therefore act in accordance with the Constitution.

The affidavits revealed that when Sassa had become aware that it would not be able to meet the 1 April 2017 Court-ordered deadline to award a new tender for the payment of social grants to another service provider, it obtained legal advice to approach the Court to request directions as to whether it wished to resume its supervisory jurisdiction. That legal opinion was received on 10 June 2016, but the then minister averred that she only saw it after October 2016. There was no indication in the minister's affidavit what, if anything, she had done to keep up to date with the progress of awarding a new tender between April 2016 and October 2016. In her version she did not do anything because she 'assumed that the existing reporting chain and communication channels were working' and that she would be informed if anything of consequence arose.

Moreover, the affidavits exposed the minister's decision to appoint work streams and work stream leaders reporting directly to her and not to the CEO of Sassa. In doing so, she had bypassed the Sassa executive committee, including the erstwhile acting CEO, and contravened governance protocol. This in turn gave the work streams, essentially independent consultants, direct access to the minister, creating parallel reporting structures.

The minister's affidavit failed to mention both of the above facts. This, according to the Court, was a strong factor in determining whether she had acted in good faith or not.

The Court held that despite the above, there was not enough information to grant a costs order against the minister in her personal capacity. The Court held that it could not make an adverse order against the minister on the basis of allegations that were untested and which she had not had the opportunity to challenge. To determine if the member of Cabinet acted in bad faith, and for the minister to explain her conduct to the Court, it was held that the parties must be given the opportunity to agree to a process under Section 38 of the Superior Courts Act (No. 10 of 2013), failing which the Court would determine the process to be followed in terms of the same provision. The Court therefore ordered that:

- The minister is joined as a party to the proceedings in her personal capacity.
- The parties must, within 14 days of the judgment, report to the Court whether they have agreed to a process in terms of Section 38 of the Superior Courts Act to determine the issues relating to the minister's role and responsibility in the establishment and functioning of the work streams referred to in the affidavits filed in the proceedings.

The parties agreed to participate in this inquiry process, and the Court made an order on 2 August 2017 appointing Judge Ngoepe to preside over the inquiry, described below in the context of the 27 September 2018 judgment of the Court under the same case number.

South Africa Social Security Agency and Another v Minister of Social
Development and Others (CCT48/17) [2018] ZACC 26 (Date of Hearing:
6 March 2018; Date of Judgment: 30 August 2018)

By February 2018, Sassa had made little progress in fulfilling the Court's
order for insourcing the payment system or appointing another service
provider and filed an urgent application requesting the Court to grant
another extension of the suspension of the declaration of invalidity for
a further six months. This was agreed but the requested extension was
limited to the part of the contract that dealt with the provision of the
cash payment service.

In its judgment, the Court identified the issues that required
determination:

- Whether Sassa was entitled to be heard on an urgent basis.
- Whether Sassa's request for an extension of the suspension of the
  operation of the order of invalidity of the contact between Sassa and
  CPS for the payment of social grants should be entertained.
- Whether the then Minister of Social Development and CEO of Sassa
  should pay the costs of the application out of their own pockets.

Regarding urgency, the Court noted that Sassa had not explicitly set
out circumstances that rendered the matter urgent. Rather, the so-called
urgency was self-created by Sassa's own delays and failure to make
significant inroads during the 12-month period that the Court had
afforded it with the extension of the suspension of the order of invalidity.
No case was made for urgency.

Nonetheless, the Court held that the absence of urgency did not
necessarily mean that Sassa's application should be dismissed. The
Court had to consider whether in the special circumstances of the case
there were reasons which otherwise justified the granting of a further
extension of the suspension of the order of invalidity. The Court noted
that the extension of a declaration of invalidity cannot be had for the
asking – a proper case justifying the extension must be made. The

objective of the suspension of the declaration of invalidity of the Sassa/CPS contract was to:

- Avoid disruption in the payment of social grants that would have caused intolerable suffering to social grant beneficiaries and their dependants.
- Afford Sassa the opportunity to put matters right by concluding a fresh contract.

Despite being afforded time to sort out the problem, Sassa had failed to do so. The question was therefore whether the balancing of the relevant factors favoured the granting of a further extension.

In considering the sufficiency of the explanation furnished by Sassa as to why a further extension ought to be granted, the Court found Sassa's explanation 'utterly inadequate' and neither candid nor complete. The Court also considered that in its papers, Sassa did not assure the Court that if the further extension for six months were granted, the defect would be remedied in that period. The Court also highlighted the principle of finality in litigation that promotes certainty and forms part of the rule of law, a founding value of the Constitution. In this regard the Court noted the acute need for finality with regards to the social grants crisis. The Court found that the uncertainty in relation to whether social grants would be paid must come to an end.

Nonetheless, the Court held that while the factors discussed above warranted the refusal to grant a further suspension, there were other factors that strongly supported the granting of the extension requested. These included the approximately 2.8 million social grant beneficiaries who would have been left without their grants and have their right to social security, to food and to human dignity violated if the extension were not granted. Furthermore, social grant beneficiaries were not to blame for Sassa's failure to act diligently and comply with the extended period previously granted by the Court.

The Court therefore held that it was just and equitable in the circumstances to extend the suspension of Sassa and CPS's invalid contract for a further six months.

Black Sash Trust (Freedom Under Law Intervening) v Minister of Social Development and Others (CCT 48/17 C) [2018] ZACC 36 (Date of Judgment: 27 September 2018)

This judgment considers the question of whether the erstwhile Minister of Social Development, Minister Dlamini, ought to pay, in her personal capacity, for the costs involved in the case of Black Sash Trust v Minister of Social Development[4] in which the issue of costs was left open and reserved.

In order to ascertain whether the minister ought to pay for the costs out of her own pocket, the parties agreed to participate in a process in terms of Section 38 of the Superior Courts Act whereby retired Judge President Ngoepe conducted a fact-finding inquiry for two weeks during January and April 2018 to determine Minister Dlamini's role and responsibility in creating a parallel decision-making and communication process at Sassa and the DSD that contributed to the social grants crisis; and as to whether the minister had misled the Constitutional Court on her role in the crisis. The Black Sash participated as a party in the proceedings, where the minister was called to give an account of the crisis, the appointment and reporting of the work streams, and her reporting to court, and where she was subjected to cross-examination by the Black Sash and Freedom under Law, a legal NGO. Judge Ngoepe further called Mr Dangor and Mr Magwaza to give evidence.

A full investigation took place and the Section 38 inquiry report authored by Judge President Ngoepe was released to both the parties and the public at the beginning of May 2018.[5] The report in essence found that Minister Dlamini had failed to make a full disclosure to the Constitutional Court, in that:

- The minister did appoint individuals to lead parallel work streams.
- These individuals reported directly to the minister.
- The reason the minister did not disclose this information to the Court was that she was afraid that she would be blamed for the social grants crisis and that a personal costs order would be awarded against her.

The parties were thereafter invited to make submissions to the Constitutional Court on whether, in light of the inquiry report, Minister Dlamini ought to be liable for costs out of her pocket. Minister Dlamini argued that holding her personally liable to pay the costs of the proceedings would constitute a breach of the principle of separation of powers, and that the Constitutional Court lacked the authority to hold a member of the executive to account by ordering them to pay legal costs out of their pocket. The Black Sash Trust as the applicant and Freedom Under Law as the intervening party both argued that the minister acted in bad faith by failing to disclose the truth about her interference with the governance of the work streams, despite filing affidavits under oath to the Constitutional Court.

In its judgment, the Constitutional Court held that the minister's argument that a personal costs order against her would offend the separation of powers had no merit. Instead, the test for holding public officials personally responsible for costs is simply bad faith and gross negligence in the context of litigation. Accordingly, the Court held that the contents of the Section 38 inquiry report were sufficient for a personal costs order against the minister.

The conduct of the minister was held to be reckless and grossly negligent. She occupied a position as Minister of Social Development that demanded a greater commitment to ethical behaviour and required a high commitment to public service. The minister failed to honour this commitment when she used her position to place herself between constitutionally enshrined rights and those entitled to them, in this matter social grant beneficiaries. The report by Judge President Ngoepe revealed that the minister misled the Court to protect herself from the consequences of her behaviour. She allowed a parallel process to occur knowing that she withheld information that would lead her to being held personally liable for the social grants disaster.

In determining the extent of the personal costs order, the Court emphasised that this was a discretionary determination which required considering Minister Dlamini's personal responsibility arising from the parallel processes she had set in motion, and her shielding this truth from the Court, against the fact that ordinarily state officials do not bear personal responsibility for the good faith performance of their official functions. The Court then, historically and for the first time, ordered that Minister Dlamini pay 20 per cent of the taxed costs.

The Court also found that the inquiry report strongly suggested that Minister Dlamini had lied under oath in her affidavits filed in the Constitutional Court and orally in evidence to the Section 38 inquiry. The Court thus directed the Registrar to forward a copy of the inquiry report to the National Director of Public Prosecutions to determine whether to prosecute the minister for perjury.

After this judgment, Sassa paid its 80 per cent legal cost. After a media campaign the minister finally paid her legal cost in May 2021. Later in 2021 the Director of Public Prosecutions in Gauteng successfully prosecuted Ms Dlamini for perjury.

THE PROFITABILITY OF EXPLOITING THE POOR

While the numbers of social grant beneficiaries have grown exponentially since democracy, these gains, such as they are, have been under attack. Quite apart from the mess surrounding the actual payment of grants, the award of a government tender to a private company to distribute social grants demonstrated a lucrative market for CPS/Net1, its subsidiaries, associates, and other unrelated companies, to target arguably exploitative financial products and services to social grant beneficiaries.[6] As the Court later found in *Net1*, debit order deductions 'affect the operation of over 10 million beneficiary bank accounts that translate into a value of approximately R550 million per month'.[7]

The exploitative practices have ranged from targeting multiplicities of funeral policies to individual beneficiaries, to high cost 'pay day' loans, exploiting a particularly vulnerable group of people by burying them in intractable debt cycles and further poverty. While both the illegality and fact of these practices were heavily contested by the companies implicated, the widespread reporting on them, and complaints to Sassa, led to government slowly waking up to this crisis by attempting to implement a 'funeral clean-up' process (see Chapter 2).[8] This clean-up process itself was then attacked by the vested corporate interests.

Notwithstanding the constitutional obligation on private actors not to interfere with or undermine the state's efforts to protect social assistance, several companies, including CPS/Net1, brought legal challenges opposing the government's funeral clean-up attempts through regulatory amendments. In doing so, they themselves relied on the Constitution, arguing that any government attempts to limit grant beneficiaries' contractual freedom is an infringement of beneficiaries' right to dignity and equality.

CHALLENGE TO THE CLEAN-UP OF FUNERAL POLICY DEDUCTIONS

Funerals and funeral policies are a lucrative business where there is a cultural imperative on many South Africans to have dignified funerals for their relatives, which transpire into large and costly funerals.[9] Funeral insurance is by far the most common form of insurance in South Africa.[10]

Channel Life Limited and Sanlam Developing Markets Limited v South African Social Security Agency and Others, North Gauteng High Court, Pretoria, case number 79112/15 (Unreported) (Date of Hearing: 10 May 2016 [matter postponed without a future date])

In October 2015, insurance and funeral policy providers Channel Life and Sanlam Developing Markets brought an urgent High Court application to interdict Sassa's funeral clean-up process, arguing that Sassa had an obligation to effect deductions against social grants pursuant to private insurance contracts between them and grant beneficiaries.[11] Sassa argued it had a legislative discretion whether or not to allow deductions, which flows from a legitimate purpose to protect grant beneficiaries from improper and coercive business practices aimed at securing their consent. Sassa argued the regulations afforded it no discretion to permit a deduction without written consent from the beneficiary given to Sassa (as opposed to the written contract between the beneficiary and the insurer) to attenuate the harm of numerous complaints that policies are ascribed to grant beneficiaries without their informed consent or knowledge of the terms and conditions of such policies, and to clamp down on the harm of multiple funeral policies per beneficiary. The Social Assistance Act and regulations allow for only one deduction per month, not exceeding 10 per cent of the value of the beneficiary's social grant, for a funeral policy only, to be deducted from social grants.[12]

The Black Sash intervened as *amicus curiae* to demonstrate the negative impact of deductions from children's grants, arguing private companies should be prohibited from interfering with the state's duty to provide social assistance.

Shortly before the matter was scheduled to be heard on 10 May 2016, the minister promulgated amended regulations[13] aimed at cleaning up and restricting further deductions from social grants and enforcing the clean-up process. The matter was postponed indefinitely for Channel Life to consider its position in relation to the amended regulations. It has not to date re-instituted proceedings, but the matter has arguably been overtaken by the Net1 group, as described below.

CHALLENGE TO THE EXCLUSION OF CHILD SUPPORT GRANTS FROM PERMITTED FUNERAL POLICIES

Prior to the May 2016 amendment to the regulations, direct funeral deductions were arguably permissible from all grants, including children's grants. The value of the child support grant at the time was R380 per month. The maximum of one deduction of no more than 10 per cent of the total amount, for a funeral policy, only applies to direct deductions. In practice, it is not limiting the sale of further funeral policies to grant beneficiaries after they have received their grants. The amended regulations introduced a blanket prohibition on direct funeral policy deductions from child support, foster child and care dependency grants.

Lion of Africa Life Assurance Company Ltd v South African Social Security Agency and Another (97973/2015) [2016] ZAGPHC 550 (Date of Hearing: 17 December 2015; Date of Judgment: 15 March 2016)

The case was heard in the North Gauteng High Court in December 2015 prior to the regulations amendment, after insurance company

Lion of Africa received a letter from Sassa indicating that 'in order to ensure that protection against the rights of the children is adhered to, the Agency has placed a moratorium on the new funeral policy deductions from children's grants with effect from 01 January 2016'[14] (see Chapter 2). Lion of Africa brought an urgent interdict application to stop this moratorium on funeral policy deductions from children's grants; an application that was opposed by Sassa.

In its founding affidavit, Lion of Africa stated that it had concluded approximately 47 000 funeral insurance policies with recipients of children's grants together with application forms containing the request in writing by the beneficiary, as required by Regulation 26A of the Social Assistance Act. By 8 December 2015, Lion of Africa had concluded 14 639 new funeral insurance policies, with recipients of children's grants making up 75 per cent of these policy holders.[15]

The court found that the matter was indeed urgent and that the non-joinder of CPS contracted by Sassa to distribute social grants was immaterial as these paymasters acted on the instruction of Sassa. However, the court found it to be inappropriate to decide on a constitutional issue in the urgent court and opted not to make any finding in regard to the constitutional issues raised by Sassa, such as whether using children's grants for paying for funeral insurance cover was unconstitutional insofar as it deprives children of their constitutional right to social security. The court decided that the constitutional issue could be considered in due course as envisaged by Rule 16(A).

Instead, the court decided the applicants' case based on whether it met the threshold for granting an interim interdict. The court held that the applicants had established: a *prima facie* right; a reasonable apprehension of irreparable harm if the interim interdict was not granted; that the balance of convenience favoured the granting of the interim relief; and the unavailability of any other remedy.

In concluding that a *prima facie* right had been demonstrated by Lion of Africa, the court had considered the judgment of Judge Du Plessis in a prior Channel Life case in 2011, where the court found that 'once the requirements of Regulation 26A (1), (2) and (3) have been met, the Agency is obliged to allow deductions as provided for [in] Regulation 26A.'[16]

Secondly, the court considered the fact that a system allowing for funeral policy deductions against children's grants was already in place and therefore a *prima facie* right had been established. The court found that at the time of the application, the system allowed for the deductions of funeral policy cover from children's social grants, and therefore to grant the interim relief would only be preserving the status quo.

The judge was also satisfied that the requirement of irreparable harm had been met because of Lion of Africa's assertion that if the moratorium were granted, approximately 20 000 policies with monthly premiums totalling approximately R1.7 million would be adversely affected. Finally, the court found that there was no alternative and satisfactory remedy available to the applicant based on the irreparable harm that the moratorium risked causing as well as the urgency in which the application was brought. The court therefore exercised its discretion in favour of Lion of Africa and granted the interim relief.

Sassa appealed this interim order directly to the Constitutional Court.

South African Social Security Agency and Another v Lion of Africa Life Assurance Company Ltd CCT 07/17 (Date of Hearing: 26 May 2016)

At the time of the amendment, the appeal was already pending before the Constitutional Court. Lion of Africa had already obtained an interim order from the high court interdicting Sassa from implementing a moratorium on new funeral policy deductions from children's grants in terms of its clean-up process, pending Lion's judicial review challenge to the clean-up process more broadly. Sassa appealed the interim order directly to the Constitutional Court.

The Black Sash intervened again as *amicus curiae* to argue that the purpose of the child support grant is to provide for a child in need of care. While the grant is paid to the parent or caregiver, it is for them to utilise it as a contribution towards caring for the child.[17] The Social Assistance Act provides that a deduction from a social grant is only permissible if it is necessary and in the interests of the beneficiary,[18] which must mean the benefit of the child.

The Black Sash also sought to admit evidence to the court of an expert study it commissioned from the Chair of Actuarial Scientists assessing the benefit and value for children of Lion's funeral policies.[19] The report concluded that the need for funeral cover for children is very limited, it is not necessary, and the probability is that claims paid come to less than one per cent of premiums. This means that 99 per cent of the amount deducted from the children's grants goes towards administration expenses and profits of the insurance company, and deductions of the kind made by Lion of Africa are wholly disproportionate to the benefit received, which is neither necessary nor in the interests of the beneficiary.

The Constitutional Court invited the Black Sash as *amicus curiae* to make submissions on three points. Firstly, that the purpose of the children's grant is to provide social assistance to meet the needs and guarantee the constitutional rights of children. Secondly, that children, as those who benefit from children's grants, should be classified as beneficiaries, even though they do not physically receive the grants themselves. Thirdly, that at the highest margin it can only be claimed that deductions against funeral policies are sometimes in the best interests of children. Therefore, a blanket obligation to permit such deductions when the requirements of Regulation 26A are met is impossible.

The Black Sash argued in its papers that if such deductions do potentially fall within the ambit of the special exemption created by Section 20(4) of the Act, then the minister has a discretion whether to allow them, and the minister is entitled to make general policy as to how that discretion is to be exercised. Because of the state's obligation to provide social assistance, particularly to children, it should have the discretion to make policy decisions that protect social assistance from depletion.

Because the amended regulations were passed shortly before the hearing, on the day of the hearing the matter was rendered moot, as funeral policy deductions from child support grants were then prohibited by the amendment. Lion of Africa confirmed to the Court that it would not implement the interim order granted in its favour in December 2015.[20]

As a result, the Constitutional Court has not pronounced on the important questions of law. The outcome was nevertheless momentous for the families and children receiving grants.

CHALLENGE TO THE AMENDED REGULATIONS

Immediately following the promulgation of the amended regulations, four new legal challenges were launched by private companies to challenge the minister's interpretation of the new regulations.[21] Collectively, five companies directly linked to CPS and Net1 were part of this challenge, which involved four legal applications:

1. Net1 Applied Technologies SA and Others v CEO, South African Social Security Agency and Others
2. Finbond Mutual Bank v CEO, South African Social Security Agency and Others
3. Smart Life Insurance Company Limited v CEO, South African Social Security Agency and Others
4. Information Technology Consultants (Pty) Ltd v CEO, South African Social Security Agency and Others.[22]

The companies argued that the amended regulations do not and cannot restrict the use of debit orders from grants, which was the minister and Sassa's interpretation and the basis of Sassa's instructions to the companies to stop all debit orders from beneficiary accounts. In legal submissions to the Court the minister argued that the companies' interpretation is in direct conflict with the purpose and rationale of the amended regulations as well as the objects of the Act to protect grant beneficiaries from predatory deductions from their grants and ensure that they receive access to social assistance as a safety net against abject poverty.

This case involved three different applications brought against Sassa, its CEO and the erstwhile Minister of Social Development. All concerned the amendments to Regulations 21 and 26A of the regulations of the Social Assistance Act promulgated on 6 May 2016. Sassa, its CEO and the erstwhile Minister of Social Development interpreted the new regulations as prohibiting all electronic debits, stop orders and Electronic Fund Transactions (EFTs) from beneficiary accounts held at Grindrod Bank. This interpretation had caused Sassa to instruct CPS and Grindrod Bank to stop all debit order and USSD platform deductions being processed from the Sassa-branded Grindrod Bank accounts of beneficiaries with immediate effect.

Net1 and the other applicants contested Sassa and the minister's interpretation and resisted implementation of this instruction. It approached the court for a declaratory order that the amended regulations, in particular Regulations 21 and 26A, do not restrict beneficiaries in the way in which they operate their own bank accounts.

Sassa and the minister's court papers recorded the numerous complaints they receive from beneficiaries of unauthorised deductions which defeat the purpose of the grant system by depleting the value of the grants essential for the 'poorest of the poor in society' and the very rationale for amending the regulations to protect beneficiaries.[23]

The Black Sash Trust and six individual grant beneficiaries acting in their own names sought to be admitted as co-applicants in all four of the consolidated applications, to participate in a larger capacity than *amicus curiae*. In this they would align themselves with Net1 against Sassa to protect beneficiaries' bank accounts. The Black Sash and the grant beneficiaries sought conditional relief that should the court interpret the amended regulations in the companies' favour, the court make a declaratory order that the state is under a constitutional obligation to protect beneficiaries from exploitation that prevents them receiving their full grant benefit, and that the court directs the minister to make regulations that do adequately protect beneficiaries from this exploitation.

The South African Reserve Bank (Sarb) did not support or oppose the relief sought, although it filed an explanatory affidavit that strongly supported any initiative by government to curb debit order abuse and supported lawful measures that did not disrupt the national payment system to curb the abuse. Sarb also raised concerns about a potential conflict of interest concerning CPS as the service provider for the payment of social grants, while companies affiliated to Net1 sold products to grant beneficiaries, ostensibly through their access to beneficiaries through CPS.

On 9 May 2017, the court found in favour of the companies and dismissed the Black Sash's conditional relief seeking new regulations protecting beneficiaries.[24] The minister, Sassa and the Black Sash were refused leave to appeal and petitioned the Supreme Court of Appeal.

The court held that it was clear that once the grant was transferred into the recipient's account at Grindrod Bank, it operated as any bank account at any commercial banking institution. Sassa had no control over any such account with Grindrod Bank, just as it has no control over accounts with any other commercial banks. Therefore, the court found that there was no merit in the submission by Sassa, its CEO and the minister that the Grindrod Bank accounts were not bank accounts chosen by the beneficiaries, but a mere 'method of payment chosen by the Agency' as defined in the new regulations.

In explaining its decision, the court recalled that social grants are paid by Treasury from the budget of the DSD and administered by Sassa through CPS. In this regard, Sassa pays over the total amount of social grant payments to CPS. In turn, CPS pays the amount received from Sassa into the Sassa-branded accounts at Grindrod Bank, just as it would at other commercial banks. From those accounts, the payments to the recipients are paid into their respective personal accounts held at Grindrod Bank or any other bank. Each recipient who holds a bank account with Grindrod Bank in his or her own names has a direct client/banker relationship with Grindrod Bank, or with any other banking institution, and the grant recipients hold their accounts subject to the terms and conditions of their respective bank accounts. Furthermore, the Grindrod Bank accounts operate within the ordinary and regulated banking environment of the National Payment System (NPS).

In other words, no contractual relationship exists between Sassa and Grindrod Bank. Furthermore, Sassa does not operate the accounts held at Grindrod Bank. Each recipient of a grant is obliged to present himself or herself every month at an ATM, Sassa pay point or other merchant's point-of-sale device to authenticate the transfer of the grant into his or her bank account. This is also true where beneficiaries hold bank accounts at other banking institutions. Thus, the court held that Sassa has no control over accounts with Grindrod Bank just as it does not have control over any account with any other commercial bank.

In addition, the court noted that Regulation 21(1)(a) clearly provides for two scenarios: either payment of the social grant into a bank account, or a payment method determined by Sassa. The latter envisages a specific alternative method that is not a bank account. On a purposive reading of Regulation 21(1), the court held that it was clear that the prohibition in Regulation 21(4) was not applicable in respect of Regulation 21(1)(a). The two categories must entail different and distinct payment methods. That much is clear from the use of 'or' in the wording of Regulation 21(1). The court therefore granted the declaratory relief sought by the applicants to the effect that these regulations do not restrict beneficiaries in the operation of their bank accounts. In the event, the court did not grant the further relief sought to set the regulations aside or declare that the Minister of Social Development had no authority to promulgate the regulations.

The court also found that the applications to intervene as an applicant or *amicus curiae* could not succeed because the Black Sash sought relief relating to constitutional issues. In the court's view, these constitutional considerations were not strictly relevant in interpreting the provisions of Regulations 21 and 26A which were the subject of the main applications, and therefore these intervention applications were refused.

The Minister of Social Development of the Republic of South Africa & Others v Net1 Applied Technologies South Africa (Pty) Ltd & Others; Black Sash Trust & Others v The CEO: The South African Social Security Agency & Others (825/2017 and 752/2017) [2018] ZASCA 129 (Date of Hearing: 16 August 2018; Date of Judgment: 27 September 2018)

Notwithstanding the High Court refusing Sassa leave to appeal, the SCA determined that it would hear the matter, and dealt with two related applications for leave to appeal. The first concerned the question of whether certain amendments to the regulations promulgated under the Social Assistance Act prohibited all electronic debits, including debit orders, stop orders or EFTs from the accounts of social grant beneficiaries held with Grindrod Bank.

It was uncontested that the amendments were motivated by the concerns of the minister, Sassa and civil society about the alleged predatory marketing practices by vendors who were intent on selling their financial products within the social grant payment system to social grant beneficiaries and receiving payment by debit orders or EFTs. There were also allegations of unauthorised deductions from bank accounts of beneficiaries, and studies revealing how elderly people receiving grants were often illiterate, struggled with technology and could easily be taken advantage of. There was therefore general agreement that social grant beneficiaries should be protected against unscrupulous vendors and corrupt activities.

The SCA did not limit arguments to the appeal record and asked the parties to make submissions on the impact of the recent events that had altered many aspects of the way social grants were paid out to beneficiaries. Following the invalidation of the contract between Sassa and CPS for the payment of social grants, Sassa concluded an agreement with Sapo for the payment of social grants on its behalf. This new contract was accompanied by new payment procedures, including those that: (a) required beneficiaries to provide written authorisation to Sassa for payments to be made into their bank accounts with any commercial bank of their choice; or (b) that payments be made through a Sassa/Sapo card provided to beneficiaries linked to the beneficiary's Special Disbursement Account (SDA), operated and held by Sapo. The SDA does not allow any EFT debits, stop orders, USSD platforms or any other financial transactions, apart from withdrawals and debits for goods purchased at point of sale.

In deciding the appeal, the SCA reasoned that since it was common cause that where a grant beneficiary elected to have their social grant paid into a bank account held with a commercial bank of their choice, the grant beneficiary was at will to authorise any debit deductions. There could also be no doubt that under the new payment regime Grindrod Bank was to be considered a commercial bank through which beneficiaries might now receive payment. In the new payment dispensation, grant beneficiaries were entitled to receive payment of grants into a bank account of their choice, including the bank accounts held at Grindrod Bank. Unless the beneficiary account holder elected to close his or her Grindrod Bank account and to migrate to a Sapo account or to another bank, the Grindrod Bank account would remain open. Beneficiaries who continued to use these accounts were responsible (as account holders) for paying all bank charges associated with these accounts.

Thus, the court held that an interpretation of the amended regulations would have no practical effect as the Grindrod Bank/Sassa accounts no longer existed under the new payment regime. Therefore, the new Sapo-administered payment system rendered the application for leave to appeal by the minister and Sassa moot or of no practical effect.

To justify its decision, the court relied on Section 16(2)(a)(i) of the Superior Courts Act which stipulates that 'when at the hearing of an appeal the issues are of such a nature that the decision sought will have no practical effect or result, the appeal may be dismissed on this ground alone'. In addition, the court held that the appeal bore no reasonable prospect of success due to:

- The conditions of the Grindrod Bank account had been known to all the relevant parties. Those conditions, in clearly spelt out terms, catered for and permitted authorised debits by way of EFT and stop orders.
- Payment into the Grindrod Bank account constituted payment 'into the bank account of the beneficiary' and were therefore not subject to the debit restrictions imposed by the regulations.
- The way the minister and Sassa sought to have the regulations interpreted and applied amounted to an unwarranted interference with a social grant beneficiary's right to conduct a mainstream bank account in his or her name and to operate within the mainstream banking system.
- The new payment regime was successful as a measure to combat abuse, namely, ring-fencing, via the Sapo–Sassa Special Disbursement Accounts, which permit no deductions.

For all these reasons, the court dismissed the appeal.

The second application for leave to appeal related to the Black Sash Trust and the six other individual beneficiaries of social grants who had all applied for leave to intervene in the litigation culminating in the orders set out above. The High Court refused the applications for leave to intervene and for the Black Sash to be admitted as *amicus curiae* (despite the Black Sash not seeking to participate as *amicus curiae*, but as a co-applicant with a direct and substantial interest).

The SCA held that a primary consideration in an application to intervene is generally whether a party seeking to do so 'has a direct and substantial interest in the subject matter of the litigation'. The SCA overturned the High Court order refusing the Black Sash leave to intervene. The SCA considered the role that the Black Sash plays in relation to social grant beneficiaries and its involvement in preceding social grants litigation, which clearly indicated that the Black Sash did indeed have a direct and substantial interest in the matter, and that the interests of justice dictated that the application to intervene should have been granted.

The court held that the refusal of the application for leave to intervene was even more peculiar in the light of the fact that the Black Sash had been permitted to address the court below on the issues it considered pertinent. The appeal was therefore upheld and the Black Sash Trust's application to intervene was granted.

However, this ultimately had no impact on the outcome of the SCA's decision to dismiss Sassa's appeal on the interpretation of the legislation and regulations. Considering the Black Sash's arguments, however, the SCA did caution Sassa to ensure that the integrity of the social grant system was protected in order for grant beneficiaries to receive their grants without predatory practices. At the time, and as Sapo was taking over as the service provider, the SCA did not take the point further.

OTHER RELEVANT LITIGATION

While the Black Sash was not directly involved in this matter, it is appropriate to the discussion to include the following case.

Nohdumiso Zalisa and Others v South African Social Security Agency and Others (82073/2018) [2019] ZAGPPHC 4 (Date of Hearing: 28 November 2018; Date of Judgment: 21 January 2019)

A later matter deals with an application for urgent relief brought by 14 individual applicants and Moneyline Financial Services (Pty)

Ltd against Sassa, its CEO, the Minister of Social Development, the South African Post Office SOC Limited and Grindrod Bank. The relief pertained to a direction by Sassa and its interpretation of the amended Regulation 21(1)(a) to the Social Assistance Act whereby all valid and authorised prior decisions made by social grant beneficiaries as to where their social grants ought to be paid would be invalid as of 31 January 2019. The regulation required social grant beneficiaries to either submit a form authorising the payment of their grants into their private bank account (Annexure C Form) or by default receive their social grants at Sapo.

The court granted the interim relief on the date of the hearing in November 2018 pending the handing down of judgment in January 2019. In its judgment, the court reasoned that it had granted the interim relief on the grounds of urgency and the irremediable harm that would befall the applicants and two million other social grants beneficiaries in similar positions. The first category of applicants included those who made the choice to have their social grants paid into private bank accounts before the change to the regulations in issue took place on 6 May 2016. The second category of applicants included those who had elected to have their social grants paid into private bank accounts in the period after 6 May 2016 and up to 1 January 2018. The third category included those who, after 1 January 2018, elected to have their grants paid into private bank accounts, and informed Sassa by submitting the Annexure C form referred to above.

The social grants of the first and second categories of beneficiaries would not be paid into their chosen private bank accounts if they were operated by Moneyline. As a result, applicants would also forfeit and lose their free funeral cover worth R2 500 each, a perk of the bank account. These beneficiaries would then have to go to a Sassa office to find out what had happened to their grant payment for the month, and then go to a Sapo branch to withdraw the grant. The court considered the inconvenience, confusion, distress, time wasted and transport costs – particularly in rural areas – caused to the elderly, the disabled and those entrusted with the care of young children (that is, social grant recipients), harm that was not remediable in due course.

Moreover, the loss of some two million clients would be a devastating blow to Moneyline's business, the damage to its goodwill would be irremediable, and it would be unable to obtain substantive redress in the ordinary course. In light of these reasons, the court granted Moneyline the relief it sought.

However, when deciding whether to grant the applicants a final interdict, the court had to be satisfied: (a) of the existence of a clear right; (b) that an injury was actually committed or there was a reasonable apprehension that an injury would be committed; and (c) that there was an absence of similar protection by any other ordinary remedy.

Balancing these factors, the court held that granting a final interdict was not appropriate in the circumstances. The reasons for this decision were, firstly, that the applicants were unable to prove the existence of a clear right to have their social grants paid into a bank account of their choice and, secondly, that the applicants, by bringing their application in the form of an interdict, failed to follow the correct procedure for the review of administrative decisions as provided for in the Promotion of Administrative Justice Act (or Paja). In its reasoning, the court explained that, based on the facts, Moneyline was indeed aware that a review in terms of Paja was the only remedy available for the relief it sought. The court referred to the established principle that a litigant cannot avoid the provisions of Paja by going behind it and seeking to rely on either Section 33(1) of the Constitution or the common law, or indeed the rule of law.[25] Thus the relief sought by Moneyline was refused.

In addition, the court held that it was satisfied that a statutory system, properly authorised, had been put in place for sound reasons by Sassa. These reasons were to prevent unlawful deductions from the accounts of social grant beneficiaries. Moreover, there was no reason to disbelieve the undertaking by Sassa that social grant beneficiaries would be paid.

Ultimately the court found that it was inappropriate for it to substitute Sassa's grant payment system with its own or go against the clear wishes of a statutory authority in the absence of illegality. The application was dismissed and the interim order that the court had previously granted thus lapsed.

THE APPOINTMENT OF A PANEL OF EXPERTS UNDER THE AUDITOR-GENERAL

Because of the oversight role which the Constitutional Court took on following the Black Sash's urgent direct access application heard in March 2017, the Court appointed a Panel of Experts and instructed it and the Auditor-General of South Africa to:

- Evaluate the implementation of payment of social grants during the 12-month period.
- Evaluate the steps envisaged or taken by Sassa for any competitive bidding process or processes aimed at the appointment by Sassa in terms of Section 4(2)(a) of the South African Social Security Agency or the Sassa Act (No. 9 of 2004) of a new contractor or contractors for the payment of social grants.
- Evaluate the steps envisaged or taken by Sassa aimed at Sassa itself administering and paying the grants in the future or any parts of it.
- File reports on affidavit with this Court every three months, commencing on a date three months after the date of the order, or any shorter period as the legal practitioners and experts may deem necessary, setting out the steps they have taken to evaluate the matters referred to in the above paragraphs, the results of their evaluations and any recommendations they consider necessary.

This mandate was subsequently extended on 23 March 2018 when the Court extended its declaration of invalidity of the contract between Sassa and CPS for a further six months. The Panel of Experts operated from 6 June 2017 to 15 October 2018 and submitted 10 reports to the Court providing an evaluation of developments as mandated by the Court. (See Appendix 1 for a summary of the key issues identified by the Panel of Experts.) Some of the panel's initial recommendations were overtaken by events (for example, the decision to appoint Sapo as service provider), and many of its recommendations were not implemented. What follows is an account of the panel's recommendations, Sassa's responses to them and their outcomes.

For almost the entire duration of this litigation campaign, the Panel of Experts held a watching brief over the process and made a range of independent suggestions. While some of its suggestions were not ultimately implemented, it is nevertheless important to trace its efforts over these years and record its achievements and its unfinished business.[26] The Panel of Experts provided a useful mechanism that materially impacted on policy. Symbolically, its work also redefined public opinion on the problems within the Sassa system and in relation to the outsourcing of the payment system.

One of the measurable and important outcomes of the Panel of Experts' work was the establishment of a 'recourse forum', established because of the Black Sash's multiple representations to the panel, and which is still in place. The Black Sash, Sassa and the DSD participate in the recourse forum, which initially also included Net1, CPS and Grindrod Bank. Sapo also now participates in the recourse forum. It is a platform for beneficiary communication to Sassa, the DSD and Sapo through the Black Sash and its partner organisations, which continues to play a useful role in beneficiary concerns and systemic issues being raised before Sassa, the DSD and Sapo, and for those bodies to provide feedback on these concerns to beneficiaries.

CONCLUSION

While the panel's conclusions were extremely critical of Sassa, this chapter has recorded several legal achievements that protected and empowered the country's most vulnerable people, enabling them to make changes in their daily lives. There were a number of extraordinary outcomes from all of this litigation.

The importance of the Constitutional Court's initial *AllPay* decision, declaring the controversial contract with CPS invalid yet suspending the order of invalidity to ensure that grant beneficiaries continued to receive grants, cannot be understated. This decision remained the underlying thread woven through the Hoog campaign, that the demand for socioeconomic rights by some of the poorest and most vulnerable South Africans was a matter of national importance and public interest.

The impact of the strategic litigation on which the Black Sash embarked extends beyond the orders the respective courts made. It has had a profound impact on shifting national discussions on the Social Assistance welfare model, on the policy and actual decisions around the payment mechanisms for social grants, and, most importantly of all, on the lives of grant beneficiaries in ensuring they receive their grants and in highlighting their exploitation.

While the politics of South Africa as a 'welfare state' is heavily contested, the Hoog campaign and the intense media focus around this litigation appeared to garner much public support on the importance and value of the social assistance system, and the dire need for its lawful and effective operations. This too was a win.

Through a combination of the legal challenges in *Channel Life* and *Lion of Africa*, and the amendments to the regulations, children's grants may no longer be used to fund funeral polices. These matters are an example of the Black Sash and civil society supporting the efforts of the state to clean up the social grant system positively.

The Constitutional Court recognised the role that CPS played, stepping into the shoes as an organ of state where it had been contracted to provide a constitutional mandate. It was compelled to continue the administration of social grants until another service provider or Sassa was able to do so, unlike in ordinary commercial contracts. It was also compelled to provide audits of its profits and account for its operations. Its accounts were not beyond public scrutiny and it was recognised as publicly accountable. CPS was ordered to account to the Court to show when it broke even on the cost of its administration function, and at which point it started making a profit in terms of the allegedly unlawful contract. Starved of its ill-gotten funds, it declined rapidly and was placed under business rescue in May 2020.[27] Freedom Under Law is now pursuing litigation against CPS to seek clarity from the Court on what portion of its considerable profits were ill-gotten, and to compel it to repay those to the fiscus. In April 2021, the Constitutional Court ordered CPS to resubmit its financial statements and working papers for audit.

For the first time in South Africa, a cabinet minister was held liable for legal costs to be paid out of her own pocket, which was a groundbreaking decision, and the erstwhile Minister of Social Development, Bathabile

Dlamini, was publicly declared reckless and grossly negligent by the Court. She was subjected to an inquiry and acknowledged as having lied under oath in her affidavits filed in the Constitutional Court and orally in evidence given before the Section 38 inquiry. The Court directed the Registrar to forward a copy of the inquiry report into her behaviour to the National Director of Public Prosecutions who decided in August 2021 to prosecute the minister for perjury. This was also a first for a cabinet minister.

The Constitutional Court played an exceptional oversight role over Sassa and the Minister of Social Development in requiring them to report to the Court quarterly, and then monthly, and in the appointment of the Panel of Experts under the Auditor-General. This demonstrated to the companies involved, the public, the executive, and perhaps most importantly to grant beneficiaries themselves, the critical importance of the protection of the integrity of the social grant system.

Ultimately, Sassa concluded an agreement with Sapo for the payment of social grants on its behalf. Funds from Treasury were ring-fenced for this purpose and new payment procedures introduced, bringing to an end a fraught period that had marred the sterling record of South Africa's social welfare system.

4 *The Net1 business model*

Around the time that Cash Paymaster Services (CPS) was awarded the Sassa contract in 2012, there was a drive by many in the financial services industry, both internationally and in South Africa, for greater 'financial inclusion' of the poor.[1] Net1 appeared to be a forerunner in this wave of 'financial inclusion', particularly targeting the underbanked and unbanked market in remote rural and peri-urban areas in South Africa.[2] The proprietary Universal Electronic Payment System (UEPS) technology was Net1's competitive advantage and offered digital connectivity outside the National Payment System (NPS) infrastructure.

Research by the FinMark Trust in its 2013 FinScope Survey found that 'financial inclusion' did not deliver on the promise of sustainable livelihoods for the poor.[3] In fact, indebtedness dramatically increased, and it was found that in the case of microloans, 45 per cent of borrowers were 90 days or more in arrears on at least one account. The most vulnerable in society were carrying the burden and consequences of what had been sold as 'financial inclusion'.

A study from India showed that the hidden cost of 'financial inclusion' lay in the challenge and the cost incurred in addressing complaints and accessing recourse.[4] Financial Service Providers (FSPs) in South Africa did not provide accessible mechanisms to ensure their target markets' right to administrative justice.[5] Most grant claimants know where to find a Sassa office in their area, but the locations of CPS offices were largely unknown.[6] The only mechanism available to register complaints with CPS was a call centre. However, the number was toll free only from a landline, and most grant beneficiaries rely on mobile phones.[7] The call centre provided the illusion of accessibility, but the ability to access redress remained out of reach.

Net1 and its subsidiaries were able to take advantage of the law's inability to keep pace with the changing uses of technology; the consolidation of the outsourcing of grants to one company; uncertainty about the bounds of privacy and personal information; and the murky realm of information swapping and sharing that subsidiary companies allowed.

A BRIEF HISTORY OF NET1

Net1 was founded in 1989, the brainchild of Mr Serge Belamant, a South African IT specialist. In the early 1990s, Mr Belamant tried to persuade South African banks to use his UEPS. His breakthrough came in 1995 when Visa hired Net1 Technologies, or more specifically Mr Belamant, to create a new application based on his proprietary UEPS technology. By May 1997, Mr Belamant had incorporated Net1 UEPS Technologies Inc. in Florida, USA.[8]

In 2004, Net1 UEPS Technologies Inc. acquired Aplitec, a public company listed on the Johannesburg stock exchange. Aplitec was delisted and renamed Net1 Applied Technology Holdings Limited. Net1 UEPS Technologies Inc. listed on the New York Nasdaq stock market in 2005, and the company made a secondary listing on the Johannesburg stock exchange in October 2008.[9]

The acquisition of Aplitec was strategic as it owned a subsidiary, CPS, which was founded in 1971 in South Africa. CPS was previously owned by First National Bank, with contracts worth R54 million to distribute social grants to approximately 1.2 million grant beneficiaries in four provinces.[10] Aplitec acquired CPS from First National Bank in 1999 and continued to deliver cash at pay points in rural and peri-urban areas on behalf of South Africa's social security administration.[11]

NET1'S STRATEGY FOR GROWTH IN SOUTH AFRICA

In 2006, Net1 identified Sassa as a key source of future earnings.[12] In 2012, Sassa issued a tender for the national distribution of social welfare grants. Net1 told its shareholders that because of the South African government's intention to increase the size and scope of social welfare grants, the company was well-positioned to expand its current market share as well as to diversify the types of financial products it provided to social grant recipients.[13] For Net1 to expand, it needed to win the 2012 Sassa contract and leverage this contract to deliver on its promised increase in earnings. (How Net1 won the CPS contract, and the litigation that followed, is described in detail in Chapter 3). Since 2009, Net1's South African operations through its subsidiary, CPS, were its bread and butter.[14] The majority of earnings came from the Sassa contract, inherited through the Aplitec acquisition. By this time, CPS was delivering social grants to over 3.5 million beneficiaries in the Eastern Cape, Limpopo, KwaZulu-Natal, Northern Cape and North West provinces.[15] Net1 further leveraged this contract by selling microloans and life insurance products, on behalf of registered underwriters, to cardholders who received social welfare grants. As later became apparent, this 'diversification' into loans and life insurance was to become the cornerstone of Net1's profiteering off its social grant contract after 2012, through its Financial Services Unit.

In its 2009 annual report, Net1 outlined its structure, in which all of its operations, including its technology and subsidiary companies, were grouped into 'business units'. These business units had operational headquarters in different South African cities, but its 'suite' of products were everywhere (to maximise commercial gain) and at the same time, nowhere (that is, mostly online, which meant there was no specific location from which beneficiaries could access recourse).[16]

The anchoring business units in Net1's South African operations were:

- EasyPay,[17] based in Cape Town, through which Net1 owned the largest independent financial switch[18] and merchant processor in South Africa for credit and debit card transactions.[19] This allowed

Net1 to provide a variety of additional payment services, such as bill payments, prepaid mobile top-ups and prepaid utility services.

- CPS, based in Johannesburg, which was the social grant unit that deployed the UEPS/EMV or smart credit card technology to distribute social welfare grants on a monthly and rotational basis.
- The Financial Services Unit that offered cardholders microfinance, life insurance, and transactional and money transfer products.

In the lead up to the awarding of the 2012 Sassa contract, Net1 consolidated its Financial Services Unit. Net1 also built a network of subsidiary companies that offered financial products exclusively targeted at social grant recipients. Moneyline extended unsecured loans; Smart Life sold funeral insurance; and Manje Mobile supplied prepaid airtime and electricity (see Appendix 2). One of the ways that Net1 solidified its presence in the South African business landscape, continually growing a basket of products,[20] was by using social grant payments as a springboard for the introduction of further products and as a way to amass biometric data.

For Net1 to trade its financial products legally in South Africa, it had to register as a bank or have access to a banking licence. In January 2007, Net1 signed a co-operation agreement with Grindrod Bank, a small retail bank, to establish a retail banking division. Grindrod Bank was responsible for the day-to-day running of the retail bank, while Net1 was responsible for the supply and maintenance of the IT infrastructure, including the UEPS hardware and software. When CPS was awarded the Sassa contract in 2012 to administer social grants nationally, the partnership became even more significant for Net1. Grindrod Bank commissioned Net1 to design its IT system for the Sassa social grant contract.[21]

The Net1 partner bank, even though it serviced millions of social grant accounts, is not widely recognisable as a banking institution in South Africa. Grindrod Bank does not set up public interfaces through ATMs, there are no constantly revamped branch premises, no radio and television advertisements and no obtrusive branding. Rather, the bank chooses to operate in the software of the banking landscape. The reasons for this cloaking have changed over time. Initially, Grindrod Bank serviced extremely wealthy clients and businesses, and believed this lent it a veneer of exclusivity to its targeted audience.

For almost a decade after 1994, financial service providers (FSPs) targeted employed, particularly white, middle-class South Africans. Hull and James explain that FSPs realised the saturation of this market after 2004 and, in their search for new markets and greater profit, began to target 'riskier gap markets' composed of poor people, who often did not have bank accounts.[22] It was in this setting that financial institutions such as Grindrod Bank saw the potential profit of scooping up previously unbanked populations into formalised banking systems. The bank redirected its focus from the rich towards the very poor. Despite changing their target market, the bank continued to choose to operate relatively 'undercover' while courting and being courted by Net1.

NET1'S 'FIRST WAVE/SECOND WAVE' BUSINESS MODEL

In 2009, Net1 first proposed its 'first wave/second wave' approach to expanding into new markets.

> In the 'first wave,' we seek to identify an application for which there is a demonstrated and immediate need in a particular territory and then sell and implement our technology to fulfil this initial need. As a result, we achieve the deployment of the required technological infrastructure as well as the registration of a critical mass of cardholders. During this phase, we generate revenues from the sale of our software and hardware devices, as well as ongoing revenues from transaction fees, maintenance services and the use of our biometric verification engine. Once the infrastructure has been deployed and we achieve a critical mass of customers, we focus on the 'second wave,' which allows us to use this infrastructure to provide users, at a low incremental cost

to us, with a wide array of financial products and services
for which we can charge fees based on the value of the
transactions performed.[23]

When CPS was awarded the Sassa contract in 2012, the first wave/second
wave business model came into effect and was key to Net1's earnings
and growth. One of the strengths of the company in terms of meeting
the contractual requirements for the 2012 tender was its experience in
the use and implementation of biometric services in the global south.
During the first Sassa national contract, using Net1's technology, CPS
facilitated the collection of grant beneficiaries' and recipients' personal
data and opened approximately 10 million Grindrod Bank accounts.[24]
The bank account included debit order and USSD[25] facilities. The Sassa-
branded Grindrod bank card had an embedded chip that could function
offline and that stored the personal and biometric data of each grant
recipient, a crucial feature for the implementation of the second wave.

When the second wave began, Net1 subsidiaries started to sell an
array of financial products to grant recipients, using the technology
embedded in the bank card, which gave them access to the personal and
biometric data of grant recipients, as well as their bank accounts for debit
order and USSD deductions. Every subsidiary within the Net1 group
– including Smart Life (life and funeral insurance), Moneyline (loans),
and Manje Mobile (prepaid airtime and electricity) – accessed the same
smart card reader. When grant beneficiaries put their cards into card
readers and placed their thumbs on the biometric scanners, owned and
controlled by Net1, their entire bank account history and other personal
information was made available to a subsidiary.

Net1/CPS's 2012 biometric identification technology system used
to register, administer, and pay grant claimants was promoted as the
most innovative advancement in banking and biometric machinery.
Yet the CPS national payment system differed from previous payment
programmes not in its use of biometrics, but in the organisation and scale
of enrolment. A year after the initiation of the large-scale registration
drive, 19 million people (40 per cent of the total population) had had

their fingerprints documented, their voices recorded, their photographs captured and their signatures digitised.[26]

Biometric enrolment and verification works by developing a physical characteristic, for example a fingerprint, into an 'electronic digital template' (a computer code that corresponds with that fingerprint) and this information is then stored in a database. This stage is called enrolment/registration.

Once a grant beneficiary or recipient has registered, their biometric information is stored. The process of verification begins every time someone presents their biometric information (most commonly a thumbprint) and their identity needs to be confirmed. The thumbprint is compared to the one already in storage. A match or a mismatch is the biometric method of confirming the identity of the person who has registered.

Net1 and its subsidiaries' processes show how little protection there is from the widespread distribution of personal data through private entities and even within many state institutions and departments. Even though there may be legal protections in place for the use of biometric data by the institution collecting the information, once this information is spread those protections are diluted, and it is less clear who has access to this information and what they might do with it. In the case of social grants, during the enrolment onto the new system after 2012, grant beneficiaries were informed that if they did not provide their biometric data they would not receive their grants.[27]

THE EASYPAY EVERYWHERE CARD

In 2015, in the *AllPay 2* case (described in Chapter 3), the Black Sash intervened before the Constitutional Court to address deficiencies in the new tender process.[28] This action spotlighted the effects on grant beneficiaries of CPS's (and therefore Net1's) phenomenal growth and increased revenue. The Court ordered Sassa to implement a new tender process within a given timeframe and report on its progress. If a suitable service provider could not be found, it was incumbent upon Sassa to insource the administration of social grants.

In May 2015, coinciding with the launch of the new tender process, Mr Belamant told investors that despite having created a world-class payment system that brought 10 million poor South Africans into the formal banking economy, CPS (and therefore Net1) had decided not to participate in the new Sassa tender process for the national distribution of social grants.[29] Mr Belamant said that he was intent on developing the 'largest rural banking infrastructure in South Africa' without the restraints imposed by Sassa.[30] In June 2015, Net1 launched the EPE Grindrod Bank account.

EPE sales agents aggressively promoted the EPE Grindrod Bank account as a better alternative to the Sassa-branded Grindrod Bank account. The EPE or 'Green Card' was also sold as a requirement for accessing a loan. The Black Sash and its partners have documented cases where EPE sales agents, operating at or outside Sassa pay points, convinced recipients that the EPE card was the Sassa card, and that the loans they were applying for would be granted by Sassa (see Chapter 1).

The EPE account was a 'parasitic' bank account that was linked to the Sassa-branded Grindrod Bank account. As soon as the recipient's social grant was deposited into their Sassa account, it was automatically transferred to the Green Card account, from which the Net1 subsidiaries immediately made debit order and USSD platform deductions. Recipients were told to keep their Sassa-branded Grindrod Bank account cards while transacting with the EPE Green Card.

The CPS had been responsible annually for the distribution of approximately R150 billion in social grants. For Net1, it was a highly profitable contract, reporting double-digit revenue growth every quarter. Payment plus interest (for ancillary products offered by Net1's affiliates) was instantly deducted from a social grant, paid reliably every month, with no risk to the lender. Furthermore, when grant monies were transferred from a Sassa account (for which Sassa paid CPS R16.44) to the EPE account, it cost the beneficiary an additional R10. The EPE card also incurred bank charges for withdrawals and statements, securing Net1 a very lucrative double-dipping deal, made easy by the technology that allowed instantaneous payments at the click of a button.

THE END OF AN ERA FOR NET1

In September 2018, after almost seven years, the constitutionally invalid CPS contract with Sassa finally ended.

In a letter to shareholders, Mr Belamant said that it was with much excitement that CPS had finally exited a six-and-a-half-year contract with Sassa. 'We are privileged to have run one of the world's largest and most successful social grant distribution programs, consistently paying on time and without disruption, using our biometric technology.' [31] Mr Belamant also noted that his company's Sassa contract had caused considerable reputational damage based on 'unfounded media allegations'.[32] But he said he now believed that Net1 finally had the freedom and the bandwidth to focus on its financial inclusion initiatives in South Africa and abroad. Mr Belamant assured shareholders that Net1 would return to being a consistently profitable company.

However, both this optimism and Mr Belamant's involvement with Net1 came to an end. CPS was involved in continual litigation in relation to its contract with Sassa. Two of these cases presented a substantial risk to Net1 if the Court were to hold it responsible for CPS's liabilities.

1. The February 2020 order of the Constitutional Court rejected CPS's appeal of a lower court judgment ordering CPS to repay Sassa more than R316 million, plus interest, of contract implementation costs reimbursed to CPS in 2014.[33] Because CPS's liability substantially exceeded the value of its assets (it owed more money than it owned), CPS had been placed in business rescue and was eventually liquidated.

2. The second case arose from the 2013 Constitutional Court order declaring the 2012 contract between Sassa and CPS invalid. The Constitutional Court required CPS to file a financial statement, to be audited by independent auditors, detailing CPS's revenues earned, expenses incurred and profits derived from the Sassa contract (see Chapter 3). In 2018, CPS filed two independent audit verification reports – one by KMPG and a second by Mazars – suggesting that CPS made profits of about R252 million from April 2012 to September 2018, despite a substantial loss of nearly R557 million in

the last six months of 2018. However, in 2020, Sassa filed an audit report by Rain Chartered Accountants establishing that CPS made R1.1 billion profit for the same period. Freedom Under Law, a South African non-governmental organisation, made an application to the Constitutional Court alleging that CPS under-reported its profits from the Sassa contract and requested the Constitutional Court to order CPS to repay such profits. CPS opposed Freedom Under Law's request on the basis that Freedom Under Law was asking for new relief that did not fall under the Court's supervisory jurisdiction. While National Treasury approved the Rain Chartered Accountants report, it called into question the 'quality of the audit work' by KPMG and Mazars. Missing information and understated profits brought the audit reports from both firms into question. Rain Chartered Accountants claims it did not receive the necessary cooperation from the CPS auditors and the Court ruled that CPS had to provide the missing information.

While no claim had yet been made against Net1 holding it liable for the obligations of CPS, in his 2020 annual report the new chairperson at that time of the Net1 board, the late Mr Jabu Mabuza, told shareholders that the board believed that there would be a legitimate legal basis for such a claim.[34] Mr Mabuza explained that 'we cannot assure you that any such claim will not be made against us. If Sassa or another third party were to seek and ultimately succeed in obtaining a judgment against us in respect of CPS's liabilities, any such judgment would have a material adverse effect on our financial condition, results of operations and cash flows'.[35]

Net1 reported an operating loss of $6.9 million (about R103 million at the time) for its 2020 second quarter financial period. From 2018, CPS saw its revenue decline by 6 per cent, to $20.4 million (about R304 million), a consistent pattern since the termination of the Sassa contract.[36]

Looking ahead to 2021, Mr Mabuza told shareholders that the company would return to its roots and focus its incremental capital and management resources on providing financial inclusion services to underbanked consumers and small businesses in South Africa. He explained that Net1 had modified its business strategy to remain focused on South Africa, and to reduce its activities outside the African continent. Key to this modified business strategy is the approximately one million EPE customers the company retained post the Sassa contract.[37]

However, even if Net1 can successfully implement its new business strategy, future losses from adverse court rulings and other operational losses may prevent Net1 from sustaining or expanding its business. In the 2020 annual report, Mr Mabuza told shareholders that Net1 could not assure them that it would achieve, sustain or increase profitability in the future.[38]

THE VITAL IMPORTANCE OF INVESTIGATIVE JOURNALISM

Once alerted to the unfolding social grant crisis, journalists did sterling work in providing the details to the public. Investigations into the Sassa crisis by *amaBhungane*, an independent, non-profit newsroom based in South Africa, were key. Craig McKune of *amaBhungane* was one of the first to investigate the unauthorised and allegedly fraudulent and unlawful deductions experienced by grant recipients. His investigations demonstrated that Net1 and its subsidiary companies showed little regard for regulations designed to protect customers from abuse. As a result of his exposés, the Financial Services Board (FSB) investigated allegations that Net1 was abusing clients – mostly social grant beneficiaries – and breaking financial laws.

McKune began his investigations in 2012. Through introductions by the Black Sash, he interviewed beneficiaries who told him that money was taken from their Sassa-branded Grindrod Bank accounts without their authorisation and that they were powerless to stop this. McKune made contact with a whistleblower, a salesman for one of the Net1 subsidiary companies selling financial products to social grant beneficiaries. The whistleblower was instrumental in getting the financial services regulator to investigate Net1. McKune reported that this probe came after he and the whistleblower separately presented evidence to the FSB suggesting Net1's sales staff might not be properly accredited to sell some of its financial products.[39] McKune's article for *amaBhungane* is provided below.

Reporting by Craig McKune for *amaBhungane*

Critics have accused Net1 of abusing grant beneficiaries through its business of debiting money from social grants to pay for financial products. Many beneficiaries say money is taken without their authorisation and that they have no clear way to stop this.

Net1 vigorously disputes this, but my investigations show the company has a long history of flouting financial regulations designed to protect clients from abuse. Its executive chair Mr Serge Belamant did not answer detailed questions, but said: 'We follow all of the rules and regulations by all authorities.'

The regulator

My attention was first drawn to Net1's financial regulatory problems in January [2012]. I was investigating the complaints of the company's alleged abuse of grant beneficiaries.

Wanting to know what steps an aggrieved beneficiary should take, I looked up the terms and conditions for the Sassa grant bank cards on Net1's website. They say that complaints can be directed to Net1's outsourced FSP, a company called Eledon Project Management. Eledon accounts to the FSB, a statutory body established to regulate people who sell insurance, financial advice and related services. Such FSPs fall under laws like the Financial Advisory and Intermediary Services (FAIS) Act (No. 37 of 2002) and the insurance acts. The FSB's overall job is to make sure FSPs treat their customers fairly.

It is common for companies like Net1, who don't have their own FSP licence, to outsource the role to a licenced FSP like Eledon. This works well when the licenced FSP has enough staff and experience to keep its operating partner in check – and when the operating partner works in good faith with the FSP. Otherwise, it's a sham.

I called Eledon's phone number and reached one Lenny D'Onofrio. I lied to D'Onofrio, telling him I was calling on behalf of my domestic worker who was having troubles with her Net1 bank account – Net1 was debiting money for a loan she had repaid a long time ago. What's more, she had lost her bank card and could not get her Sassa grant anymore. These are stories I have heard from a few beneficiaries. D'Onofrio told me I had reached the wrong office. He said he was the 'compliance officer' for Eledon but that I should call the company on a different number.

A man named Carl answered. 'Hi. I'm looking for Eledon,' I said. 'What is the company he works with?' Carl said, clearly confused. 'No, it is a company,' I explained. 'It has an FSP licence for Moneyline.' Moneyline is Net1's lending subsidiary. Carl put me on hold for a minute to consult with his colleagues. When he returned, he said: 'I think you have an incorrect number,' and ended the call.

I tried a second number for Eledon's Daniela Anderson. On social media, she uses the surname D'Onofrio. I was later told she is D'Onofrio's sister, although Eledon did not confirm this. Anderson dutifully listened to my story. She said I should speak to Lenny D'Onofrio. Completing the circle, I called D'Onofrio again, revealed that I was a journalist and recounted my experience trying to lay a complaint with Eledon. It appeared likely that grant beneficiaries with real problems would be given the run-around when they tried to sort out financial problems through Eledon, I said.

I told him that Net1 was distributing terms and conditions for one of its bank cards that erroneously listed someone else, not Eledon, as the FSP. It was Eledon's job to fix this – so beneficiaries knew who to contact with problems – and it had clearly failed.

I said that Net1 had hundreds of salespeople through the country. They are convincing grant beneficiaries to open new bank accounts, where their social grants are automatically transferred every month. To protect consumers, the FSB requires anyone dispensing financial advice to obtain certain qualifications. Yet Net1's salespeople are not accredited with the FSB, as Eledon's profile on the FSB website suggests.

The bottom line, I said, was that Eledon appeared to be ill-equipped to make sure Net1 treated grant beneficiaries fairly when it sold them financial products. I also suggested to Lenny D'Onofrio that the family relationship between Eledon's compliance officer (him) and a 'key individual' (Daniella Anderson aka D'Onofrio) might be a conflict of interest – these are statutory positions. FSPs are supposed to have their own checks and balances to further protect consumers, including a compliance officer that oversees the FSP's operations. And I pointed out that a third D'Onofrio – said to be Lenny's wife – was a senior manager within Net1 and, according to a press release, 'has worked with Net1 for the majority of her tenure in banking, which has allowed her to establish working relationships with executive and management teams across most business units'.

How, I wondered, did all the D'Onofrios and Eledon act impartially when dealing with each other and Net1?

Report to the headmistress

Lenny was outraged. He emailed me: 'Your line of questioning and reading of the facts and the law regarding, amongst others, a perceived conflict of interest and any wrongdoing on behalf of any of the parties mentioned in your questions are at best misstated, speculative and at worst baseless. To my knowledge, no client has been prejudiced or "given the run around".'

He concluded: 'Your self-confessed conduct in pretending to be the employer of a client with a legitimate complaint to elicit information is both unethical and a potential breach to the [press code]. In light of your actions to date, I have no confidence that you will report on the matter in a fair and unbiased manner, and accordingly do not intend making any further comments.' The press code permits misrepresentation if in the public interest.

I sent similar questions to the FSB and within days Net1 and Eledon were in trouble. The FSB demanded documents and contracts from them and, in short order, Net1's top managers and Lenny D'Onofrio were on a plane from Johannesburg to Cape Town, where they endured two days of tense interviews with regulators. FSB spokeswoman Tembisa Marele told me: 'The FSB has already begun its engagement with Eledon regarding the allegations. A regulatory onsite visit has been scheduled to determine, among others, Eledon's operational ability to oversee the financial services activities rendered by [Net1].'

But the D'Onofrios are by no means the beginning of Net1's dubious relationship with South Africa's financial laws.

Licence fail #1

Net1 launched its plan to leverage South Africa's welfare system by founding the Smart Life Insurance Company in 2011. At the time, Net1 was hoping that its subsidiary, CPS, would win the Sassa contract to distribute social grants nationally.

Mr Belamant cut in financial services consultant Chris van der Walt to Smart Life in 2011 as Van der Walt held an FSP licence. Van der Walt, who later became embroiled in litigation with Belamant, explained in a sworn affidavit how it was Smart Life's initial business plan to leverage CPS's expected Sassa contract to sell funeral insurance policies to grant beneficiaries. He said: 'It was envisaged that CPS's infrastructure, such as its staff members who effect the payment of government benefits at payment sites across the country, could simultaneously market and sell long-term insurance products, notably funeral policies.'

Van der Walt's job was to make sure Smart Life obeyed the financial regulations. His FSP licence meant that he had to account personally to the FSB if anything went wrong. He said: 'CPS confidently expected that it would be awarded the tender,' and in February 2012, it was – although the constitutional court later ruled that the contract was invalid because Sassa badly botched the tender in favour of CPS.

Things quickly went wrong for Smart Life. By early 2012 Van der Walt had received legal advice that Smart Life's strategy might be anti-competitive. CPS also did not have an FSP licence. So, Van der Walt and the Smart Life board changed tack and started to roll out a Smart Life branch network completely independently of CPS and the Sassa contract. But Belamant stopped this, Van der Walt said, and a power struggle ensued with Net1 as the controlling shareholder versus Van der Walt, the FSP.

In a letter to his regulator, the FSB, Van der Walt complained that Net1 would 'steamroller' decisions 'through the board at threat of dismissal of the directors'. Van der Walt recounted one board meeting: 'Belamant expressly told the independent directors that if they can't keep him out of regulatory trouble, they serve no purpose on the board and they can F*&^ off.'

Van der Walt claimed that Belamant and Net1's chief financial officer, Herman Kotze, 'hold the FSB in low esteem and have been very vocal about what they believe to be undue interference in Net1's right to conduct business'. He said Belamant routinely referred to a certain financial regulatory framework as 'that b##^sh*t'.

One of Van der Walt's Smart Life co-directors resigned in protest over similar complaints, while CPS continued to sell Smart Life policies without a licence. Then the FSB intervened. In February 2013, its long-term insurance registrar, Jonathan Dixon, ordered Smart Life to stop selling insurance policies immediately. Dixon pointed at Belamant, who he said 'does not function within the confines and parameters of the [Smart Life] board as a collective and unilaterally approves or rejects key decisions'. Dixon said Belamant was conflicted as both Smart Life chair and Net1 executive chair, and this endangered Smart Life's clients' policies, which had to be sustained for the rest of their lives.

Not long after, Belamant fired Van der Walt. 'During a board meeting, Belamant admitted that he simply wanted me "out",' Van der Walt said in a letter to the FSB. '[Belamant said] he had instructed attorneys to find contractual reasons for it regardless of merit, and if the independent directors did not support his resolution, he would convene a shareholder meeting and dismiss them all.' Van der Walt sued Belamant, who countersued. Net1 also laid criminal charges over documents Van der Walt removed from Smart Life. Ultimately, they settled out of court and the charges went nowhere, Van der Walt said.

Meanwhile, the FSB continued its own probe, finding that both Smart Life and CPS contravened financial regulations. Van der Walt was in trouble because Net1's breaches happened on his watch as the FSP licence holder. The FSB also found that Van der Walt provided contradictory versions on other matters. It decided that he 'does not comply with personal character qualities of honesty and integrity' and debarred him.

Van der Walt appealed to an FSB panel, but Judge Yvonne Mokgoro upheld the decision. She ruled that Van der Walt's duty was to make sure Net1 obeyed the law. He knew 'that none of the people employed by CPS who sold the Smart Life policies had been duly qualified and authorised by Smart Life or any FSP for that matter, to serve as representatives. Besides, CPS was not an authorised FSP.'

Van der Walt has applied to have Mokgoro's decision reviewed in a high court.

Licence fail #2

Then Net1 signed on with a new FSP, Libra Financial Services. Libra's people refused to speak to me, but I was otherwise able to collect enough information to piece together some of their story. It is no less worrying than Van der Walt's. Starting late in 2013, Libra put together an emergency rescue plan for Net1. It assessed Net1's compliance with the FAIS Act and other laws and took steps to fix problems.

Under Libra's watch, Net1 was able to resurrect Smart Life and get the insurer its own FSP licence. Libra used its own FSP licence to cover for CPS, Net1's loan company Moneyline and Net1 Mobile Solutions, which sells electricity and airtime. The latter is responsible for many grant beneficiary complaints about unauthorised deductions.

But by late 2015, Libra – like Van der Walt before them – was battling to keep Belamant and Net1 on the straight and narrow. In one email, a Libra staffer notified Net1's executives that Net1 found itself in a 'high risk position' because it was 'non-compliant' with financial laws. According to the email, Net1's managers improperly bypassed Libra to instruct financial staff 'in direct and flagrant disregard of the FAIS Act'. The Libra staffer also wrote that when grant beneficiaries complained about Net1's debits from their accounts, they were 'not being responded to within mandated timelines', and Net1 had been 'extremely reticent' to provide information about the complaints to Libra.

Libra also complained that Net1's hundreds of sales employees were giving financial advice – as defined by the FAIS Act – when they convinced beneficiaries to open new accounts so that they could take loans. To give such financial advice, the salespeople must be properly FAIS accredited, a cumbersome and expensive process involving exams, training and monitoring. According to Libra, Net1 didn't want to get them accredited.

Grace Bonokwane (with her daughter), a social grant beneficiary, who attended the first engagement with Minister Dlamini, DSD and Sassa officials in Feb 2014. Photo: Thom Pierce

Mr Sipho Bani sharing his struggles to get recourse, St George's Cathedral, 2016. Photo: Eric Miller

Dorena and Jacob Juries (Franschoek), behind the scenes of the Grant Grabs 1 documentary – exposing coercion into purchasing funeral policy. Photo: Thom Pierce

Jakob Fortuin (Op Die Berg, Ceres) warning beneficiaries about the pitfalls of the Green Card, 2017. Photo: Erna Curry

Black Sash paralegal Vincent Skhosana facilitating an information and education session, Gauteng 2017. Photo: Erna Curry

Members of the Seitebaleng Service Club, Soshanguve; Grant Grabs 3 documentary, 2017. Photo: Erna Curry

TransAfrica Life representatives refunding grant beneficiaries from Tweefontein (Mpumalanga) for fraudulent funeral deductions, October 2017. Photos: Evashnee Naidu

Hoog picket at St. George's Cathedral, October 2015. Photo: Ashraf Hendricks (GroundUp)

Discussing first MTT report with Minister Dlamini, Parliament, 21 August 2014.
Photo: Black Sash archives

DSD's Brenton van Vrede receiving the memorandum during the picket outside St. George's
Cathedral, October 2015. Photo: Eric Miller

Nomonde Nyembe (Cals attorney) and Lynette Maart (BS Director) explaining the outcome of the
Black Sash ConCourt hearing to Hoog activists, March 2017. Photo: Black Sash archives

Thandiwe Zulu (Black Sash Gauteng Regional Manager) and Lynette Maart - Black Sash ConCourt Victory, March 2017. Photo: Black Sash archives

Hoog activists and ANC Women's League members outside the Constitutional Court for the Black Sash case, 15 March 2017. Photo: Ihsaan Haffejee (GroundUp)

Minister Dlamini appears before Scopa, Parliament, 24 March 2017. Photo: Ashraf Hendricks

Witzenberg Rural Development Centre paralegals, Black Sash, DSD and Sassa negotiating recourse and refunds for grant beneficiaries with CPS/Net1, Grindrod Bank officials, Ceres, May 2017. Photo: Leopold Podlashuc

Second recourse and refunds session for grant beneficiaries with CPS/Net1, Grindrod Bank, Sassa Ceres, June 2017. Photo: Esley Philander

Paralegal Janaap Odendaal (Hope4 Destiny, Delft) monitoring CPS officials during the second recourse and refunds session for grant beneficiaries, Ceres, June 2017. Photo: Leopold Podlashuc

When I asked one Net1 salesman if he and his colleagues had been accredited to give financial advice, he said: 'No, we don't have that ... None of us has ever been trained with FAIS. We were not even given some sales training, including the one which is FAIS. None of us ever attended or have got any certificates of FAIS compliance.' I asked if his Net1 branch manager was trained in financial services. He said: 'Nothing, nothing.'

However, FSB spokeswoman Marele said: 'The question whether or not financial services are being rendered is both a factual and legal question which should be answered on a case-by-case basis. This will also be looked at during the regulatory onsite visit [of Eledon].' I received separate correspondence from a senior FSB manager who explained that in her opinion Net1's staff were indeed dispensing financial advice, so they should be properly accredited.

In the Libra staffer's email to Net1, he said: 'This has unfortunately become an untenable situation, as no remedial action, nor response to our communications, has been forthcoming.' Not long after, Libra fired Net1 – and the D'Onofrios stepped in.

If at first you don't succeed

Two years ago [in 2015], Net1 applied to the FSB for CPS, Moneyline and Net1 Mobile Solutions' own FSP licences. If successful, Net1 would no longer need to use outsiders like Van der Walt, Libra and Eledon. To get its licences, Net1 needs to demonstrate to the FSB that its managers and staff are fit and proper for the job, that it can stick to the rules and that it will treat its clients fairly.

The FSB was expected to decide on these licences but this appears to have been delayed by the probe. FSB deputy executive officer Ms Caroline da Silva told me that Net1's applications were taken to a licence committee in March 'and are still under consideration'. In a separate reply, FSB spokeswomen Ms Marele said: 'It would be inappropriate to make any comments in a public forum in respect of the applicants' appropriateness to hold FSP licences.'

In response to detailed questions for this article, sent in February, Net1's Belamant said: 'This week is not good for me to respond as it is the week of our board meetings and investors update. I can assure you however that all is good on our front and that we follow all of the rules and regulations by all authorities.' Through a new PR advisor, Bridget von Holdt, Net1 responded to follow up questions last week. She said: 'The comments made by the individuals concerned are false, misrepresented or inaccurate. Net1 has referred to the relevant reports, judgments and affidavits regarding the disciplinary action taken by the FSB and criminal charges brought against these individuals and FSP for dishonesty, fraud, etc. Based on this, it is not recommended that you rely on their interpretation of events (sic).'[40]

CONCLUSION

As a financial writer, Ann Crotty tracked the Net1 story over a number of years – how it operated, its business model and how it ended. Here, to conclude this chapter, she provides a hindsight overview of that history.

Many in the investment community regarded the Net1 business model as the holy grail of banking – it was an opportunity to bank the unbanked. The end of financial exclusion for millions of poor South Africans was on the horizon, some investors believed. Their enthusiasm reflected the widely held view that the only thing preventing millions of people across the globe from enjoying better standards of living was the lack of a bank account. In 2018 a World Bank report estimated that 1.7 billion adults across the world are 'unbanked'; the World Bank stated that its vision was to achieve universal financial access.[41] By one estimate, banking the world's unbanked population has the potential to increase the global economy by over $600 billion per year.[42]

Investor enthusiasm saw the Net1 share price surge from R58 in 2012 when CPS was awarded the Sassa contract to a high of R165 in early 2015. Institutional fund manager Allan Gray was one of the early backers, taking up a hefty 16 per cent stake in 2012. Remarkably, World Bank associate, the International Finance Corporation (IFC), only piled into Net1 shares in 2016. Driven by the alluring opportunity of 'banking the unbanked' it acquired 20 per cent of Net1, making it the single largest shareholder in the company.[43]

So much for how Mr Belamant's plan looked on paper. The reality, which was evident from conversations in the snaking queues of grant recipients that popped up across the country on the first day of every month, was starkly different. It quickly became apparent that the new Net1-backed system for distributing social grants was not a passport to life-enhancing financial inclusion, but a hook to trap recipients into a spiral of reckless borrowing and, in a disturbing number of cases, apparently fraudulent deductions for services never purchased.

While Net1's contractual obligation with Sassa was to ensure that 10 million recipients received their grants every month, its focus was on devising ways of marketing this gamut of 'financial products' including funeral policies, microloans, and prepaid cellular airtime and electricity. The company's technology was designed to enable it to deduct payments for these services every month from the social grant that was due. In many instances, the desperately poor recipients had nearly all their grant money deducted to pay for these products; some were even unaware of having purchased them.

In 2014, the Black Sash issued a media release[44] urging the government to investigate and stop the abuse, where it appeared that service providers within the Net1 group were able to access personal information from the database controlled by Net1 subsidiary CPS and appeared to be using dubious marketing methods to market loans, airtime, funeral insurance and other financial products to grant recipients, through their indirect access to beneficiaries as a result of the payment contract.

As became apparent through Net1's annual reports and earnings calls, marketing these financial products was part of Mr Belamant's plan for Net1. He is quoted as saying that it was 'ethically defensible' to market loans to grant beneficiaries, and 'people are free of mind, and you still have to allow them to do what they want with their grant money. If they want to spend money on airtime, they're going to'.[45] He said in the same article that 3.2 million grant recipients had used Net1's cell phone service to buy airtime and electricity and argued, 'We're giving them something they need, and we're giving them something better and cheaper than they could get elsewhere'.[46]

This was evidently the line Mr Belamant had sold to his shareholders, around 60 per cent of whom resided outside South Africa. For some, such as the IFC and possibly Alan Gray, Mr Belamant's notion of financial inclusion might have been sufficient enticement. For others, Mr Belamant's promise that the business would generate profit margins of 20 per cent or higher was the standout attraction – it was significantly above the sort of profit levels achieved by most listed companies. 'We've said from the beginning with this particular contract, we would make an average of 20 per cent bottom-line profit which is not unreasonable, if you think about it', Mr Belamant told News24. 'In fact, that's actually low for my investors. They would prefer a 30 per cent or 40 per cent profit', he added.[47]

The deeply troubling aspect of the Net1/Sassa grant debacle is that Mr Belamant's version of reality for 10 million grant recipients was backed by powerful forces because it fitted comfortably into their 'free-market-financial inclusion' narrative. These forces were able to take solace from the fact that oversight entities such as auditors KPMG and the National Consumer Tribunal had raised no concerns. Indeed, as Allan Gray pointed out in March 2017 in defence of its continued investment in Net1, neither KPMG nor the National Consumer Tribunal had found evidence that Net1 was using the Sassa database of grant recipients to illegally and/or improperly sell a range of additional services to them. As far as Allan Gray was concerned this meant their investment in Net1 was sound. 'On the whole, our society seems to believe that more financial inclusion for the poor is good, despite the harm that can be caused by entry-level consumers buying policies or borrowing money on terms they don't fully understand', said Allan Gray's chief operating officer Rob Dower in a public letter on 9 March 2017.[48]

Despite the seriousness of the situation, it appeared Mr Dower had not looked too closely at KPMG's links with Net1, in particular the fact that KPMG was Net1's internal auditor and had a history of generating less than vigorous findings on its client. (By early 2017 KPMG's reputation had already been damaged – almost irreparably – by its close ties to the Gupta family.) If Mr Dower had looked more closely at the National Consumer Tribunal's finding in a 2015 case, he would also have realised how tenuous and limited in application it was. To its credit, Allan Gray did significantly revise this view and later dissociated from Net1, making its position clear by posting a statement on its website under the heading 'Net1: Do the right thing'.[49] There was no such revision of the IFC's determination to stick by Mr Belamant, and ignore growing evidence that his efforts to 'bank the unbanked' was further impoverishing them while enriching wealthy investors.

What is really troubling is the fact that had any of these powerful players bothered to attend a payout session, they would have quickly been jolted out of their faith in Mr Belamant and 'financial inclusion'. As far back as 2014, in a case brought by Absa (*AllPay* case), the Constitutional Court had found that the contract with Net1 subsidiary CPS with Sassa was invalid. Surely that should have set off alarm bells and encouraged investors to treat cautiously any claims the company made?

Had it not been for NGOs such as the Black Sash, Freedom under Law and Corruption Watch – with outstanding support from the Panel of Experts appointed by the Constitutional Court – millions of this country's poorest would have remained unprotected from the determination of corporate executives to 'bank the unbanked' at any cost.

Acknowledgement
The Black Sash is grateful to journalist Ann Crotty for her assistance with this chapter and for writing this conclusion.

5 *Tackling state capture at Sassa*

As the Hoog campaign progressed, it became apparent that Sassa was part of a far broader political project. This chapter places Sassa and the grants crisis in a broader context of state capture, which had a direct negative impact on and consequences for the poorest and most vulnerable in our society.[1]

In 2017, 'state capture' was announced as the South African phrase of the year by the Pan South African Language Board (PanSALB).[2] The term found its way into the public lexicon following the release, in 2016, of the Public Protector's State of Capture report. The report detailed the findings of an investigation into the allegedly corrupt relationship between senior government officials at various state institutions and parastatals and the Gupta family, who were personally connected to then President Jacob Zuma.[3]

In this chapter, various research documents are considered to locate Sassa within the state capture milieu. The Public Affairs Research Institute (Pari), in its publication titled *The Contract State: Outsourcing & Decentralisation in Contemporary South Africa*, argues that South Africa has become a contract state, with state institutions being hollowed out and outsourced.[4] Two reports by The State Capacity Research Project,[5] an interdisciplinary inter-university research partnership, aimed to stimulate public debate about state capture in South Africa, are also considered. Lastly, we discuss remedies that were sought to address the constitutionally invalid 2012 contract between Sassa and CPS (see Chapter 3).[6]

In May 2017, the first report by the State Capacity Research Project, *Betrayal of the Promise: How South Africa is Being Stolen*, was released. The report defines the phenomenon of state capture as

> the formation of a Shadow State, directed by a group of power elites, which operates within and parallel to the constitutional state (in both formal and informal ways) and whose objective is to repurpose state governance in order to derive benefits that align with the power elite's narrow financial or political interests – which are often in conflict with public norms and not aligned with the principles of the constitution.[7]

The report notes that understanding state capture purely as corruption does not explain the full extent of the political project underpinning it. Institutions were repurposed not only for looting on a vast scale, but also to consolidate political power that ensured the long-term survival as well as the maintenance of a 'political coalition'. Public benefit narrative masked private enrichment.[8]

The authors of *Betrayal of the Promise* explain that the emergence of a 'Shadow State' should be viewed in the context of the slow pace of black ownership of the economy during the Mbeki era (1999–2008).[9] The central critique of the black economic empowerment (BEE) route to transformation is that 'white monopoly capital' was left intact. Due to the loopholes in BEE legislation, white businesses were able to 'front' (the practice of appointing black people to positions without decision-making authority or bringing in 'empowerment partners' on terms that did not alter the balance of economic power in commercial companies). BEE during the Mbeki era only produced a small black elite, while excluding ordinary people, especially women and youth, from the economy.

In the run-up to the 2007 ANC conference in Polokwane that elected Jacob Zuma as ANC president, there was a basic conviction within the ruling party that the economy remained in white hands and the 'people' did not share in the wealth of the country. Hence the transition from traditional BEE to Radical Economic Transformation (RET), which is driven by transactors in the form of a black capitalist class that is not dependent on 'white monopoly capital'. Zuma's election resulted in the rise of preferential procurement practices in state-owned entities as the primary means for creating a powerful black business class. This was at the epicentre of the political project mounted by the Zuma faction: to address the slow pace of economic transformation under Mr Mbeki, BEE could be advanced through the procurement spend of state institutions and parastatals, particularly through large-scale tenders and contracts. The government's procurement systems therefore became central to state capture.[10]

The 2014 Pari publication argued that South Africa has become a 'contract state'.[11] The country's public procurement system was exposed to the risks of corruption and patronage due to the lack of capacity within the contract state. These risks were exacerbated by political interference. Politicians placed associates in senior positions and manipulated public servants, eroding administrative checks and balances and undermining consequence management. Furthermore, this removed procurement decision-making from those with the expertise needed to make the technically appropriate decisions.[12]

In October 2018, the State Capacity Research Project released a new report, *How One Word Can Change the Game: A Case Study of State Capture and The South African Social Security Agency.*[13] This is a sequel to the *Betrayal of the Promise* report. Using Sassa as a case study, it provides a detailed example of the modus operandi of the Shadow State. It demonstrates that state capture is a political project that has had a direct negative impact on the poorest and most vulnerable in society.

Foley and Swilling, the authors of *How One Word Can Change the Game,*[14] explain that the power elite consists not only of individuals who are employed in government, but also includes external actors outside government within the ruling party, family and tribal affiliates, and a wide array of other actors. Most often this will also include at least one powerful individual in the private sector, through which the intended benefits (financial, political or both) can be derived.

The power elite are the 'drivers' or managers of the activities of the Shadow State. These individuals are in positions that yield exclusive powers within the constitutional state. They are ministers, deputy ministers, board members and hold senior administrative positions such as chief executive officers (CEOs) of state-owned enterprises. These are positions of oversight and ultimate accountability with exclusive executive authority.[15]

Supporting the power elite are the 'fixers' who are involved at an administrative or operational level in government. Their function is to infiltrate and manipulate the processes and functioning of the state. They serve as an accountability buffer between the power elite and any illicit activities that are taking place within the government.[16]

The 'broker or middleman' serves as a secondary buffer, residing in the Shadow State and falling outside of any formal engagements or exchanges. Without having any direct involvement in any of the formal contracting, the middleman is free to interact with and between the various members of the Shadow State, both within and outside of the government, and the external benefitting party (be it a company, political party or a select group of individuals).[17]

In terms of the modus operandi for 'capturing' a government agency like Sassa, the Shadow State undertakes the four core tasks or actions from within the government itself, as directed by the power elite:

1. Secure control – It secures control over the public service through the appointment of cabinet ministers, board directors at state institutions and heads of strategic agencies.
2. Secure access – It secures access to opportunities for repurposing the state by manipulating or changing the directives or objectives of government. In cases where the objective of the Shadow State is to accrue wealth, this often centres on large-scale tenders and contracts.
3. Weaken governance – Key technical institutions and formal executive processes are intentionally weakened. This entails removing key senior officials and replacing them

with pliable people, or people in 'acting' positions, thus limiting their ability to make long-term strategic decisions.

4. Secure patronage – Creating parallel political, governmental and decision-making structures that undermine the functional operation of government institutions. This would secure the patronage network.[18]

HOW SASSA WAS CAPTURED BY THE SHADOW STATE

The first tender to appoint a national grant paymaster

In 2004, legislation was promulgated to formalise South Africa's social security systems and establish the national entity responsible for administering social grants. A central pillar was the establishment of Sassa to standardise grant payment nationally, consolidate and maintain a registry of all grant beneficiaries, and minimise losses to the state due to fraud and corruption.[19] On 23 February 2007, Sassa issued its first Request for Proposals (RFP) for the 'provision of a payment service' (see Chapter 3).[20] Nine bids were received for the tender, but concerns emerged about lack of clarity in the RFP requirements. These could not be resolved, and the RFP was cancelled by the Bid Adjudication Committee (BAC) on 25 September 2008, almost a year and a half after it was issued.[21]

In response to media speculation about why the tender was cancelled, then Minister of Social Development Mr Zola Skweyiya commissioned a report, *Narrative Report of the Adjudication Committee in Respect of Payment Tender Service*,[22] which raised concern about the development of a private sector monopoly over the grant payment system and Sassa. It proposed dividing the bid into nine provincial tenders.[23]

The minister and Sassa are also concerned about the fact that certain service providers have dominated the social grants payment market since the service was opened up. In the current bid process, instead of looking for one service provider to ensure uniformity of services nationwide, Sassa decided to subdivide the bid into nine provincial tenders.

This will prevent the development of a monopoly and allow opportunities for new entrants into the market.[24]

However, this impacted on the tender specifications, which were unclear. How many service providers was Sassa aiming to appoint? How would the services be allocated should there be more than one service provider? Should they be allocated according to province, or based on the method of payment?[25] Further to this, it was determined by the BAC that bidders 'did not provide standardised payment services; [services] were offered via merchants and were thus not safe and secure for beneficiaries; were not cost effective; did not transfer maximum risk to the private sector; and were not in line with principles of Black Economic Empowerment'.[26]

The Department of Social Development (DSD) was forced to extend the existing contracts with the grant delivery agents, CPS, Empilweni, and AllPay, following the cancellation of the tender in 2008.[27] Sassa and the South African Post Office (Sapo) continued their discussions under Minister Skweyiya, resulting in an agreement in 2009 to delegate a number of social grant payment services to Sapo.[28] However, CPS wanted to retain its dominance in the social grant market and challenged the Sassa/Sapo agreement in the High Court, winning an interdict to halt this decision.[29] Significantly, the Supreme Court of Appeal overruled this order, effectively validating the Sassa/Sapo agreement. In 2009, when Mr Jacob Zuma became President, Mr Skweyiya – the first Minister of Social Development of democratic South Africa – was replaced by Minister Edna Molewa, and Ms Bathabile Dlamini was appointed deputy minister. The Sassa/Sapo agreement became moot as it failed to secure the new minister's approval.

On 23 April 2010, Sassa CEO Mr Fezile Makiwane was dismissed.[30] Mr Coceko Pakade, then Chief Financial Officer of the DSD, was appointed acting CEO of Sassa.[31] Mr Makiwane was part of the team that had finalised the Sapo agreement in 2009.[32] After his dismissal there was a strategic shift in approach to the distribution of social grants and Sapo was expunged. President Zuma reshuffled his cabinet later that year, appointing Ms Bathabile Dlamini as Minister of Social Development and retaining Mr Pakade as acting CEO of Sassa.

Manoeuvres by the Shadow State

A 2012 an *amaBhungane* article by Craig McKune[33] publicly revealed for the first time a bribery attempt that took place during the 2007 Sassa tender adjudication process. Advocate Norman Arendse, chair of the BAC and author of the *Narrative Report* commissioned by former Minister Skweyiya,[34] alleged that while deliberating on the R7 billion state tender in 2008 he was offered an 'open chequebook' bribe by an individual claiming to represent CPS. Advocate Arendse named prominent sports administrator Mr Gideon Sam when he reported the incident.[35] No official investigation or follow-up was ever undertaken.[36]

Foley and Swilling suggest that Net1/CPS enjoyed access and influence at the highest level, which explains the consistent support of CPS, particularly by Ms Bathabile Dlamini, a Zuma loyalist.[37] This support was made clear at an interview with Mr Zane Dangor, who was a member of the Bid Specification Committee (BSC) that prepared the Request for Proposal (RFP) for the 2011/2012 tender. He referred to a meeting that took place in August 2009 just three months after President's Zuma's inauguration. It was arranged by Deputy Minister Dlamini and was attended by Mr Michael Hulley, then personal lawyer of President Zuma, Mr Duduzani Zuma, President Zuma's son, Minister Molewa and Mr Dangor, who was then Chief Operations Officer at DSD and was responsible for negotiating the extension of contracts for payment of service providers.[38]

The purpose of the meeting was to consider the 2007/2008 cancelled tender and the litigation challenges the DSD and Sassa were facing with CPS. Mr Hulley and Mr Duduzani Zuma suggested working with CPS to find a solution, on the understanding that Advocate Arendse's earlier recommendation – to retain provincial service providers for the payment of social grants – not be implemented.[39] Dangor flatly rejected this, advising

Minister Molewa that this would be in direct contravention of the legal procurement processes. The meeting ended shortly thereafter. Minister Molewa agreed with the recommendations made by Dangor. An article in the *Mail & Guardian* newspaper suggests this led to her being moved sideways to the position of Minister of Water and Sanitation in 2010.[40]

SASSA'S SECOND TENDER

Under Minister Dlamini's leadership, the payment of social grants moved away from a fragmented system of multiple provincial services providers to one service standardised under a national paymaster. This new direction impacted on the method of payment into a bank account (see Chapter 4) and seemed to benefit from economies of scale.[41] On 17 April 2011, Sassa issued the second RFP that encapsulated this new direction. However, these tender specifications did not deal with the concern raised in the Narrative Report about being held ransom by the private sector's monopoly.

Four days after the new RFP was released, on 21 April 2011, Minister Dlamini appointed Ms Virginia Petersen as Sassa CEO.[42] On 10 January 2012, Ms Petersen issued Bidders' Notice 2 'clarifying' the requirements for biometrics. The tender specification was changed by deleting the word 'preferred' and stating instead that the service provider 'must' have biometric capabilities. As CPS was the only bidder who had this capability at the time, it won the tender.[43] Seven days after the notice was issued, on 17 January 2012, CPS was awarded the five-year contract to distribute social grants nationally. Foley and Swilling's analysis provides insight into how Sassa's tender process was seemingly manipulated to benefit a specific bidder and disqualify others, which is one of the important tools used in state capture.[44]

SASSA/CPS CONTRACT CONSTITUTIONALLY INVALID

The Constitutional Court declared the award of the tender to CPS constitutionally invalid on 29 November 2013 (see Chapter 3). At the heart of AllPay's argument for the CPS contract to be set aside was the claim that Sassa had imposed an 11th hour change to the tender specifications, fatally prejudicing its bid.[45] The Court found the contract awarded to CPS irregular as Bidders Notice 2 constituted a significant change to the RFP.[46] The Court also took exception to the fact that little consideration was given to CPS's BEE model.[47] It would later emerge, through investigative reporting by *amaBhungane*,[48] that the agreement between CPS and its consortium partners (not submitted to the courts) provided an empowerment model that was an 'empty shell'.[49] The lack of consideration for the principles of BEE was a concern that was also initially raised in the *Narrative Report*.[50]

During her tenure as Sassa CEO, Ms Petersen undertook specific actions that seemed to aid the Shadow State in gaining control over Sassa's procurement processes. On 25 April 2014, Ms Petersen authorised an irregular payment of R316 million to CPS for the 're-registration of grant beneficiaries'.[51] This payment seems to coincide with the settlement of the broad-based black economic empowerment (BBBEE) consortia (comprising Mosomo and Born Free Investments) loan agreement for its shares in Net1, resulting in a debt-free ownership of just under two million shares worth approximately R237 million.[52] Again, action by Ms Petersen violated Sassa's own procurement procedures and was eventually declared by the Supreme Court of Appeal 'irregular and unlawful' in a challenge brought by Corruption Watch.[53] On 23 March 2018, Judge Moroa Tsoka ordered CPS to pay back the R316 million, plus interest, from June 2014 to the date of payment, to Sassa.[54] On 30 September 2019 the SCA dismissed CPSs' appeal, upholding the order of Judge Tsoka.[55]

In the *AllPay* case, evidence was submitted to indicate the role played by politically connected private individuals in manipulating the tender process in favour of CPS. Further to this, Foley and Swilling, in an interview with Mr Dangor, were told that upon the insistence of Deputy

Minister Dlamini the meetings and preparation of the tender documents took place in Mr Michael Hulley's offices. It was during these meetings that the biometrics issue was first introduced. It was apparently agreed within the Bid Specification Committee (BSC) that biometrics could be included in the tender. It was not, however, a mandatory requirement. Once the tender was issued, the BSC's involvement ended. The BSC was not part of the decision to make biometrics a requirement to issue Bidders' Notice 2.[56]

Mr Hulley's involvement in the Sassa tender evaluation process became public with the inclusion of the Tsalamandris transcripts[57] in the *AllPay* case. In a recorded conversation Mr John Tsalamandris, a Sassa employee, who was secretary to the bid committee at the time, accused Mr Hulley, Sassa's 'strategic adviser' on the tender, of being on CPS's payroll, implying that some officials were bribed. The rot, he said, 'links right to the top, that's why Hulley is there'.[58]

Mr Hulley's involvement was later confirmed by Sassa.[59] It would appear that Mr Hulley played multiple roles in the process, first advising Sassa on how to settle the law suits with CPS and then switching to a new role in which he earned R21 000 per day for providing 'commercial, financial and legal advice' to Sassa.[60] A *Mail & Guardian* investigation went further, revealing that in an interview, Mr Serge Belamant, CEO of Net1, had said that Mr Hulley had been brought in before the tender in an attempt by Sassa to settle various lawsuits CPS had brought against it.[61] If true, the *Mail & Guardian* noted, it was remarkable that after investigating the possibility of settling CPS's cases against Sassa, Mr Hulley was drafted as an adviser on a tender the company later won.[62]

THE NEW TENDER PROCESS

The 2013 Constitutional Court order made it clear that Sassa was to issue a new tender for the national payment of social grants for five years. Sassa was to insource the payment of social grants should a service provider not be appointed (see Chapter 3). To comply with the order, Minister Dlamini appointed a Ministerial Advisory Committee (MAC) to investigate and advise her on the best payment options for social security. Amongst other things, the committee was asked to explore the existing market for a suitable payment model that would make it possible for Sassa to pay social grants in-house.

In December 2014, the MAC submitted a report in which it recommended that Sassa should develop its own payment system and that work streams should be established to facilitate the implementation of the committee's recommendations. Coinciding with this, Sassa was in the process of advertising a new tender in line with the court order. There were, however, disputes around the RFP. CPS took exception to the lack of clarity around the technicalities of the tender and the use of beneficiary data, which the Black Sash Trust had also raised concerns about. The Constitutional Court was required to provide guidance, in the form of a follow-on judgment to the *AllPay 2* case, on the revision of the RFP and set out the timeframes by which Sassa and the DSD were required to complete the process.[63] The RFP was revised and issued again on 24 March 2015.

In October 2015, the new tenders were adjudicated, in line with the Constitutional Court timelines, and on 5 November 2015, Sassa filed a progress report to the Constitutional Court informing it of the outcome of the tender process and outlining the steps that Sassa proposed to take over the payment function after 31 March 2017. On 25 November 2015, the Court issued an order indicating that it was satisfied with the proposal put forward by Sassa to take over the payment of grants and the Court discharged its supervisory jurisdiction over Sassa as it was no longer viewed as necessary (see Chapter 3).[64]

THE FORMATION OF A PARALLEL STRUCTURE

In July 2015, Minister Dlamini sent the CEO of Sassa, Ms Petersen, a letter instructing her to appoint various work streams, based on the recommendations of the MAC. In the letter, the minister gave the following instructions:

> I have decided that in order to roll out implementation process diligently, we need to retain the collective knowledge and

institutional memory of the key members of the Committee.
Given their knowledge and expertise, these members will
lead the work streams and work jointly with you and the
Sassa Executive Management team to ensure that the various
work streams are adequately resourced to execute [sic]
their respective mandates in a speedy manner without any
disruption, and to minimise delays in the implementation of
the third recommendations.[65]

A year lapsed between the minister's 2015 letter and the appointment of
the work streams by the new acting CEO, Ms Raphaahle Ramokgopa,
in July 2016. Foley and Swilling explain that it is unknown why there
was this delay in appointing the work streams, but one possible reason
could be that their appointment (for which R47 million was budgeted
over three years) was not in line with a Public Finance Management
Act (PFMA) (No. 1 of 1999) requirement for an open tender process.[66]

Ms Zodwa Mvulane was appointed as project manager for the
payment system. She had no prior experience of complex payment
systems. The work streams reported directly to the minister through
Ms Mvulane, thus bypassing departmental and Sassa processes. This
meant the work streams were elevated above DSD and Sassa officials,
which limited Sassa officials' ability to carry out their mandates. Foley
and Swilling note that the appointment of advisory committees may
exacerbate the weaknesses of key state institutions, creating a powerful
network of seemingly 'independent' experts and advisors.[67] The line
between advising and decision-making tends to fall away with the
emergence of a Shadow State. This is where the decisions made by
so-called 'kitchen cabinets'[68] are carried through into state institutions
and legitimised via repurposed tender procedures for the appearance
of upholding the constitutional state facade.[69]

The work streams ultimately delayed the process of Sassa taking
over the payments of grants, thus benefitting CPS, and came at a cost
of R40 million.[70] They appeared designed to benefit the independent
consultancies owned by members of Minister Dlamini's hand-
picked MAC who were irregularly procured to run the process. One

such consultant was Mr Patrick Monyeki, a close associate of fired Sars Commissioner, Mr Tom Moyane, and a man who had bagged significant government contracts over the years. Mr Monyeki's company, Rangewave Consulting, was also exposed as having scored an R80 million windfall for an IT strategy review at Sars, as part of Mr Moyane's illegal R200 million deal with global advisory firm Gartner. (While Mr Monyeki resigned as director of Rangewave in March 2018, he remained a shareholder.[71]) In addition, a 2012 investigation by *amaBhungane*[72] revealed that Mr Monyeki served as the IT technical advisor on the Bid Evaluation Committee (BEC) in 2011 for the R10 billion tender and was alleged to have swung the tender in favour of CPS.

In April 2016, Ms Mvulane became aware that Sassa would not be able to take over the payment of the grants within the timeline mandated by the Constitutional Court. She concluded that Sassa would probably require two more years, which meant continuing payment to CPS in the interim. The technical work stream would later advise that 'the plan [presented in the progress report] was overly optimistic, unrealistic, and underpinned by insufficient research'.[73]

Concerned by the apparent lack of progress, Mr Dangor (who was then special advisor to the minister and co-chair of the Ministerial Task Team regarding deductions from grants), together with Mr Sipho Shezi (also a special advisor to the minister), met with Ms Mvulane and the acting CEO of Sassa, Ms Ramokgopa, at the beginning of October 2016. It became clear that the acting CEO had very little knowledge of the work streams' plans or what Sassa intended to do.[74] In November 2016, Mr Thokozani Magwaza took over as CEO of Sassa, replacing Ms Ramokgopa. Previously Mr Magwaza was the acting Director General at the DSD, and Mr Dangor replaced Mr Magwaza in this position. Both Mr Magwaza and Mr Dangor raised concerns about the work streams reporting directly to the minister and not to Sassa, which in effect 'created parallel reporting structures'.[75]

Testimonies given at the Section 38 inquiry mandated by the Constitutional Court to determine Minister Dlamini's role and responsibility in creating a parallel decision-making and communication process made it clear that within the government there was no agreement on a future payment system or how a crisis was going to be averted.[76] There was a stark contrast between the different approaches of the officially recognised state that is set up in compliance with constitutional requirements and the covert, unconstitutional Shadow State.

The first option (promoted by DSD officials Mr Dangor, Mr Shezi and Mr Magwaza) was to limit the reliance of Sassa on CPS as much as possible, in order to remove CPS from the grant payment system within a year, and, importantly, to approach the Constitutional Court to inform it that Sassa could not meet its undertaking to the Court to insource the social grant payment system. The second option (preferred by Minister Dlamini and enabled by the parallel work streams of external consultants) was to enter into a new (invalid) contract with CPS, with newly negotiated higher rates for at least two more years. An important aspect of this second approach was that Sassa would not seek to approach the Constitutional Court prior to entering into a new, invalid, contract with CPS. It would instead inform the Court after the fact. This was in direct opposition to the recommendations presented to Sassa and the DSD in three separate written legal opinions.[77]

Through later court filings it came to light that Minister Dlamini had travelled to KwaZulu-Natal to meet President Zuma.[78] A media report[79] alleged that at the meeting the minister also met with Mr Hulley, among others. It is not clear if it was Mr Hulley's advice that Sassa did not need to seek direction from the Constitutional Court for extending CPS's payment services, but should rather inform the Court once negotiations for a new contract had been finalised. There appeared to be no written legal opinion justifying this new approach, which was in stark contradiction to the other three legal opinions that had been attained.

Minister Dlamini's decision to act against the advice given in three separate legal opinions to approach the Constitutional Court regarding the extension of CPS's services was thus based on an unseen 'new legal opinion'.[80] Significantly, this decision appears to have been made outside the formal government structures of Sassa and the DSD.

UNRAVELLING THE CAPTURE OF SASSA

In response to the uncertainty around the continued payment of social grants after the invalid contract between Sassa and CPS was due to come to an end, the Black Sash (then joined by Freedom Under Law) approached the Constitutional Court as an applicant. The outcome of the litigation – the extension of the invalid contract by the court to ensure beneficiaries would receive payment, the appointment of a Panel of Experts and the section 38 enquiry which was a mechanism to hold Minister Dlamini to account (see Chapter 3) – was critical in exposing state capture at Sassa.

South Africa is a constitutional democratic state in which public norms are based on the Constitution and all the citizens of the country are expected to act in accordance with the rule of law. The Shadow State, however, does not subscribe to the principles on which the Constitution is based. The Shadow State strives not only to subvert the Constitution but, if allowed, to replace it – hence reference is made in the *Betrayal of the Promise* report to a 'silent coup'.[81] This can only be achieved by changing public norms, often through deception that is rooted in populist politics.[82]

In the run-up to and following the March 2017 Constitutional Court ruling, those who had opposed Minister Dlamini's approach resigned or were removed from the offices of the DSD and Sassa. Mr Dangor[83] resigned from the post of Director General of the DSD in March 2017 (four months into his appointment) and by 10 April 2017 Minister Dlamini's long-time special adviser, Mr Sipho Shezi, had been fired.[84]

With the crisis averted, and just prior to leaving Sassa on 17 July 2017, Mr Magwaza terminated the contracts of the members of the work streams after National Treasury had declared their appointment irregular. At the same time, Mr Magwaza also received approval from National Treasury for a deviation from the standard procurement process for provisioning services between and within different government entities. This enabled him to sign the cooperation agreement between Sassa and Sapo.[85]

However, on 19 July 2017, Minister Dlamini replaced Mr Magwaza with one of her close supporters and a fellow member of the ANC Women's League, Ms Pearl Bhengu.[86] With all three opponents (Mr

Dangor, Mr Shezi and Mr Magwaza) out of the way and an ally now appointed as acting CEO of Sassa, the Shadow State's modus operandi of removing key senior officials and replacing them with pliable people, or people in 'acting' positions, in order to further its agenda, was still in play. Long serving civil servants such as Mr Dangor, Mr Shezi and Mr Magwaza, who understood their roles and responsibilities as governed by law, had the ability to push back against instructions that were in contravention of the required governance standards. However, Ms Bhengu had limited experience as a civil servant, which may have made her less able to do so.

Towards the end of October 2017, the Panel of Experts established by the Constitutional Court in 2017 presented a damning report to the Court regarding the conduct of Sassa officials who were responsible for ensuring that a grant payment system was in place by April 2018. The panel indicated that the absence of a comprehensive implementation plan for Sassa's stated objectives providing adequately for risk management, risk mitigation and proposed alternatives should the course of action fail, or an exit plan in respect of CPS, presented a serious risk.[87] The panel had not received a copy of the Sapo RFP, despite requesting it on numerous occasions from the department.

Alarmed by the Panel of Experts' report and the fact that Sassa had missed four self-imposed deadlines for signing a contract with Sapo, the Standing Committee on Public Accounts (Scopa) and the Social Development Portfolio Committee called on the DSD, Sassa and Sapo to update Parliament (see Chapter 6). As meeting after meeting unfolded, it became clear that the divide between Sassa and Sapo would require an intervention. After Mr Magwaza's exit from Sassa, the two state entities could not reach an agreement. The portfolio committees combined their efforts supported by National Treasury to remedy this situation.

On 8 November 2017 Minister in the Presidency Jeff Radebe, who was the chairperson of the Inter-Ministerial Committee (IMC),[88] reported back to Parliament that the committee had set up a task team to intervene and that an agreement would be concluded by 17 November (see Chapter 6).[89] However, at this meeting copies of a letter from the Director General of National Treasury to the CEO of Sassa outlining serious flaws in Sassa's handling of the matter were distributed to Members of Parliament. It stated that 'Sassa should not have approved the disqualification of Sapo on three areas but rather seek to engage and explore options on possible ways to close the capacity gap or seek the intervention of the Inter-Ministerial Committee' (see Chapter 6).[90]

It is unclear who supplied this letter to the MPs. The Director General of National Treasury found that the BEC and BAC did not appear to have used the Centre for Scientific and Industrial Research's (CSIR's) due diligence report in reaching its conclusions and recommendations, and that the RFP specifications were 'biased'. This letter, together with the history behind the invalid contract between Sassa and CPS, caused many of the MPs to raise concerns that Sassa was deliberately attempting to delay a takeover of payment services, leading to yet another self-created crisis in April 2018. Once again, the debate was whether the contract with CPS would be extended or if CPS would be contracted again, under a different name, through 'the back door'.[91]

On 17 November 2017, at the 11th hour, the IMC on Comprehensive Social Security under the leadership of Minister Jeff Radebe agreed upon an implementation protocol between Sassa and Sapo (see Chapter 6).[92] This agreement came eight years after Minister Skweyiya's agreement with Sapo in 2009.[93]

In December 2017, at the ANC national conference, Mr Cyril Ramaphosa was elected president of the ANC. In February 2018, Mr Jacob Zuma resigned, and Mr Ramaphosa was elected President of the country. Shortly thereafter President Ramaphosa made significant changes to the Cabinet and removed Ms Bathabile Dlamini as Minister of Social Development. She was redeployed to the Presidency, as Minister of Women, Youth and Persons with Disabilities, and Ms Susan Shabangu became Minister of Social Development. This event marked a turning point for Sassa and the social grant payment system by removing the apparent internal obstacles that were delaying the transition to Sapo supporting Sassa with the grant paymaster function.

Following Minister Dlamini's transfer out of the DSD, there was a marked change in how the DSD and Sassa approached the transitioning of the grant payment system from CPS to Sapo. Still under the watchful eye of the Constitutional Court's Panel of Experts, both Sassa and Sapo continually reported on the progress of the transition, leaving little room for any deviations that might derail the process. From the Black Sash's perspective, the principle goal for the period of transition was to monitor, report, and propose remedies for challenges as and when they arose.

By the time Parliament intervened in November 2017, Sapo had less than five months to meet the looming deadline of 1 April 2018 for taking over the payment of social grants. A contract between the DSD, Sapo and Sassa was signed on 10 December 2017 and the difficult task of transitioning the grant payment system commenced.[94]

Of the four principle functions outlined in the original RFP from Sassa, Sapo was awarded three: the development of an integrated payment system; the provision of banking services; and the management of card production, all of which required beneficiaries' biometric data.[95] The only remaining function was the servicing of cash pay points. With only a few months to finalise the procurement process and contract negotiations, it was highly unlikely that a replacement for CPS would be in a position to take over cash payments from April 2018. Sassa, however, only approached the Constitutional Court with this information on the eve of the deadline. On 23 March 2018, to ensure that beneficiaries continued to receive cash payment services, the Constitutional Court extended the suspension of the order of invalidity, and the contract between Sassa and CPS was extended for an additional six months.[96]

Ruling in favour of the extension sought by Sassa, the Constitutional Court again levied significant criticism against both Minister Dlamini and Ms Bhengu. Both were instructed to explain why they should not be held liable for the costs related to the second extension of the CPS/Sassa contract. Ultimately, both were found to be responsible for the extension, but only Minister Dlamini had a personal costs order placed against her following the outcome of the Section 38 inquiry (see Chapter 3), and not in respect of the 2018 extension.[97] In handing down judgment, the court said:

> It has been a sorry saga and it is proper that Minister Dlamini must, in her personal capacity, bear a portion of the costs. It would account for her degree of culpability in misleading the

Court – conduct which is deserving of censure by this Court
as a mark of displeasure – more so since she held a position
of responsibility as a member of the Executive. Her conduct is
inimical to the values underpinning the Constitution that she
undertook to uphold when she took up office.[98]

In May 2021, Dlamini complied with a payment of the portion for
which she was held personally liable for the taxed costs of Black Sash
and Freedom Under Law in the amount of approximately R650 000. Ms
Nicole Fritz, CEO of Freedom Under Law, said in response that it was
essential that government leaders entrusted with important positions
of care and responsibility on behalf of our society's most vulnerable
members 'be required to face real reckoning when they so starkly fail
to discharge their responsibilities'.[99]

Shortly after Minister Dlamini's departure from the DSD, Minister
Shabangu swiftly removed Ms Bhengu from the role of acting
CEO of Sassa. In May 2018, it emerged at a Scopa meeting that in
December 2017 Ms Bhengu had signed off on payments of almost
R20 million for four seemingly unscheduled events. All the payments
fell under the R5 million ceiling for authorising expenditure without a
competitive bidding process. The dates of these events coincided with the
run-up to the ANC elective conference.[100] However, in November 2018 Ms
Bhengu was appointed CEO of yet another state-owned entity, the Ithala
Development Finance Corporation.[101]

Following the extension permitted by the Constitutional Court,
Minister Shabangu cancelled the cash payments bid and added the
cash payment function to the Sapo contract. This sudden addition to
the scope of Sapo's services meant that Sapo would need to take over
additional aspects of the payment of social grants at very short notice.
Sapo, it seems, did not have the capacity to meet the logistical and
regulatory requirements of providing beneficiaries with the option of
receiving their grants at pay points. This led to the closing down of
hundreds of pay points across the country, in contravention of long-
standing payment standards and policies such as the 5 km maximum
travel distance for beneficiaries to access their social grants.

Providing cash payment services was not Sapo's only challenge. New Sassa/Sapo Special Disbursement Account (SDA) cards needed to be produced and distributed. The process of issuing the new cards was initiated in May, but only completed in December 2018.[102] When the initial deadline for the extension of the CPS contract was reached in April 2018, an agreement was made with Grindrod Bank that beneficiaries could continue to use the old Sassa-branded Grindrod Bank cards until they either registered on the new system or had indicated a preferred private bank account to which their grants could be transferred.

This arrangement, however, came at a cost to beneficiaries, with a R10 monthly service fee charged to those still using the old bank card.[103] Based on the expert panel's reports, it seemed there was no plan in place for Sassa to seamlessly migrate electronically paid grant recipients who were using the old CPS Sassa-branded Grindrod Bank cards into the new system by September 2018.

The panel reported allegations that Net1 was intentionally attempting to sabotage the migration from CPS to Sapo by conducting a misinformation campaign to encourage grant recipients to open EasyPay Everywhere (EPE) bank accounts, and refusing to allow Sassa and Sapo employees to access the sites where grant recipients received their cash payments.[104] By the time the Sassa crisis reached its peak at the beginning of 2017, Net1 had managed to sign up approximately 1.95 million beneficiaries for EPE bank accounts since its launch in June 2015.[105] It was estimated that by 2020 more than two million grant recipients (approximately 20 per cent of total recipients) had opened EPE accounts. Regulation 21(1)(a) stipulates that grant beneficiaries wishing to have their grants paid into a private bank facility of their choice are required to provide such authorisation in writing, on a prescribed form.[106] This requirement, however, does not appear to have been applied to the numerous social grant beneficiaries who were receiving grant payments in EPE accounts. Net1 argued that the 'biometric authorisation' attained using Net1's proprietary technology was a sufficient indication of beneficiaries' preference for payment into EPE bank accounts.

This indicates yet again how Net1, through CPS, leveraged its biometric technology and access to the beneficiaries' data to evade national government regulations. In June 2018, Sassa began to automatically transfer beneficiaries who had not signed the required forms into new Sassa/Sapo accounts.

THE COST OF SASSA'S CAPTURE

It is not possible to provide a comprehensive, accurate estimation of the cost that resulted from the state capture of Sassa. However, the cost of the 2012 case which declared the contract constitutionally invalid was estimated at R10 billion over five years.[107] In addition, there were the other legal costs of litigation. The opportunity cost to the state is also difficult to calculate. Would Sapo have been in a better position to disburse grants efficiently and effectively had seven years not been lost to the invalid CPS contract? There is no way of knowing.

Over and above the constitutionally invalid CPS contract and subsequent irregular payment for the re-registration of grant beneficiaries, various instances of fruitless and wasteful expenditure, maladministration and possible fraud/corruption were ongoing concerns for Parliament (see Chapters 4 and 6).[108]

The following information illustrates the escalation of irregular expenditure: in 2010/2011, the year in which Ms Dlamini became minister and Ms Petersen become CEO of Sassa, the accumulated amount of irregular expenditure from 2007 stood at R8.8 million. In the 2012/2013 financial year, the amount recorded as irregular expenditure was R47.4 million. In the 2016/2017 annual report it was recorded that the closing balance of irregular expenditure stood at a staggering R1.4 billion.[109] In 2017, Sassa CEO Mr Magwaza told Parliament that much of the irregular expenditure happened on Ms Petersen's watch, and did not follow due process as required by the Public Finance Management Act.[110] In this meeting the following issues were flagged:

- R4.4 million was spent on damaged vehicles and R1.2 million on the 'Mikondzo event'.[111] No details were provided for the expenditure of a further R3.5 million.

- Ms Petersen backed a bid by audit firm SAB&T for a R74 million contract despite the BAC recommendation that the competing bidder, that scored the highest points, be awarded the contract.[112]
- R414m was spent on hiring private security companies for Sassa staff over a four-year period (2012 to 2016).[113]
- The work streams cost R40 million, and very little evidence can be provided on what work was actually done by them.[114]
- R233 million was spent on a lease paid to convicted fraudster and former Northern Cape ANC chairperson John Block, and R74 million was paid irregularly to audit firm SAB&T.[115]

Most important is the cost to beneficiaries. In 2017, CPS submitted an audit statement, as required, declaring that the company had made an estimated profit of R1.1 billion (see Chapter 2). However, this amount was contested as it did not include profits that had accrued to Net1 from the sale of financial and other products to social grant recipients, and the monies lost through unauthorised and allegedly unlawful deductions from grants. In May 2016, Mr Magwaza reported, 'the total monetary loss due to the unlawful deductions was close to R800 million'.[116] In addition, beneficiaries were forced to pay transaction fees by Grindrod Bank and bear the high costs incurred in attempts to access recourse.

CONCLUSION

Emerging from the Panel of Expert's assessments of the events that unfolded during the capture of Sassa, the need for a structural review and reform of the entire social grants payment system was deemed necessary. The two main issues identified were the systemic risk that was present with social grant payment being serviced by a sole supplier[117] (with an extremely wide scope without proper controls and supervision), and the way Sassa was structured – and continues to be structured.

In terms of the Sassa Act, the minister may override any decision taken by the CEO. Sassa CEO's decisions were overturned by Minister Dlamini, and she assumed the de facto role of chief accounting officer of Sassa. For example, during the Sassa crisis the CEO was not able to veto the minister's decision to appoint the work streams that created a parallel reporting structure, and the minister overrode the CEO's decision to file a report with the Constitutional Court about the necessity for the Court to consider an extension of the period of invalidity of the CPS contract. The minister instructed the CEO to withdraw the application which he filed. This amply demonstrated the conflict between the Sassa CEO and minister, where the minister took the approach that it had not been necessary to approach the Constitutional Court. This nevertheless coincided with the urgent direct access application which the Black Sash had launched, whereby the minister was still obliged to account to court.

Unlike state-owned entities, which are generally governed by a board of directors that provides a degree of separation between the administration and management of the entity and the executive, the CEO of Sassa reports directly to the minister of the DSD. There is no board or any other governing body that could enable recourse for the CEO as the accounting authority.[118] While a CEO was appointed in 2019, there are various positions, particularly regional executive managers, that in 2021 remain vacant.

At the time of writing in 2021, Sassa still had a way to go to re-establish its credibility and to play its part in ensuring that the Sassa/Sapo grant payment system is fully functional. Its reputation has been severely damaged in the process of state capture. However, with new leadership and the determined efforts of civil society organisations, Sassa is in the process of reasserting its independence and integrity.

6 *Parliamentary oversight of Sassa*

Parliament is mandated to conduct oversight of the national executive and organs of state. The committees – portfolio, select and standing – can be considered the engine of Parliament's oversight and legislative work. Committees – comprising multi-party Members of Parliament (MPs) – scrutinise legislation; oversee annual reports and spending by departments, state entities and Chapter 9 institutions; and engage the public, among other roles. They also have the power to summon any person or entity to give evidence and/or make submissions. Committee meetings and proceedings are open to the public. The Portfolio Committee on Social Development[1] as well as the Standing Committee on Public Accounts (Scopa)[2] oversee the Minister of Social Development, the Department of Social Development (DSD) and Sassa.

The Parliamentary Monitoring Group (PMG) plays an important role in making public recordings, transcripts and summaries of parliamentary committee meetings as well as submissions and documents tabled. It also publishes all the written questions submitted by MPs to ministers; and parliamentary questions provide another form of oversight of the executive. This chapter draws substantially on PMG's public records of meetings held by the Portfolio Committee on Social Development and Scopa, as well as questions and replies between MPs and the minister. It speaks to the efforts by MPs to hold the minister, the DSD and Sassa to account for the ongoing unauthorised, fraudulent and allegedly unlawful deductions from social grants, the crescendo to and beyond the 2017 social grant crisis, and finally the termination of the CPS contract.

ALLEGATIONS OF DEDUCTIONS

The Portfolio Committee on Social Development first became aware of the concerns about deductions from social grants as early as 2010, when MP Ms Semakaleng Kopane of the opposition Democratic Alliance (DA) asked the Minister of Social Development:

1. Whether she has been informed that a certain company (CPS), Northern Cape allegedly granted loans to recipients of state grants at an interest rate of 50%; if so,
2. whether any investigation has been launched into these allegations; if not, why not; if so, what are (a) the findings, (b) the recommendations and (c) the further relevant details;
3. whether she has taken any action against the company; if not, why not; if so, what are the relevant details?[3]

The minister's office submitted the following reply:

1. No, the minister has not been informed of allegations of the CPS (Northern Cape) granting loans to recipients of State Grants at an interest rate of 50%.
2. Yes.
    (a) During our investigation into the practice by CPS, it transpired that (according to CPS) its holding company is registered with the National Credit Regulator (NCR) to operate a loan scheme. However, the certificate provided by CPS was questioned by the region as CPS was not listed on the NCR credit provider database and Sassa Northern Cape regional office is in possession of a copy of the alleged proof of registration that belongs to another business entity going under the name of Friedland 035 Investments

(Pty) Limited. This is contrary to the provision of the schedule that gave the entitlement to Cash Paymaster Services (Pty) Limited/Aplitec.

(b) In terms of the current Service Level Agreement the CPS is contracted to render only the cash payment service to the Agency. Schedule 2 – RDP Program of Action of the previous SLA provides that the Service Provider will make a loan facility available for the beneficiaries on a market related basis to counteract local 'loan sharks'. However, the current SLA has no similar provision. It is our conviction that the schedule 2 was ultra vires in that Section 20 of the Social Assistance Act, Act 13 of 2004, provides that a beneficiary must without limitation or restriction receive the full amount of a grant to which he or she is entitled before any other person may exercise any right or enforce any claim in respect of the grant amount. Only the minister may sanction deductions from a beneficiary's social grant, which deductions must be necessary and in the best interest of the beneficiary.

3. Yes, action has been taken as outlined below:
   - A formal investigation into the matter has been instituted;
   - The matter has been reported to the National Credit Regulator; and
   - Sassa has ordered CPS or Friedland 035 Investments (Pty) Limited not to pursue the practice and to comply with the 100 m radius applicable to all unauthorised vendors.[4]

It was unclear from the records whether the actions listed by the minister's office under (3) were undertaken or enforced.

ESCALATION OF UNAUTHORISED AND ALLEGEDLY UNLAWFUL DEDUCTIONS

In 2012, when Sassa awarded a contract to CPS for the national payment of social grants, MP Michael Waters (DA) asked – in April – if the minister was aware that a certain company was offering loans to pensioners and deducted fees (loan repayments and interest) from social grants before they were paid out to the pensioners.[5] Mr Waters asked if the minister intended to take steps to combat this practice. The minister responded that she had not been informed about the company's alleged activities. She reiterated that, in terms of Regulation 26(A) of the Social Assistance Act (No. 13 of 2004), no loan deductions were allowed. Only deductions relating to funeral policies or schemes were authorised.[6] Despite these legislative provisions, unauthorised, fraudulent and allegedly unlawful deductions continued.

In June 2013, the issue of deductions was raised again by Ms Helen Lamoela (DA) who wanted to know if Sassa and the DSD had investigated claims of fraud and exploitation of the elderly when they accessed their grants.[7] The minister replied that neither CPS, Sassa nor the DSD were aware of any cases of fraud and exploitation of the elderly. She encouraged MPs to submit evidence to the DSD of such cases for further investigations.

An article by *Business Day* journalist Ms Linda Ensor was circulated at the committee meeting of 22 October 2013 which referred to an alleged legal dispute over loan repayments to CPS, which the Legal Resources Centre (LRC) said left many grant beneficiaries with little to live on.[8] Sassa CEO Virginia Petersen reported that the agency's 2012/13 annual report recorded complaints of ongoing deductions from the Sassa-branded Grindrod Bank cards.[9] She stated that according to Regulation 26(A) of the Social Assistance Act, deductions of no more than 10 per cent of the value of grants were permitted, and only for funeral cover.[10] She said when Sassa tried to close a micro-loan service, the 'loan sharks immediately came up with a triple amount that beneficiaries had to pay'.[11] Sassa engaged the Financial Services Board (FSB) to assist in conducting a survey of all deductions, as well as the funeral benefits on offer.[12] Ms Petersen explained that a definition was required – whether a grant or pension was considered an income – to stop people from using social grants as collateral.[13]

At a committee meeting on 15 October 2014, Ms Evelyn Wilson (DA) advised that she was aware of illegal deductions – for airtime and electricity – made from a Sassa card in Limpopo.[14] She asked when the corruption would stop. The minister retorted that the issue of corruption was not only a problem in Sassa. 'Communities also contribute to corruption. They are squandering their own money. The most robbed grant recipients are older persons.'[15] The chairperson said the matter of illegal deductions required legal action. The minister again acknowledged that there was a problem.[16]

In 2014 the Ministerial Task Team (MTT) was established comprising senior executives of Sassa and the DSD working together with civil society organisation under the auspices of the Black Sash. On 17 October 2014 committee member Ms Veronica van Dyk (DA) enquired:

1. When will a recourse system – which is owned and controlled by Sassa – be designed and implemented to ensure that unlawful debit deductions are stopped and refunded with interest and bank charges?
2. How will Sassa and her department ensure that CPS, which according to the Constitutional Court judgment is performing a state function through the payment of social grants, complies with all the relevant legislation and regulations and what measures will be included that will restrict third party creditor access to the social grant beneficiaries' bank account?
3. Will the payment systems be designed in such a manner that social grant bank accounts are off limits to creditors; if so, (a) how will this be done and (b) by when?
4. Has her department and Sassa blocked and reversed with immediate effect any debit deductions for (a) Umoya Manje services, (b) loans and (c) any other financial service

providers other than legal 26(A) deductions; if so, what are
the relevant details?

5. Did she engage the SA Reserve Bank to issue a directive in
    terms of Section 12 of the National Payment System Act,
    no 78 (1998), in the public interest to protect the Sassa bank
    accounts and confidential information of grant recipients?[17]

In her response, the minister informed MPs that Sassa was in the
process of issuing a new tender for the payment of social grants that
would resolve some of the critical issues. With regard to illegal or
unauthorised deductions, she referred MPs to a media statement
dated 27 August 2014 about measures the DSD together with Sassa
had already embarked on to address this and other related challenges
(also see Chapter 3).[18]

On 22 October 2014, in response to the Auditor General's report on
Sassa, the committee asked for an update on progress the DSD and Sassa
had made in addressing the deductions problem.[19] Sassa reported that
the MTT was tasked with exploring ways to address deductions from
social grants. In a written question on 31 October 2014, Ms Liezl van
der Merwe (IFP) asked the Minister of Social Development:

> What (a) is the status of the report of the Ministerial
> Committee that was appointed to (i) investigate illegal
> deductions from the Sassa grant recipients' accounts and
> (ii) advise on a future payment model for social assistance
> benefits, in view of the fact that a preliminary report was
> expected to be submitted before the end of July 2014? (b)
> were the report's findings and (c) remedial action has her
> department taken?[20]

In her reply the minister indicated that she had published the content
of the report during a media briefing:

> I outlined both preventative and remedial action. The
> programme of action, which the Department and key

stakeholders will embark on to address the identified challenges has been made public and the Honourable Member can familiarize herself with the content thereof.[21]

While the minister had indicated to the committee in July that it would receive a preliminary MTT report, it would appear from the line of questions to the minister that MPs did not receive the report that was released to the media. The requests by MPs to be briefed and receive progress reports on compliance with the constitutional court order and the work of the MTT became an ongoing struggle.

PROGRESS TOWARDS A NEW GRANT PAYMENT SYSTEM

In March 2015, MP Mncedisi Filtane of the United Democratic Movement (UDM) asked the minister if she had completed the process of designing and implementing a (recourse) system owned and controlled by Sassa to ensure that unauthorised and allegedly unlawful deductions from a large number of pensioners' grants was stopped and affected pensioners were refunded with interest and bank charges; and if not, why not and what was the timeframe for the implementation of the specified system.[22] The minister said Sassa had drafted a Request for Proposal (RFP) for a new payment service provider that had been published on 28 October 2014. She continued that the RFP prohibited any deductions from social grants, except for the permissible deductions as per 26(A) of the Social Assistance Act.

In June 2015, Sassa updated the committee on its plans to take responsibility for the payment of social grants by April 2017.[23] Ms Petersen explained that a feasibility report – outlining technological solutions required for insourcing social grant payments – had been completed by the Ministerial Advisory Committee (MAC) and work streams had been proposed to facilitate the implementation of the MAC's recommendations.

In October 2015, Ms Petersen advised the committee that while the new payment tender was in progress, as per the Constitutional

Court order, there were further legal challenges during implementation that required a change to the revised RFP and an extension of the bid deadline (see Chapter 3).

In November 2015, Ms Deidre Carter of the Congress of the People (Cope) asked the minister whether the request for a meeting with her to discuss the concern regarding deductions had been granted.[24] Media articles had started surfacing, raising concerns about the progress Sassa was making in addressing unauthorised and allegedly unlawful deductions. The minister, apparently irritated, replied:

> As I have stated previously, I have set up a Ministerial Task Team made up of senior officials from the Department, Sassa, Black Sash and community organisations to look into this matter of illegal or unauthorised deductions and to recommend possible remedial actions, some of which we are currently implementing.
>
> When I received the Honourable Member's correspondence on this issue, I accordingly advised that we join our efforts by working jointly with the Task Team in order to avoid unnecessary duplication. This would have enabled the Honourable Member to familiarize herself with the work of the Task Team and the various measures we are currently implementing to address this matter. An impression created through sensational and misleading media articles that I don't take this matter seriously is very unfortunate, especially from the Honourable Member who knows that we have been constantly briefing the portfolio committee about various measures we are implementing in this regard.
>
> Unfortunately, the Honourable Member chose to conveniently hijack this serious matter in order to score cheap and unwarranted political points by publishing false media articles about how the Department and Government as a whole is handling this matter. This is an act of extreme political

desperation for a political party that does not have a political agenda. I take this matter seriously and I have instructed both the Department and Sassa to take necessary legislative measures to swiftly clamp down on illegal and fraudulent deductions.[25]

It appears from the meeting summaries that little information was provided to the committee on what was implemented and achieved with regard to the new payment system. It seems that during 2014 and 2015, the only detailed information provided to MPs was through their written questions to the minister.

By the third quarter of 2015 Sassa summited a report to the Constitutional Court indicating that it was not appointing a new service provider, therefore CPS would be completing its five-year contract on 31 March 2017. On this basis the Constitutional Court terminated its supervisory obligations.

RED FLAGS AND A LOOMING DEADLINE

During 2016 it was hoped that some of the concerns around deductions were at least partly resolved when the minister published amendments to the Social Assistance Act regulations (Sections 21 and 26).[26] The agency was to put in place a 'Sassa owned and controlled recourse system' with refunds for beneficiaries, backdated to 2012.[27] However, the implementation of the new grant payment system by the March 2017 deadline was running into difficulties. Members became increasingly concerned after repeated requests by the committee for Sassa and the minister to provide it with updates and deadlines on the insourcing as per the Constitutional Court's order.

At a committee meeting in August 2016, the chairperson, Ms Rosemary Capa, said that Sassa and the DSD had failed to give a straightforward report on the issue of deductions.[28] She said that MPs were angry that they were receiving incorrect information that might raise questions about their integrity; and that issues were not discussed in the committee because they were said to be *sub judice*, but were apparently discussed elsewhere.[29]

In the DSD's 2016 Budget Review and Recommendations Report released in October, Ms Wilson (DA) noted the DSD and Sassa had not reported on insourcing the payment of social grants (as contained in Sassa's report to the Constitutional Court).[30]

SCOPA WEIGHS IN ON IRREGULAR, FRUITLESS AND WASTEFUL EXPENDITURE

At the end of 2016, the issue of inappropriate expenditure surfaced. The Standing Committee on Public Accounts (Scopa), on 23 November 2016, requested the Minister of Social Development and Sassa officials to account for the irregular expenditure flagged in the Auditor General's report in Sassa's 2013/2014 annual report.[31] Of specific concern was the irregular payment of R316 million to CPS. In addition, there was the R414 million spent on physical security, R233 million spent on an office lease with the Trifecta group of companies, R75 million paid to SAB&T auditing and consulting services, and R20 million on other irregular expenditure, including R4.4 million on damaged vehicles, R1.2 million on the cancellation of a meeting for the department's Mikondzo Project on social delivery and R3.5 million for which no details were provided.[32] Mr Thokozani Magwaza,[33] CEO of Sassa, said most of these contracts were concluded by former employees including Ms Virginia Petersen and Mr Frank Earl.[34] Scopa told Sassa and the DSD that investigations would be held with consequences to follow.

LOOMING 1 APRIL DEADLINE

By November 2016, it was evident that the Portfolio Committee on Social Development was losing patience with both the minister and Sassa.[35] In its judgment, the Constitutional Court ordered Sassa to report on seven deliverables. The minister admitted that the deadlines for the seven deliverables had not been met. She asked the committee not to 'push [Sassa] to reveal its contingency plans in public as this might jeopardise the work it has done already'.[36] What mattered, she stated, was that grants would be paid on 1 April 2017.

Responding to the minister's request, Ms Sibongile Tsoleli (ANC) replied that the committee was a constitutional structure, a portfolio committee of the Parliament of the Republic of South Africa, and to claim that when the committee requested information it put the work of the department at risk was unacceptable, unless the information was classified. The information requested from the DSD and Sassa was not classified and the committee wanted to exercise its oversight freely. The committee asked for a report on Sassa's implementation of the new grant payment system, as the current presentation was not responding to this request. The committee wanted Sassa to come clean and alleviate the public's fears. Was Sassa ready to take over insourcing of grant payments? Members of the committee said they needed to be able to tell their constituents that they would receive their grants and to answer their questions.[37]

Ms Bridget Masango (DA) raised the concern that nothing was said about the deliverables being accomplished. She reminded the committee that the Constitutional Court had discharged its supervisory role on the basis of the list of deliverables with timelines. This raised a number of questions. What informed the timelines for the deliverables? Why was the post office, which had a footprint throughout the country, not included in any of the options?[38]

MPs noted that Sassa's presentation suggested that the agency was not ready to take over (insource) grant payments from 1 April 2017. Ms Wilson noted that five deadlines had been missed and Sassa had not returned to the Constitutional Court to explain why.[39] Towards the end of the meeting MPs wanted Sassa to confirm that CPS would continue the service until the agency was ready to insource grant payments and that social grants would be paid on 1 April 2017. The chairperson therefore instructed Sassa to prepare a progress report that clearly outlined its plan, timelines and challenges to meet the Constitutional Court order deadline.[40] This was the final meeting for 2016 before Parliament closed for its annual recess.

BUILD-UP TO A SELF-MADE CRISIS

As the 1 April 2017 deadline loomed, Parliament became increasingly alarmed at how little Sassa had done to take over grant payments. In its first meeting for the year on 1 February 2017, the committee ordered the minister, the DSD and Sassa to brief it on a weekly basis.[41] Ms Dlamini was absent for this briefing and MPs refused to accept the minister's apology, insisting she was not taking a matter of national importance seriously. In its report, Sassa acknowledged it had failed to do the work required by the Constitutional Court, and provided short, medium and long-term plan(s) for future grant payments.[42]

While ANC MPs accepted Sassa's report, opposition MPs expressed their dissatisfaction.[43] Some asked if a national emergency had been manufactured so that the CPS contract could be extended. Ms Liezl van der Merwe (IFP) referred to comments in the media by the CEO of Net1 (and CPS), Mr Serge Belamant, that he would continue to work with Sassa only under 'favourable' conditions.[44] She questioned whether Sassa was under political pressure to extend the contract. She noted that Sapo had been begging for this contract, yet Sassa planned to extend a lifeline to CPS instead. Sassa CEO Mr Magwaza denied there was political pressure to extend the CPS contract.[45] He had pushed for CPS and Net1 to be charged for their 'criminal act[s]' of facilitating and/or benefitting from allegedly unlawful deductions from social grants.[46] He further advised that CPS had been doing a good job paying grants and said it was Net1 that was responsible for the alleged deductions. He said that if CPS was the 'only option' that guaranteed payment of the grant on 1 April, 'so be it'.[47] He noted:

> Even though CPS is arrogant; however, it is the media that decides on their own that there is a crisis. Grants were paid before CPS, [they were] paid during CPS and will be paid after CPS. Grants must be paid on 1 April.[48]

It appears that in this meeting, ANC MPs decided to close ranks around Minister Dlamini, which was in stark contrast to the previous year when most expressed concern and frustration with Sassa's lack of progress. For example, Ms Pulani Mogotsi (ANC) said she was encouraged by the presentation and felt it showed that there is a way forward. She added the ANC government was doing a good job and expressed her support for the Ministerial Advisory Committee (MAC), the interim task team and the work streams.[49] Ms Wilson (DA) in rebuttal held that it was absolutely 'staggering' to say that a lot had been done when none of the seven deliverables had been met. Sassa had always known that it could not deliver or pay grants come 1 April, she noted.[50]

At the committee meeting held on 22 February 2017, the minister acknowledged that the DSD was still consulting its legal advisors.[51] A letter had been sent to National Treasury (dated 7 February 2017) requesting a deviation order – from the procurement requirements of the Public Finance Management Act – to enter into an extended contract with CPS. Treasury responded that such a request could only be considered with Constitutional Court support.

Sassa proceeded to present its plan to ensure that social grants would be paid on 1 April 2017 and advanced the options below:[52]

- Option 1: Procuring the service from the current service provider (CPS).
- Option 2: Procuring the service from Grindrod Bank, which serviced the majority of the beneficiaries.
- Option 3: Procuring the services of all banks wishing to comply with Sassa requirements.
- Option 4: Procuring the services of all banks wishing to comply with Sassa requirements for those beneficiaries who have access to banking infrastructure and procuring the services of the current service provider for grant recipients who are currently using cash pay points.
- Option 5: Procuring the services of Sapo.
- Option 6: For cash beneficiaries, appointing a service provider for cash distribution to grant recipients who are currently using cash pay points; and for banked beneficiaries, utilising existing bank accounts to disburse grants through the banking sector.

Sassa was in favour of option 1, saying it carried the least risk in terms of potential service delivery failure. Ms Zodwa Mvulane, Sassa grant payment transition project manager, explained that the intention was to have a Sassa card in five years. Sassa required two to three years to achieve this and the current service provider would be taking Sassa through this transition period. Sassa was in discussion with the post office to explore how it could assist with this in the long run.[53]

Option 5 made provision for the appointment of Sapo as the new social grant paymaster, an option that had been raised in previous committee meetings during 2016.[54] DA MPs asked why the post office had not been included in any of the options. Officials explained that Sassa wanted to work with the post office as it had a large countrywide footprint, however there were challenges with the post office that Sassa could not talk about. In addition, Sassa expressed concern about the possibility of post office workers going on strike and grant recipients not receiving their money.[55] Sassa outlined to MPs the pros and cons of the Sapo option:

> Sapo has a network infrastructure of 2 700 post office outlets which could be utilised for beneficiaries to go and collect their money. However, the cash pay points are working at ±10 000 pay points. Beneficiaries may not be reached especially those in the rural areas. There is also the need for a mechanism for transportation of money. Government to government collaboration is a good idea but the readiness of the post office to render the services is not clear.[56]

MPs of opposition parties expressed concerns, pointing out that there were only five weeks left before 1 April and the DSD had not begun negotiations with CPS nor had it approached the Constitutional Court. They also raised concerns about the work of the MAC – the precursor to the work streams – enquiring what it had been doing all these years. ANC MPs, in their responses, defended the DSD, arguing that the presentation demonstrated progress. They expressed the view that there was no national crisis on the horizon.[57]

SCOPA AND THE SASSA CRISIS

On 28 February 2017, the DSD and Sassa appeared before Scopa on the termination of the CPS contract.[58] The minister was absent, and Sassa CEO, Mr Magwaza, was on sick leave. Acting Sassa CEO, Ms Thamo Mzobe (also the CEO of the National Development Agency),[59] had been appointed that morning. Members were sceptical about the timing and expressed even greater disappointment that the minister was not present at such a critical hearing. They wanted to know if the representatives at the meeting had sufficient information to answer detailed questions. Scopa members decided they would confine themselves to asking questions about the CPS contract only, as the only other official present with relevant knowledge was Sassa Programme Manager, Ms Zodwa Mvulane.

Scopa asked why Sassa did not have contingency plans in place when the CPS contract was deemed invalid (and the period for the suspension of invalidity was about to expire). Sassa acknowledged its failure to meet the deadline and insisted that extending the irregular CPS contract was 'the safest option' to ensure that grants would be paid on 1 April 2017.

Members asked why CPS wanted a 30 to 50 per cent increase in its R16.44 fee per grant per month. The 30 per cent option would amount to a total payment of R3 billion and the 50 per cent option to R3.4 billion. Both were well over the 2017/18 Sassa budget of R2.6 billion. Most members expressed concern about the additional cost and where the budget would come from. They expressed doubt that National Treasury would make available additional funds, or that it would support an extension of the CPS contract unless the Constitutional Court permitted it to do so.[60]

Mr Mkhuleko Hlengwa (IFP) said they were on the eve of a crisis and pleaded with the chairperson, as a matter of urgency, to have the minister appear before the committee because the irregularities of this entire transaction were escalating.[61]

In closing, the chairperson, Ms Capa, said to the Director General, Mr Zane Dangor, that 'the CPS thing is a ruse which we are being given here. They are creating an emergency to put a gun to South Africa's head. The critical questions are why? What interest and whose interest? Whatever is going to be negotiated with CPS, we cannot stomach anything beyond 12 months'.[62]

On 7 March 2017, Scopa and the Portfolio Committee on Social Development convened a joint meeting.[63] The room was packed. The Scopa chairperson, Mr Themba Godi, said that Scopa was determined to find out how Sassa had reached this point. Minister Dlamini arrived 20 minutes late. She then requested to leave this meeting early, to attend a Cabinet meeting, and this was refused. The committees were adamant that she account in person.

The minister stated that 'the issue of grants was very important' and she did not want South Africans to think that she was arrogant. She objected to talk of a national crisis as grants would be paid on 1 April. She said that Sassa had underestimated the magnitude of the task and the time required. Sapo had been considered, but had been unable to cope with the enormity of the task. Sassa had 9 000 payout points, while Sapo had only 2 600 offices. Besides, most Sapo offices were found in the old apartheid towns and some areas did not have Sapo offices at all, she said.[64]

MPs were unimpressed with Ms Dlamini's explanations. They accused her of being unable to manage Sassa and some called for her to resign. She was also accused of misleading Parliament because National Treasury had not approved deviations made by Sassa and was unlikely to give approval.

On 8 March 2017, Sassa presented its weekly progress report to the committee. Sassa confirmed that it had held negotiations with CPS from 1 to 3 March 2017 and that they had reached an in principle agreement which would be made public once the negotiations had been finalised.[65]

Sassa informed the committee of the urgent application lodged in the Constitutional Court by the Black Sash, joined by Freedom Under Law. The court hearing was set for 15 March 2017. Committee chairperson Ms Capa said that the issue was now a national matter.[66] The committee had not known about the litigation and welcomed the information.

Sassa's next weekly meeting with the committee took place on 15 March 2017,[67] which was the day of the Court hearing of the Black Sash case. At this meeting Ms Dianne Dunkerley, Sassa's Executive Manager for Grants, gave the presentation in the absence of the CEO who was attending the Constitutional Court proceedings. Ms Dunkerley explained that an Inter-Ministerial Committee (IMC) was established after a Cabinet meeting on Wednesday, 8 March 2017.[68] The IMC would guide the process and ensure social grant payments were made in April 2017, as well as oversee the transition going forward.

The committee was informed that the negotiations with CPS had stalled and the IMC would identify a new team to negotiate with CPS, once the Constitutional Court had provided direction and after the National Treasury had approved the deviation from normal procurement processes.[69]

On 14 March, Net1's Mr Serge Belamant had warned that if there was no signed deal in place between Sassa and CPS by 15 March 2017, which was also the date of the committee meeting, grant recipients would not be paid on 1 April.[70] Speaking to the *Mail & Guardian* outside the Constitutional Court during a 15-minute break in the legal application brought by the Black Sash, Mr Belamant said:

> Is there anyone else right now who can do the job? The answer is no, except for the post office and the pigeons that they want to use. You know, I think they want to fly the money with pigeons and that might work better than the way they do the letters at the moment.[71]

Ms K Jooste (DA) sought clarity on Mr Belamant's statement that if the contract was not finalised that day, it would not be able to render the services again. If this was true, she asked, what should be done? The chairperson suspended any further discussion on the matter, as CPS was not present at the meeting to account for the comment.

THE TRANSITION TO THE NEW GRANT PAYMASTER

On 10 May 2017, Sassa and the minister appraised the Portfolio Committee on Social Development on the implementing of the court order made in the Black Sash's case.[72] In March, the Constitutional Court extended the declaration of invalidity of the prior CPS contract, so that it could be phased out over 12 months and reinstated its supervisory role for the duration of this period, with support from a Panel of Experts. Sassa noted that it was unclear at this stage who would take over the national payment of grants.

Ms van der Merwe (IFP) asked if Sassa was considering working with all banks, or only with Sapo, and whether the post office would be ready to take over the payment of grants within the stipulated time.[73] Sassa's CEO Mr Magwaza explained that Sassa would hold a workshop with Sapo the following week to explore whether and how the two entities could collaborate.[74] Ms Tsoleli (ANC) welcomed the presentation as a step in the right direction, but felt it lacked specific timeframes. She stressed that twelve months was not a long time. For oversight purposes, Sassa should ensure that the next presentation to this committee included timeframes.[75] Ms van der Merwe agreed the presentation lacked timeframes and also sought clarity on a statement made by the minister that the court order was unfortunate.[76]

In response, the minister took issue with the judiciary and the media:

> The most worrying aspect of this whole thing is that while waiting for the Court, newspapers are raising issues that are aimed to influence the entire process. One of the Judges (allegedly) said, 'we read what is in the newspaper'. This means that they are influenced by what is in the newspaper. What this also means is that whatever decision will be reached will be influenced by public opinion. Public opinion that is not tested is sometimes used as part of arguments, because it was said so by a judge. DSD is not the first department to miss deadlines for targets set. It is understandable that this issue brought so much attention because it involves payment

of grants to vulnerable people in the country. Sassa must be given the benefit of doubt whenever issues are raised. Hearsay should not be used to judge officials' performance.[77]

The minister's comments can be perceived as an astonishing attack on the independence of the judiciary.

SCOPA DEMANDS ANSWERS

During the first part of the meeting on 16 May 2017, Scopa's chairperson, Mr Godi, stated that the committee needed to know what measures they (Sassa and the minister) had taken to take over payments or, should Sassa not be ready in 12 months, would it be taking on a (new) service provider, he asked. Would Sassa have a legal contract within 12 months? A specific answer was required. What was the process? Secondly, the committee wanted to know about the working relationship between the Sassa CEO and the minister.[78]

CEO Magwaza replied that Sassa would take over in three to five years, and that costing was incomplete which meant he was unable to confirm the estimated R6 billion stated by the minister the previous day. At the end of 12 months, CPS would not be managing the payment system, he assured the committee. The data concerning beneficiary information would be migrated from CPS to Sassa between October 2017 and January 2018; if not Sapo it would be someone else, he said. A workshop with Sapo will take place the next day, after which they could report on progress. He confirmed that as CEO, he had a cordial employer-employee relationship with the minister. He said he went to court against the minister as he could not be held accountable for what happened prior to his arrival at Sassa.[79]

Mr Ezekiel Kekana (ANC) stated that it seemed as if the Court hearing was only yesterday as Sassa seemed to have accomplished so little in the interim. What about the filing on 17 June?[80] Mr Magwaza responded that Sassa was confident that it would file on 17 June. They were developing a business plan, which would be clearer following the meeting with Sapo. All the parties in the legal process filed names of technical and legal experts and the Constitutional Court would revert with selected names.[81]

In the second half of the meeting, Scopa focused on accounting for the R1.1 billion irregular, fruitless and wasteful expenditure highlighted in Sassa's 2015/16 audit report. Scopa continued to place pressure on Sassa to account for this.[82] The committee was informed that efforts had been made to locate former Sassa CEO, Ms Virginia Petersen, to provide information, but she could not be found.

Throughout the meeting MPs repeatedly expressed annoyance at the lack of detail in the financial report to the committee and the incomplete responses to questions. In conclusion, the MPs impressed on Sassa executives that they should apply themselves more diligently to the task of financial and consequence management, and insisted that information should be submitted promptly to finalise the report on the R1.1 billion irregular, fruitless and wasteful expenditure. In addition, Sassa was to submit a report on timelines for the implementation of the Constitutional Court order.[83]

MINISTER BRIEFS COMMITTEE ON SAPO'S ENGAGEMENT

On 31 May 2017, Sassa officials and the minister briefed the committee on its engagement with Sapo. In Sassa's presentation, it listed Sapo's capabilities:

- It had already established pay channels and was effecting payment.
- It had known experience as a payment provider of social assistance.
- It had experience of operating as a bank (Postbank).
- Beneficiary data would be secured as it would be managed within government.
- Reliable and trusted Telkom support would be provided on technology and connectivity.
- Government would be investing in its own infrastructure through this collaboration, thereby supporting the broader state infrastructure development plan.

- It provided an opportunity to mobilise within government for support, such as from the State Information Technology Agency, the Council for Scientific and Industrial Research (CSIR) and the Government Printing Works, to increase their capacity for the greater good of government.
- It had a sophisticated payment infrastructure.
- A letter of agreement with the agency was in place which provided opportunities for collaboration.[84]

Members were encouraged by the progress made with Sapo. However, they felt that the presentation still lacked the detail they needed to understand the status of the transition to a new service provider. Mr Solomon Mabilo (ANC) pointed out that the presentation did not contain specific and realistic timelines that would enable oversight by the committee. The minister agreed that Sapo must present a full report to this committee. She confirmed that before submitting the June progress report to the Constitutional Court, Sassa would bring it to the committee so that the legislature was aware of its content. Sassa would also submit this progress report to the IMC.[85]

Several MPs asked about how Sassa would ensure the protection of beneficiaries' confidential data. In response, Sassa's Chief Information Officer, Mr Abraham Mahlangu, said that the issue of data was pervasive across the board because it is related to the fine print. Beneficiaries' data would be protected between Sassa and government existing repositories such as the trust centre. The trust centre has various layers of security and Sassa would use beneficiaries' data to effect payment only, and not for any exploitative motive or financial benefit. He noted it was unfortunate that beneficiaries' data was used when it was in the hands of the agent that was trusted by Sassa to pay grants.[86]

SASSA FAILS TO PRESENT ITS WEEKLY PROGRESS REPORT

On 14 June 2017, Ms Nelisiwe Vilakazi, the DSD's Acting Director General, said Sassa would not be able to present its weekly progress report, but would soon do so in writing. She explained that the agency was overwhelmed with work as it had to submit its first report on 15 June (the following day) to the Constitutional Court.[87]

Ms Masango (DA) said the CEO of Sassa had assured the committee that it would see the report before it was submitted to the Court. The chairperson, Ms Capa, then asked the committee secretary to read out the committee's resolution that stated that the Sassa progress report was a standing item that must be presented at every one of its meetings with the committee. Ms Tsoleli (ANC) expressed concern, saying that not presenting the weekly report was 'surprising' and 'unacceptable'.[88] The committee's weekly progress meetings with Sassa appeared to have failed in yielding clear results. The problem was at another level.

On 21 June 2017, in the presence of Minister Dlamini, CEO Magwaza explained that Sassa had submitted its first report to the Constitutional Court and also held a meeting with the Panel of Experts.[89] After frank examination of the agency's internal capacity, time and the process required to take over the payment function from CPS, Sassa was convinced that it would not be ready to take over the full payment function value chain after the 12-month extension. However, CPS would be replaced by a new service provider within this period. Acknowledging the complexities related to the insourcing of the payment system, Sassa, in consultation with the DSD, would focus on a hybrid grant payment model, as illustrated at the centre of Figure 6.1, which would include the following:[90]

- Sassa would insource certain components of the payment process.
- Sassa would procure the services of a payment service provider as an interim solution through a competitive bidding process.
- Sassa would engage with other organs of state involved in the payment space for possible collaboration in line with approved prescripts.
- Sassa would continue with efforts to build internal capacity to take over the payments.

Figure 6.1 Summary of Sassa's plan

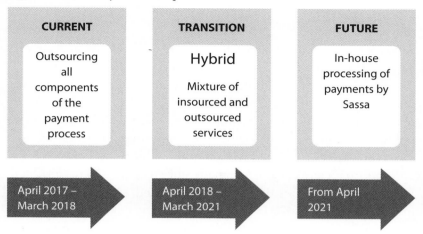

Source: PMG, 21 June 2017, see Sassa presentation

Pursuing partnerships with other government entities, committee members were not confident that Sapo would be ready by April due to the pressing timeframes provided by Sassa. Sassa indicated that Sapo had developed its concept following the joint workshop in May and would be ready to present its model by the deadline of 25 August. Until then, Sassa was unable to determine which services Sapo would be able to provide.[91]

On 5 September 2017, Sassa and Sapo were scheduled to brief Scopa on their agreement.[92] However, Acting Sassa CEO, Ms Pearl Bhengu, informed Scopa that Sapo could not present its plan as Sassa was instructed by the IMC to perform a due diligence on Sapo's proposal before an agreement could be finalised. The CSIR was appointed from among three submissions and its report would be completed by the end of September.

Scopa chairperson, Mr Godi, asked National Treasury whether, in the event that Sassa was going to use Sapo, Sassa would identify what Sapo could do and not do. The National Treasury official replied that the legislation stated that if the service cannot be provided by a government entity, it has to be advertised. But if it is entity to entity, both entities have to approach National Treasury. Sassa raised concerns about engaging Sapo. Treasury advised Sassa to follow the Demand

Management guidelines. The Treasury official also stated that a due diligence performed on a government entity is different from a due diligence conducted on a private company. Sassa needed to verify what Sapo could deliver in relation to the scope of work. However, it appears Sassa never followed Treasury's advice and regulations.[93]

Mr Hlengwa (IFP) commented that it appeared as if alternatives were being made to avoid working with Sapo that would allow CPS to enter through the 'back window',[94] and stated that there was no political or administrative will to work with Sapo. He requested that the committee be furnished with minutes of meetings between Sassa and Sapo to review the progress made since their joint May workshop. He asked that the transition process be detailed, so as to see who was involved in the process. The committee ran the risk of being lost and seeing many players on the field and many cooks in the kitchen, he said.[95]

On the whole, members were unhappy with the answers it received from Sassa in this meeting. They felt Sassa was not enthusiastic about working with Sapo. This meeting also did not give them confidence that Sassa would meet the Constitutional Court deadline.[96]

CONTESTATION OVER MANDATES AND REPORTING LINES

The following day, on 6 September 2017, the minister, together with Sassa officials, met with the committee.[97] The minister introduced Ms Pearl Bhengu as the new Acting CEO of Sassa. The minister complained about the route for reporting on Sassa work. She said Sassa was expected to report to Scopa as well, while they scarcely had time to meet with this portfolio committee. She had written to the Speaker of the National Assembly about reporting to two committees. Chairperson Capa replied that due to the recess, the portfolio committee had not met with Sassa for 11 weeks (since 21 June) for a progress report. However, she agreed with the minister that Scopa was overreaching its mandate and said she would consult Parliament's legal unit about this.[98]

The chairperson was of the view that Scopa should engage only on the findings of the Auditor General. It was a political management situation that she as the leader would take up. The committee allowed the Sassa officials to attend a meeting with Scopa the day before the committee met. Scopa could not be prioritised over this committee's agenda. The political organisations expected reports from MPs deployed to this committee.

Ms Masango (DA) recalled that former Sassa CEO, Mr Magwaza, had promised the committee the first bite at the report before it went to the Constitutional Court, but the committee had not seen the report.[99] Sassa officials also attended a meeting with the Panel of Experts, instead of meeting with this committee. Only one official met with the portfolio committee and presented a one-page report. She wanted to know why that was allowed to happen.

The chairperson revealed she had written to the Auditor General as the committee wanted a copy of the recent quarterly progress report. However, the Auditor General was explicit that Sassa's progress reports were to be tabled with the Constitutional Court first. The chairperson was of the view that the Auditor General had to report to the committee, as a legally constituted platform. She contacted the legal unit of Parliament for clarity on reporting lines. It was explained that in this case the Auditor General and the Panel of Experts (comprising 10 independent legal and technical experts) were monitoring and reporting to the Constitutional Court only and not to the committee. Their scope of work was to monitor and evaluate Sassa's compliance with the Constitutional Court order, including steps for competitive bidding and a determination of the steps taken by Sassa to appoint a new contractor. Lastly, responding to the concerns of MPs, the chairperson clarified that Sassa was responsible for the remuneration of the Panel of Experts.[100]

New committee member Dr C Madlopha (ANC) expressed concern that the Auditor General and the Panel of Experts would not report to the portfolio committee but directly to Constitutional Court, and about what seemed to be an adjustment of the committee's powers.[101] She suggested engaging the Auditor General, National Treasury and Scopa to discuss the situation. She further observed that there appeared to be no difference between the scope of work of the Panel of Experts and the work streams. In addition, government paid for the work of the work streams, and she asked that the Auditor General, Treasury and Scopa compare respective remunerations of the Panel of Experts and the work streams.

The chairperson informed MPs that the Panel of Experts' evaluation on Sassa's first progress report was due in September 2017. The minister informed the committee that she was to brief the IMC on 13 September 2017 on Sassa's Constitutional Court report and committed to briefing the committee the day after, on 14 September.[102]

ANOTHER SOCIAL GRANT CRISIS ON THE HORIZON

On 16 October 2017, a media report revealed that the Auditor General and the Panel of Experts warned of another looming social grant crisis.[103] 'The agency has repeatedly failed to provide the panel with the documents it needs to assess its progress, and keeps missing its deadlines … It's yet to sign an agreement with the South African Post Office (SAPO) to be the new payment distributor, which means SAPO cannot invest in the infrastructure it would need to undertake this massive task.'[104] It was further reported that Minister Dlamini seemed to obstruct Sassa's efforts to appoint a new payment service provider.

Two days later (18 October 2017) the committee was due to receive a progress report from Sassa and the DSD on their plan to implement the Constitutional Court order, but the minister, the DSD and Sassa failed to attend this meeting. On enquiring, the chairperson received a letter from Sassa stating it was not ready to report.

Ms Tsoleli (ANC) said that this committee was at a critical moment when it came to its oversight role of Sassa. The Constitution had spoken about the power of the National Assembly[105] to hold government entities to account and gave provision for summoning the minister, the DSD and everybody concerned. She believed the summoning should start right away. Another Sassa disaster was looming, and the integrity of the committee was at stake, she said.[106]

Ms Masango (DA) reminded the committee that earlier in the year (in March 2017), questions had been raised about where this committee was in the lead-up to the 1 April deadline. The report of the Panel of

Experts on a television news report[107] was shocking, she said. It was 'embarrassing' to hear that Sassa had not provided them with 90 per cent of what it asked for, and it was 'frightening' that none of the timelines were met.[108] Ms van der Merwe (IFP) confirmed that the Auditor General and the Panel of Experts' report said, 'they [Sassa] will not meet the Constitutional Court deadline'.[109] Therefore, it was of great concern that Sassa told this committee it had nothing to report. She described this as another looming disaster.[110]

Ms Mogotsi (ANC) said the minister should have tabled the report before the committee because it, and not the Court, conducted oversight. The committee should not be reading about the report from the media.[111] The chairperson said there was no need to get the report from the media – it must be tabled before the committee by the relevant bodies. She would contact the Auditor General to request the report. She believed the committee had reached a cul de sac and had used all relevant instruments and corporate principles to engage with the DSD and Sassa to give it this report. She said Sassa's failure to be at this meeting was embarrassing and disappointing. It was agreed that as Sassa had also failed to meet with Scopa, the committee would organise a joint meeting to question the minister and her officials about the findings of the Panel of Experts.[112]

The joint committee sitting took place on 24 October 2017. The minister did not attend. MPs expressed frustration that yet again Minister Dlamini was absent, but they decided to continue the meeting regardless of her absence as there was an urgent matter to be dealt with.[113]

Sassa came under scrutiny for offering Sapo only one of the four possible services in implementing the new grants payment system. Sapo was to provide an integrated payment system that could handle beneficiaries' biometric data but was unsuccessful in its bid for the other three services, namely: providing banking services, card production and cash payments at pay points.[114]

Sassa Acting CEO Ms Bhengu told the committee that Sapo had until 26 October 2017 to respond. However, Sapo did not wait that long. In a letter dated 20 October 2017, Sapo said it found Sassa's offer unacceptable and insisted on being awarded all four services. This letter was brought to the committee's attention by Ms van der Merwe (IFP). Ms Bhengu reiterated that, despite Sapo's letter and its conditional acceptance, the planned phase-out of the current payment system would continue.[115] Ms N Mente (EFF) from Scopa said that all the information received related to the shortcomings of Sapo and that she felt it was unfair that Sapo was not present to answer for itself. She thus requested a meeting with the Sapo team together with Sassa as a meeting in Sapo's absence was fruitless. Mr Tim Brauteseth (DA) from Scopa said that he had been in communication with the CEO of Sapo and he could categorically state that the committee was being lied to by Sassa's representatives. The CEO had agreed to take the stand and be cross examined on the issue before the committee. Mr Vincent Smith (ANC) from Scopa agreed with Mr Brauteseth that the committee was being misled.[116]

Another joint meeting with all stakeholders, including the Minister of Social Development, the House Chairperson, the National Treasury, Scopa, Sapo and Sassa was scheduled for Tuesday, 31 October 2017.[117] A day before the meeting (30 October 2017), Minister Dlamini released a media statement in which she announced that Sapo did not meet the requirements to fully take over the distribution of social grants.[118] The DA responded immediately, saying that it was now clear that Minister Dlamini was yet again trying to manufacture another situation where the country was forced to accept another extension of the CPS contract.[119] The opposition party said that 'dodging Dlamini' had continued to sideline Parliament as she had throughout the entire procurement process, and she had repeatedly failed to account to the Portfolio Committee on Social Development.[120] DA Shadow Minister of Social Development Brigitte Masango said that Dlamini's 'actions are in violation of her oath of office and are in defiance of the Constitutional Court order'.[121] Minister Dlamini 'can expect a grilling for failing to put the vulnerable people of our country first' at the joint committee the next day.[122]

At that joint parliamentary meeting, both committees wanted answers. Co-chairperson Godi (from Scopa) said that he did not wish to engage in meaningless talk. 'The committee needed a demonstration from the DSD and Sassa that they were, indeed, taking active measures to comply with the terms of the judgement of the Constitutional Court.'[123]

Mr Godi said that Sassa's presentation was the same one it had given the previous week, and therefore it would be better to answer MPs questions directly. After some engagement with the minister, the chairperson summarised the situation: 'there was no agreement between Sassa and the Post Office since the SCOPA meeting on 24 October.'[124] The minister objected to Sapo making a presentation at this meeting, as there was no agreement in place. However, both chairpersons agreed that Sapo should present.

Sapo told the committee it had previously paid social grants and that the post office had capacity which had been tested. Secondly, in July 2017, Sapo had received a letter from former Sassa CEO (Mr Magwaza) confirming its appointment, following advice from the National Treasury. Sapo CEO, Mr Mark Barnes, told the committee that six weeks earlier he had downloaded the CSIR Due Diligence Report received by Sassa that was not shared with Sapo. Of the 218 criteria in the report, only eight had not been met. That gave Sapo a 97 per cent pass rate. Of those eight, Sapo would contest six criteria and two criteria were not applicable.[125]

Sapo's primary focus was its banking service with Postbank, a designated service provider in the National Payment System, which performed its own interbank transaction clearing.[126] It could provide all grant recipients with fully interoperable access to all ATMs, retailers and point-of-sales purchases. Postbank was sponsored by Standard Bank and had recently applied for its own banking licence. Sassa had excluded Sapo from delivering banking services as it had determined that the process of paying social grants should be divided into four areas and it had awarded Sapo only one of those areas. Mr Barnes pointed out that it was preferable for state entities to engage in inter-governmental processes. In this way they became an asset to the state by contributing to the fiscus, instead of outsourcing functions to the private sector. Of course certain services had to be outsourced, such as the transit of cash, but working together meant the entities would benefit from economies of scale.

With regard to the tender process, Ms Bhengu, Sassa Acting CEO, said she was not permitted to depart from the decisions of the Sassa Bid Committee. In his rebuttal the Minister of Telecommunications and

Postal Services, Mr Siyabonga Cwele, expressed the view that the process should be open as this was a collaboration between two government entities, guided by the Intergovernmental Relations Framework Act.

In order to break the deadlock, MPs suggested that the IMC should be requested to intervene. Some members requested a parliamentary inquiry into the matter. This request had support but the timeframe was problematic, as Parliament was due to go into an extended December recess.

Minister Dlamini persisted in saying that Sassa would work with Sapo, but there was no empirical evidence that Sapo should be given all the services of the paymaster. She stated Sassa was not going to be challenged by Sapo. They needed advice from Parliament and not enquiries that assumed that Sassa was not doing its work. Minister Dlamini also believed that National Treasury should give guidance. She felt that Sassa and the post office were still too far apart. The process was paralysed because Sassa depended on Sapo having clear timeframes and a way forward. Sapo was not going to move, and Sassa had said that the information was too scanty, she said. Both CEOs should tell the meeting how to deal with the impasse.

Dr Mnyamezelezi Booi (ANC) said he supported Sapo and that the members were not interested in CPS. The joint committee had to accept the report of the panel appointed by the Constitutional Court which had said that Sassa and Sapo were to work together. The Sassa CEO had been asked to tell the committee exactly what the problems were, but she had not done so. The Panel of Experts had concerns about the leadership of Sassa as the locale of the problem. Co-chairperson Capa cautioned MPs about supporting a particular organisation. The co-chairpersons then requested the Sassa and Sapo CEOs, with their teams, to meet that afternoon and the following day, and report back the following evening on a way forward. The ministers agreed to this and National Treasury stated it would be prepared to observe.

The following day, 1 November 2017, Scopa and the Portfolio Committee on Social Development met with Sassa and Sapo to discuss progress in overcoming the deadlock on the social grant contract.[127] The Director General of the National Treasury reported that despite two meetings in the last 24 hours, Sassa and Sapo had not reached an agreement. It had been decided to set up a task team co-lead by National Treasury and the South African Reserve Bank to find a resolution for the deadlock. It was agreed that Treasury would review Sapo's capacity to implement the national payment system for social grants. National Treasury would also facilitate discussions between the technical teams of Sassa and Sapo and bring on board the Reserve Bank to ensure collaboration and that deadlines were adhered to.

MPs made it clear that the committee favoured neither Sassa nor Sapo.[128] They expressed concern that despite 14 meetings between Sassa and Sapo, the technical teams had never met. Members said as far as possible the grant payment system should be kept intergovernmental, and a public procurement process was therefore entirely unnecessary and time-consuming. The approach should be investing in and capacitating the state rather than outsourcing a service that ought to be in the hands of the state. Members added there needed to be a clear indication of how long the review and mediation process would take as there were only 100 working days left until the 1 April 2018 deadline. Members also asked the IMC, led by the President, to account for how social security had become a protracted crisis.

At a meeting on 8 November 2017, Minister Jeff Radebe, chairperson of the IMC on Comprehensive Social Security, briefed a joint meeting of Scopa and the Portfolio Committee on Social Development.[129] Minister Radebe said that the IMC had noted the intervention of the parliamentary committees and also noted the public anxiety that had arisen due to the delay in the finalisation of the appointment of an entity to pay social grants after the current service provider's contract expired. The IMC had considered Treasury's review of the engagement between Sassa and Sapo and had taken a decision to fast track the introduction of an integrated payment system that would be provided by a partnership between Sassa and Sapo. This included the establishment of a dedicated team from Sassa, Sapo, the Department of Home Affairs and the State Security Agency (SSA) to review and strengthen the project plan which would outline a detailed plan for execution, resource requirements, critical milestones and a communication strategy. The roles and responsibilities of each party would be detailed in the implementation protocol.

The members welcomed the intervention by the IMC, but a heated discussion ensued about a letter from the National Treasury addressed to the Acting CEO of Sassa which was circulated to MPs prior to the meeting. The letter stated that Sassa should not have approved the disqualification of Sapo; that the specifications developed by Sassa were biased; that the CSIR report was not used for its intended purpose; and that Sassa took more than 60 days to evaluate and adjudicate one proposal.[130]

Members felt that these statements by the National Treasury should be discussed in the meeting and that the Minister of Social Development and other relevant officials should answer to the allegation that Sassa and the department had created this crisis. The co-chairpersons cautioned, however, that the letter had not been addressed to the committee, it had been unofficially circulated and it was not a report to the committee. This led some committee members to protest that oversight was being suppressed. They wanted a commitment that the National Treasury findings would be considered once the IMC process was in place.

Mr Hlengwa (IFP) warned that the committee had been down this road before with regard to timelines and commitments. He argued that the IMC was dealing with people who lacked the political discipline to adhere to their own commitments. This process was initiated by members and it would only be fair if Treasury briefed the committee on the outcomes of the review. The country had spent almost R500 000 on the CSIR report, which was supposed to be an upfront assessment of what was possible and not possible. It was making a mockery of oversight if the report was not addressed.

The committee agreed it would invite the IMC to address them on 21 November. The committee wanted to hear from the IMC as the political leadership, and co-chairperson Godi thanked the IMC for being responsive to Parliament's call.

Finally, on 21 November 2017, the IMC briefed a joint committee meeting on the agreement between Sassa and Sapo on the payment of social grants.[131] Minister Radebe spoke about
- the Constitutional Court directives;
- why the IMC, on behalf of the state, had to intervene;

- the technical committees' mandate for finalising the agreement between Sassa and Sapo;
- the public sector-led hybrid model that allowed a set of public and private sector service providers to offer social grant beneficiaries maximum choice, access and convenience; and
- the conclusion of the agreement between Sassa and Sapo.

The IMC had also organised a signed implementation protocol, an approved communication strategy and the implementation plan itself.

In the new agreement, Sapo was to provide four functions: the corporate control holding account; the Special Disbursement Account (SDA); the production and distribution of cards (subject to price competitiveness); and the on-boarding of new beneficiaries (subject to cost effectiveness). The agreement also allowed external parties, including commercial banks, to assist with the social grants payments. Minister Radebe said the new system was designed to ensure that no single service provider had a monopoly. The IMC was also able to align the implementation plan with the timeframes of the Constitutional Court and to synchronise the work programmes.

The committees were pleased with the IMC's work and appreciated the leadership of the IMC chairperson in resolving the impasse between Sassa and Sapo, but remarked that if the IMC had done its work from the start, the challenges would not have escalated.[132]

At a press briefing on 10 December 2017 Minister Radebe said that the government was delighted to announce that it had reached a landmark agreement between Sapo and Sassa to bring to life a new grants payment system:

> This new system while drawing on the resources and capabilities of the South African democratic state, will also make allowance for the participation of other partners such as enterprises and commercial banks, in the payment of social grants to beneficiaries.[133]

CONCLUSION

In its yearly review, Parliament described 2017 as a bumper year of parliamentary business, court battles, internal squabbles, jousting, brinkmanship, attempts to remove the President from office, and many parliamentary inquiries.[134] The review also described how Scopa, together with the Portfolio Committee on Social Development, had led the charge in running battles with Social Development Minister Bathabile Dlamini and Sassa in finding a new distributor of the more than 17 million social grants.[135]

This chapter shows that it was almost impossible for Parliament's Portfolio Committee on Social Development to exercise oversight and hold Minister Bathabile Dlamini and Sassa to account for the CPS contract. Often Ms Dlamini did not attend or arrived late or excused herself early from meetings. This led to the perception that she did not take Parliament or the looming social grant crisis seriously. The committee's oversight mandate was severely curtailed by its inability to access information and adequate progress reports from the minister and senior executives of the DSD and Sassa. It did not help that in some instances, ANC MPs shielded the minister and Sassa in their attempts to comply with Constitutional Court orders, particularly during 2017.

The Portfolio Committee on Social Development's line of oversight and accountability became blurred and diluted when Scopa, National Treasury and the IMC joined the fray to hold the minister and Sassa to account. This occurred concurrently with the Constitutional Court exercising its oversight role. The effective functioning of the committee, its instruments for oversight and accountability as well as its impact on social development was brought into serious question. It was a Constitutional Court order in March 2017, with supervision by the Auditor General and the Panel of Experts, that ultimately relieved the country of the CPS contract and the threat of unauthorised, fraudulent and allegedly unlawful deductions from the Sassa-branded bank accounts. The Constitutional Court set a precedent when it successfully held a member of Cabinet, Minister Dlamini, liable for the 2017 social grant crisis, which cemented her removal from office.

7 Black Sash's advocacy through partnership

The Black Sash Hoog campaign, from 2013 to 2018, played a significant role in the evolution of South Africa's social security system. The campaign adopted a variety of strategies to achieve its advocacy objectives. Key to these were the principle of giving beneficiaries the opportunity to speak for themselves, using their own power and agency to get the attention of the government. Amplifying the voices of grant beneficiaries also aimed to foster greater public awareness. This chapter explores elements of the Black Sash's advocacy campaign and its impact:

> Black Sash is recognised for its ability to have on-the-ground knowledge and expertise, to research and ground campaigns in a good understanding of legislation, and to be able to elevate issues through advocacy activities.[1]

COMMUNITY MONITORING

In 2009, with European Union funding, the Black Sash initiated and developed the Community Monitoring and Advocacy Project (CMAP). The Community Based Monitoring (CBM) programme works with community partners across the country to monitor and gather evidence about the quality of service delivery. Information is collated, analysed and compiled into reports. These reports provide strong evidence that is presented to the government and other significant stakeholders and, where necessary, released into the public domain, to acknowledge good service and improve delivery. The CBM programme helped shape and was invaluable in the Hoog campaign.

Following the awarding of the Sassa contract to Cash Paymaster Services (CPS) in 2012, the Black Sash noted the significant spike in irregular and allegedly illegal deductions and, with its community partners, began to focus on collecting, correlating and documenting the information it received from affected grant beneficiaries. This rigorous research process was crucial for relaying the various grievances experienced to the government.

Between 2012 and 2018 the Black Sash contracted 20 to 30 community partners every year to monitor Sassa's service and its pay points and other payment channels. The Black Sash compiled numerous reports and case studies that were presented to officials from Sassa, the Department of Social Development (DSD), the office of the Minister of Social Development and the Department of Planning, Monitoring and Evaluation (DPME). Key challenges during the CPS contract period included:

- ongoing unauthorised deductions from the Sassa-branded Grindrod Bank accounts;
- lack of recourse available to recipients;
- lack of recourse for EasyPay Everywhere (EPE) bank account holders, including where and how to close EPE bank accounts;
- faulty CPS machines and insufficient funds at pay points, with grant beneficiaries being subjected to long waiting periods;
- the lack of commissioners of oath at pay points, in violation of the national Sassa instruction; and
- inadequate maintenance of infrastructure and buildings by the Department of Public Works.

THE TRANSITION TO THE NEW PAYMASTER

In 2018, the CBM programme shifted its focus to the transition to the South African Post Office (Sapo) as the new social grants paymaster,[2] and the new Sapo/Sassa Special Disbursement Account (SDA). An implementation plan with timeframes was agreed upon as well as the facilities to be monitored, which included Sassa cash pay points, Sassa local service offices (where card swaps took place), Sapo/Postbank outlets, ATMs, and commercial banks and retailers. Monitoring started in the first week of June 2018 and continued until November 2018, with 20 community-based organisations (CBOs) monitoring 32 sites in six provinces.

The CBM programme in 2018 conducted 6 127 surveys, an average of more than 300 surveys per site. In June, 990 beneficiaries were interviewed at the 32 sites. In July, 912 beneficiaries were interviewed at 25 sites. In August, 1 184 beneficiaries were interviewed at 18 sites. In September, 1 037 beneficiaries were interviewed at 17 sites and in October 410 beneficiaries were interviewed at 20 sites.

Despite letters granting access from Sassa and the support of Sassa and Sapo staff, CPS refused to allow Black Sash staff and community partner monitors to enter Sassa pay points. CPS threatened to cancel payments if Black Sash monitors did not vacate the premises. Although agreements and monitoring had been conducted for a while, CPS claimed that there was no national written agreement between Sassa and CPS to allow monitoring to take place.

During the first week of card swapping, the system was very slow and frequently experienced problems with internet connectivity across regions. In the second week of June, Sassa/Sapo removed biometric verification on the Home Affairs National Identification System (Hanis), which radically increased the number of card swaps that could be completed. Biometrics were re-introduced in the third week of June using thumb prints only.

The CBM monitors observed many challenges. Sapo infrastructure was highly inadequate. Several Sapo branches experienced internet connectivity problems. Cards were often out of stock. The venues were not equipped to process the high volumes of beneficiaries and recipients. Cash often ran out long before all beneficiaries had been paid. Many beneficiaries were forced to travel long distances, at their own cost, to receive their grants because many pay points had been decommissioned. Sassa failed to communicate with beneficiaries and educate them adequately. Beneficiaries were transitioned to the new SDA without documentation providing the terms and conditions of the new account. There were no flyers on the terms and conditions of the new Sassa/Sapo card and Sassa help desks were not visible at pay points.

In addition, merchants and retailers provide cash back payments to grant recipients within the National Payment System, without formal partnerships with this sector. As a result, many retailers imposed a minimum spending requirement as well as cash withdrawal limits on beneficiaries and recipients. EPE cardholders were able to withdraw cash at Sassa pay points in violation of Sassa norms and standards.

During the transition period, the Black Sash was actively engaged with stakeholders from Sassa and the DSD, as well as with the Panel of Experts appointed by the Constitutional Court, to oversee the transition to Sapo as the new social grant paymaster. The Black Sash provided reports on how the transition was unfolding on the ground, based on the feedback obtained through the CBM programme.

The Black Sash's contribution to the monitoring of the grant payment system was acknowledged when, in its final report to the Constitutional Court, the panel suggested that Sassa should draw on the monitoring reports by other organisations, including those produced by the Black Sash and community advocacy organisations. The Panel of Experts strongly recommended that Sassa establish a formal Recourse Forum. The Black Sash and its CBO partners, along with Sassa and the DSD, became founding members of the Recourse Forum when it was established in March 2018. In addition, the panel also recommended that the Department of Social Development's Inspectorate for Social Assistance should also develop a framework in respect of monitoring Sassa as an institution. In January 2021, legislation was passed to constitute the Inspectorate, which will be rolled out over the medium term.

MOBILISATION

Speak Outs

An important element of the Hoog campaign was enabling grant beneficiaries to speak for themselves. The Speak Out initiative was aimed at giving grant beneficiaries a public platform on which to engage government officials, particularly the DSD and Sassa, as well as the Minister of Social Development. These meetings, attended by between 50 and 100 people, were held at public venues in communities from which multiple complaints had been received about unauthorised deductions, alleged to be unlawful and/or fraudulent.

The first Speak Out was held on 29 January 2014 at Khotso House, Johannesburg. Officials from the National Treasury, the Office of the Public Protector and the Department of Trade and Industry heard testimony from grant beneficiaries, Black Sash and its partners as well as from other CBOs who bore witness to the impact of these deductions on individuals, households and communities.

On 16 April 2014, a larger Speak Out meeting was hosted by the Adelaide Advice Office where Mr Thokozani Magwaza, Deputy Director General for Social Security at the DSD, gave an undertaking to reopen the Adelaide Sassa office (see Chapter 3). The reopening in May 2014 was an important victory for the local community and for the Adelaide Advice Office. Beneficiaries had spoken for themselves and used their power and agency to get the attention of the government.

On 20 July 2015, the Black Sash, working collaboratively with the Paarl Advice Office, initiated a Speak Out meeting in Franschhoek, Western Cape (see Chapter 2). The Speak Out was attended by more than 50 grant recipients, Mr Magwaza, who was by then the acting DSD Director General for Social Security, and representatives from Sassa and 1Life. This was followed by a number of Speak Outs in the Western Cape, including in Genadendal and Botrivier.

This grassroots approach of enabling beneficiaries and local CBOs to use their voices became an important principle when taking up local cases and systemic issues with the Ministerial Task Team (MTT) at a national level.

Mass action

The Black Sash and its community and strategic partners staged silent public protests prior to Sassa's appointment of a new social grant service provider. On 15 and 16 October 2015, more than 1 000 people attended a silent protest organised by the Black Sash at St George's

Cathedral, Cape Town.[3] A similar protest was held at Mopanye Mall, Soweto, which 120 people attended. There was also a picket, organised with the Right2Know Campaign, outside the Sassa office in Mitchells Plain, Cape Town and at the Sassa national offices in Pretoria. The memoranda of all these events were handed to DSD or Sassa officials for the attention of Minister Dlamini. The key messages demanded

- that Sassa take over the function of the payment of social grants from CPS';
- a Sassa owned and controlled recourse system;
- a stop to all unauthorised, unlawful, fraudulent and immoral deductions; and
- protection of the confidential data of the grant beneficiaries.

This mass action was supported by civil society organisations including the Community Advice Offices of South Africa (CAOSA), Right2Know Campaign, Section 27, Equal Education Law Centre, Trust for Community Outreach and Education, Dullah Omar Institute (UWC), Social Justice Coalition, Cape Metro Health, Tshwane North Outreach, the Justice and Peace (Archdiocese of Johannesburg and of Pretoria), Tshedza Community Development, Children in Distress Network, Alliance for Children's Entitlement to Social Security (ACESS), UWC Community Law Centre, Students for Law and Social Justice, Diakonia Council of Churches, United Democratic Movement, Rural Health Advocacy Project, Khanya College, Lebaleng Advice and Development Centre, the Interchurch Local Development Agency, the U2U Foundation and the People's Health Movement South Africa.[4]

In October 2016, Sassa informed the Constitutional Court that the agency would not award the tender for the payment of social grants to a new service provider, and intended to insource the national payment of grants between March 2016 and March 2017. As a result, deductions from the Sassa-branded Grindrod bank accounts continued, and grant recipients continued to struggle with access to recourse.

The Black Sash and other civil society organisations filled St George's Cathedral again on 12 October 2016 to pray for justice for beneficiaries plagued by unauthorised and allegedly unlawful and fraudulent deductions from their grants.[5] The event came ahead of four separate court cases, ultimately amalgamated under the Net1 case, heard in the North Gauteng High Court in Pretoria on 17 and 18 October 2016. The Black Sash and six social grant recipients had applied to intervene in the court case between Net1 and Sassa over the new regulations to the Social Assistance Act (No. 13 of 2004) published in May 2016.[6] After a short mass, prayers and candle lighting by the six recipients and a few testimonies, people gathered outside the cathedral displaying posters that highlighted the key problems.

On the days that the case was being heard, the Black Sash and community partners picketed outside the High Court in Pretoria. In Durban, the Black Sash in KwaZulu-Natal, together with some of its community partners, held a picket outside the Grindrod Bank offices.

Picketing outside courts on the days the Black Sash appeared gave the Hoog campaign and beneficiaries a bigger platform to make their voices heard. Notably in the 2017 Constitutional Court case, the Black Sash's notice of the intended picket was received and permission granted without objection.[7] However, the ANC Women's League, who came out in support of Minister Bathabile Dlamini, and the Democratic Alliance (DA), who opposed this, failed to provide the necessary notice or seek permission, and the Court instructed these protesters to disperse. In a strange turn of events, these protesters decided to join the Black Sash picket. Removing their party colours and requesting the orange and black Hoog t-shirts, they chose to use their voices in support of grant beneficiaries. It also proved to be an important teaching opportunity as the Black Sash and partner organisations explained the significance of the court papers and the relevant issues.

Shareholder activism

Shareholder activism was an important element in exposing Net1's business practices and shaming some shareholders into reparative action.

The Raith Foundation, one of the funders of the Black Sash's Hoog campaign, became increasingly aware of the need to address the contradiction between the goals of its grantees and the practices of some of the investment firms from which, as a shareholder, it drew its wealth.[8]

The foundation decided to support its grantees' advocacy work through shareholder activism aimed at making financial services companies more accountable.

Allan Gray asset manager

In March 2017, in the wake of the extension of the Sassa contract with CPS, it emerged that asset manager Allan Gray held the second largest stake in Net1's listing on the Johannesburg stock exchange, with a 16 per cent shareholding.[9] In the *Business Day*, journalist Ann Crotty noted that the Net1 UEPS share price had reached a 12-month high in the week to 2 March 2017, as CPS would retain the valuable social grant distribution business for at least another year.[10] Ms Crotty wrote that this was good news for Net1's investors, in particular Allan Gray, who had been the single largest shareholder by a substantial margin since 2012.[11]

The company defended its investment in Net1. In a follow-up article, Ms Crotty quoted the fund manager who stated Allan Gray's Net1 investment was 'based on the company's track record of successfully implementing reliable and robust payment technology, which comfortably handles millions of transactions both on and offline, across various different businesses and countries'.[12] He also said that the R1.8 billion (per annum) paid to CPS was 'small' in the context of the value of the grants distributed or the harm that would be caused if they were not paid. Allan Gray stated that a fee increase for the extended contract period would not be unreasonable given it had been fixed for five years. Ms Crotty further wrote that

> Allan Gray's response was a clinical financial explanation. And tone deaf to the point of sociopathy. There was no mention of the tragic social concerns that have dogged this company for five years. It is true that Net1 has never been found guilty (not surprisingly, given its partner, the SA Social Security Agency, was the target of court action, not Net1) and it may be that the questionable deductions from grants have nothing to do with the many Net1 companies set up to sell

profitable services to grant recipients. It may even be that there's no truth to the talk of corruption in the awarding of the contract in 2012. Even if Allan Gray believes everything Net1 CEO Serge Belamant says in public is 100% accurate, it should have had the sensitivity to acknowledge there might be some issues around this company. It's sad to think that ignoring issues may have helped Allan Gray to become so successful.[13]

The following day Ms Crotty published another article about Allan Gray's response, highlighting the plight of grant beneficiaries:

Perhaps researchers at Allan Gray, the country's fourth-largest fund manager, need to get out of their ivory towers a bit more. Because those who do get out and talk to some of the 17-million recipients of social grants find there is a lot to be concerned about with Net1's handling of the contract.[14]

Ms Crotty's articles focused the media spotlight on Allan Gray and the fund management industry. The debate raged over whether investment houses were acting consistently with their social responsibility mandates by investing in Net1.[15] The articles coincided with the Black Sash's Constitutional Court case against Sassa, placing even more pressure on Allan Gray when the experiences of grant beneficiaries became known to the wider public.

Magda Wierzycka, CEO of asset management company Sygnia, pointed out:

Most asset managers forget that they are the custodians of the savings of many South Africans who would be appalled to know that they own shares in Net1 which, it appears, exploits the poorest strata of society to make a profit.[16]

According to *Business Day* columnist, Bronwyn Nortje:

> It was foolish for Allan Gray to defend Net1's business practices, but then I also think paternalism towards the poor is deeply problematic. With any luck we will, in time, find out what has really been going on, but for now, the debate has raised several interesting questions about what exactly constitutes responsible or ethical investing.[17]

In March 2017, the Raith Foundation's Ms Audrey Elster and Mr Dugan Fraser wrote an article that was published in the *Business Day* raising concerns about Allan Gray's response to its investment in Net1:

> It is important to note, as Allan Gray has done frequently, that despite several external investigations into Net1's business practices, no evidence of wrongdoing has been found. But did one of the most successful investors in this country not stop to wonder about the Constitutional Court's concerns as far back as 2013? Yes, Net1 has not been found guilty of anything, but it was party to a contract the highest court in the land deemed irregular. Was this investor even aware of the anger swelling around the social grants contract? Did it really believe 12-million children would benefit from financial inclusion and the aggressive sale of services and products?

> In its search for the facts around Net1, why did it make no effort to engage with civil society organisations such as the Black Sash or Corruption Watch? That effort had to wait until days after the finance minister slammed Net1's shareholders for doing nothing. And how bizarre is it that poorly resourced non-governmental organisations often have to clean up a mess created by powerful companies while their 'un-responsible' shareholders looked on? Now the big question is where Allan Gray will go from here. Are the circumstances around Net1 unique enough for the fund manager to justify retreating

to its ivory tower and resuming its strategy of detached compliance? Or does it now realise a new active model is needed?

Allan Gray has made fortunes for many people by being innovative, super-bright and hard-working. Those skills should now be applied to working out how to protect short-term returns, while actively managing for long-term socially sustainable profits. And doing so in a way that isn't merely designed for a marketing campaign.[18]

Allan Gray buckled under the pressure of public scrutiny, announcing in mid-March 2017 that as a shareholder it was urging Net1 to forgo all profits on the extension of the Sassa contract.[19] The asset manager confirmed it would act to remove the Net1 board should it not change its practices. This response was in stark contrast to Mr Belamant's claim that Net1 subsidiary CPS should be paid more money for a new contract because his investors were demanding more.

Allan Gray also took to heart some of the recommendations outlined in the article by the Raith Foundation. Mr Andrew Lapping, Allan Gray's chief investment officer, told the media that they had been trying to find out exactly how beneficiaries were treated. He conceded that through this investigation, Allan Gray had become increasingly concerned and its engagement with Net1 had not alleviated these concerns.[20]

Allan Gray also asked Net1 to consider cancelling all recurring monthly deductions to Net1 subsidiaries for airtime. In a move to tackle cross-selling by other Net1 subsidiaries, Mr Lapping said, 'We have also asked them to consider such measures as sending three SMS messages per month for the next three months to all Smart Life policyholders, in their home language, offering a simple, easy and button-pushing way for policyholders to cancel their policy.'[21]

Mr Lapping confirmed that the company would make changes to the way it made its investments and had hired someone to investigate Net1's social and economic impact. As part of this investigation, Black Sash and its partners received an invitation to meet with Allan Gray.[22]

At this meeting, and working with the Witzenberg Rural Development Centre (WRDC), the Black Sash challenged the Allan Gray representatives to talk directly with grant recipients in Ceres, Western Cape.

This occurred, and following email correspondence between Allan Gray, the WRDC, the Black Sash and Grindrod Bank, Net1 was asked to bring its equipment to the meetings so that the grant recipients could resolve their recourse and other issues then and there. The meetings, held in May and June 2017, were attended by over 1 000 people. Grant recipients delivered a petition to Allan Gray focusing on the EPE bank account, a product of Moneyline (a subsidiary of Net1) and Grindrod Bank. Ms Barbara October (nèe Maregele) from *GroundUp* attended the meetings and wrote the following:

> During the event, hosted by the Black Sash and the Witzenberg Rural Development Centre, beneficiaries from Ceres, Tulbagh, Wolseley and surrounding areas were given a platform to voice concerns about their social grants. Representatives from Allan Gray, then a major shareholder in Net1, also attended the meeting.[23]

One after the other, the beneficiaries – most of whom were older women – recounted being coerced into taking out multiple funeral policies to get loans. They also complained that to query other deductions, they had to borrow money to call the Sassa helpline or travel to the nearest Net1 office in Worcester, about 45 km away.

After the May 2017 event, Mr Pieter Koornhof, investment analyst at Allan Gray, promised to 'put pressure' on Net1 to resolve the issues. The beneficiaries came up with a list of demands that included:

- Free monthly statements should be provided to make tracking deductions easier.
- Beneficiaries should not be given an EPE account with Smart Life policies if they didn't qualify for loans.
- If beneficiaries wish to close their EPE accounts, this should be done within 30 days in the town in which it was opened.

- Net1 should stop selling Smart Life policies as a condition for getting a loan.
- Allan Gray was to ensure that Net1 officials went to Ceres the following month to assist personally those who wish to close their accounts.

In June 2017, Net1 appointed a seasoned financial ombudsman to oversee the company's dispute resolution processes independently. Advocate Neville Melville would be assisting the company with 'complaints from customers, including social grant recipients, outstanding information necessary for settling the complaints by way of conciliation, mediation and fact finding,'[24] Advocate Melville told *GroundUp*:

> What I've seen so far is that there is a huge problem with communication, particularly with people who are semi-literate and those who are completely illiterate. So there will obviously have to be solutions that address those problems. The biggest challenge is how do these people voice their complaints and [the current mechanism] is obviously not an adequate means.[25]

Advocate Melville told media in August 2017 that based on his research so far, he had recommended that Net1 establish an internal complaint resolution system.[26] Advocate Melville said his title would soon change to Independent Adjudicator for the Net1 Group. The Panel of Experts noted in its third report to the Constitutional Court in January 2018 that, although the Independent Adjudicator for the Net1 Group had reported a decline in complaints for November and December 2017, beneficiaries could only approach the Independent Adjudicator if they had gone through the Net1 Complaints Management Process, and their complaint remained unresolved.[27]

Reporting on the social grant crisis by Barbara October (née Maregele)[28]

Well, Allan Gray kept part of its promise by facilitating a second event with the Black Sash and its partners on 5 June 2017, attended by nearly 500 beneficiaries, mostly pensioners, from Ceres, Tulbagh, Op-die-Berg and surrounding areas. Most of them wanted to cancel their 'Green Cards' and a few others, who had been unable to finance the trip to the nearest Net1 office, just wanted to query activity on their accounts. Representatives from Grindrod Bank, Net1 and Sassa each had desks in the hall to deal with the complaints. I watched as taxis filled with people arrived throughout the day. Many elderly people, some on crutches, also queued in snaking lines to see the representatives. A group of people had also gathered outside the hall and surrounded a visibly overwhelmed Net1 official who was taking down the details of those who wanted their EPE cards cancelled.

Net1 later told me that 246 accounts had been closed that day and 149 people asked to have their Smart Life policies cancelled.

On 1 July at 5 a.m., when grants were paid, I drove back to Ceres to speak to the first few social grant beneficiaries in the queue. With help from the Black Sash and the Witzenberg Rural Development Centre, I asked whether beneficiaries who had cancelled their Green Cards were successfully getting their social grants on their reissued Sassa cards.

I spent most of the morning interviewing and photographing beneficiaries queuing outside the Shoprite in Voortrekker Road. It was a bitterly cold morning and still dark when I arrived.

When the store opened just after 7 a.m., the first ten beneficiaries were allowed inside. Inside, two tills were designated for grant payments. One of the grant recipients I had been speaking to since the first event in May 2017 was Ms Catherina Hanekom. She was one of those who had cancelled their EPE cards. Ten minutes after being let into the store, Ms Hanekom emerged with a big smile. 'I can't believe it. My Sassa card works and I got R1 470 of my [R1 600] disability grant. I just have one more payment left on a loan … that's why I didn't get the whole amount', she told me that morning.

It soon became apparent that the beneficiaries' battle for recourse from Net1 and its subsidiaries would continue beyond the end of its contract with Sassa in March 2018, when the post office began taking over the payment process. In August 2017, Net1's new ombudsman, Mr Neville Melville, told me that there were about 80 people working at Net1's complaints call centre at the time and they were overloaded with calls at month end from grant recipients. I believe that to this day, there are still people being sent from pillar to post to get their money back.

In May 2017, it was announced that controversial Net1 CEO Serge Belamant would take early retirement, prompted by the views expressed by certain of the company's shareholders.[29] This announcement came a month after Mr Belamant confirmed he would no longer be the company's chairperson. However, shareholders were up in arms after Net1 stated it would pay Mr Belamant $8 million (R105 million) for leaving the company, a figure major shareholder Allan Gray said it noted 'with outrage'.[30]

At the end of 2017, Allan Gray reported that it remained a concerned and responsible shareholder and would continue to monitor the situation closely and hold Net1 to account.[31]

PUBLIC REACH

Grant Grabs documentaries

In 2014, the Black Sash joined forces with journalist Ms Crystal Orderson to make a current affairs documentary highlighting the escalation of unauthorised and allegedly unlawful and/or fraudulent deductions from the Sassa-branded Grindrod Bank accounts into which social grants were paid. At that time, very little in-depth investigative media coverage was available. The production team comprised Ms Orderson, award-winning investigative filmmaker Mr Johann Abrahams and Esley Philander.[32]

In December 2014, the crew travelled by road from Cape Town to the Northern Cape, North West province, Gauteng and Mpumalanga to film stories of grant recipients' experiences and the impact of allegedly unlawful and/or fraudulent deductions on their lives. Particular attention was paid to grant recipients living in rural areas who struggled to make their plight heard and find recourse.

The series was titled *Grant Grabs*,[33] and the first in the documentary series was screened in March 2015 on SABC3's *Special Assignment* investigative programme. The Black Sash received requests for copies of the film from the public, including from several Members of Parliament. Over 300 copies of *Grant Grabs* were distributed. The documentary was also given to paralegals attending the Dullah Omar School. The documentary series was uploaded onto the Black Sash website to be used as an information and advocacy tool. Each episode in the *Grant Grabs* series explored a problem that was challenging the social grant system due to the Sassa contract with CPS.

The second episode produced by Ms Orderson and Mr Abrahams was completed in 2017. Entitled *Grant Grabs 2: Challenges with Seeking Recourse*, the documentary highlighted the obstacles faced by grant recipients in registering complaints and seeking recourse and refunds for unauthorised deductions from their Sassa-branded Grindrod Bank accounts. The documentary was screened on SABC 1's current affairs show, *Cutting Edge*, and had 1 113 691 viewers.

The third episode, aired in March 2018, was produced by Ms Orderson, Mr Abrahams and Ms Esley Philander from the Black Sash. Entitled *Grant Grabs 3: The Green Card*, it focused on the predatory practices associated with the EPE card (commonly known as the Green Card). The documentary revealed a dysfunctional recourse system with no refunds, resulting in perpetual indebtedness. Many recipients were misled into taking the EPE card. Sassa warned recipients against this and encouraged them to retain their Sassa-branded Grindrod Bank accounts, yet by December 2017, there were 2 016 737[34] social grant beneficiaries with EPE bank accounts.[35]

The fourth episode, produced in 2019 by Ms Orderson, was entitled *Grant Grabs 4: Stealing Grant Beneficiaries' Personal Data*. It was screened on 5 February 2019 on *Cutting Edge* on SABC 1 to an audience of 851 011. It demonstrated how Net1 subsidiaries, their network and other funeral policy service providers appeared to share and benefit from the personal and biometric information of social grant beneficiaries (see Chapters 1 and 4).

This series also gave grant recipients a voice. It contributed to public education and directed grant recipients to the Black Sash helpline and other advice offices for help in seeking recourse. It received attention from policy-makers and law enforcement agencies. Last but not least, it was a powerful advocacy tool.

Media

The media can expose issues and raise greater public awareness. By focusing on an issue, the media increases public pressure on those accountable to take action. The media focus on the social grant system was instrumental in the success of the Hoog campaign, shining a light on the plight of grant beneficiaries. Media investigations unearthed evidence of the nature and extent of the unauthorised and allegedly unlawful deductions from the Sassa-branded Grindrod Bank accounts and demonstrated the challenges in obtaining recourse. Throughout this book you will find references to articles covered by the media.

GroundUp

GroundUp is a news agency with a focus on reporting from within communities about issues that impact on their daily lives. *GroundUp* was started in April 2012 as a joint project of Community Media Trust[36] and the University of Cape Town's Centre for Social Science Research.[37] *GroundUp* amplified the voices of grant recipients and the portal remains an important source of information.

GroundUp journalists interviewed grant recipients and enabled them to tell their stories in their own words. They witnessed first hand the unfolding events and impact of the social grant crisis on the ground and through the cases they pursued. *GroundUp* established a dedicated page on its website entitled 'Everything you need to know about social grants'.[38] It is written in plain language with information on each grant, who qualifies, how to apply and what documents will be requested for the application. Some of this information is available on the official Sassa and DSD websites, but it is hard to find and often difficult to read and understand. To this day this page is still one of the most frequently visited on the *GroundUp* website.

Journalist Barbara October wrote one of the first articles that highlighted the concerns of the Black Sash's Hoog campaign in May 2014.[39] Entitled 'Now I can't afford groceries', it told the story of grant beneficiary Esme Pamplin who had unauthorised deductions taken off her account for airtime, loans and other goods. She could not afford to feed her family and embarked on the enormous challenge of seeking recourse.

Reporting on the social grant crisis by Barbara October (nè Maregele)

I decided to write two articles. In the first I would explain how these deductions were being made and to give context about the companies involved; and in the second I would interview a beneficiary, Esme Pamplin from Heideveld in Cape Town, about how the deductions affected her daily life.

When I visited her house, all her payment slips and documents were spread out on the couches in her front room. She painstakingly explained to me how she came to discover the monthly deductions of about R100 from her pension which was around R1 350 at the time. The deductions were for electricity and airtime, when in fact Mrs Pamplin didn't even own a cell phone. Her pension was the only stable income for her family of seven and the deductions left a hole in the family's shoestring budget.

By interviewing a beneficiary, we hoped to put a face to all the statistics and numbers that had been released by Sassa and other media at the time. We hoped that this would help readers understand that those affected by the problem were not 'just a small percentage of the total beneficiaries' as Sassa liked to say, but people who were among the most vulnerable in our communities.

GroundUp has since published hundreds of reports on issues related to social grants in towns and major metros across the country. We have covered what has since become known as 'Sassa-Gate' through the multiple parliamentary hearings into the problems with social grant payments and the transfer from CPS to the Post Office; the associated court cases; and the profits made by CPS and its parent company Net1 from the grant payment system. But mostly we have written articles from the ground, recording the snaking queues at pay points in rural areas and the plight of those like Mrs Pamplin for whom the social grant was often the difference between survival and starvation.

We knew that the payment of the grants was a huge operation. At the time, most beneficiary accounts were held at Grindrod Bank. The same bank was responsible for underwriting the EPE accounts, known among beneficiaries as Green Cards. These accounts enabled grant beneficiaries to withdraw their money from retailers like Pick n Pay. Like CPS, EasyPay was owned by Net1, as was Moneyline, a company that provided loans to grant recipients, Smart Life, a funeral insurance company, and Manje Mobile, a system where beneficiaries could buy airtime on credit.

Legally, the only deduction allowed from a social grant before it is paid to a beneficiary, was a single 10 per cent deduction for funeral insurance. But once the money was in the beneficiary's bank account, he or she could authorise other deductions, like any bank account holder, including deductions to Moneyline, or Manje Mobile. The problem was that many of these deductions were not being authorised – or so the beneficiaries said.

In response to the Black Sash's campaign, the then Minister of Social Development, Ms Bathabile Dlamini, set up a task team to investigate the problem. The team reported in August 2014 and the minister accepted its recommendations, including the design and implementation of a system to stop alleged 'unlawful and immoral' deductions and to make sure the money was refunded to beneficiaries.

Sassa then set up a Beneficiary Payment Dispute Resolution Mechanism. Social grant beneficiaries were required to fill out a form and the information was to be sent to the service providers, in most cases CPS and Grindrod Bank. This process meant that the burden of recourse to their own money was placed on the beneficiaries. Dozens of people I interviewed on various occasions said they were at their wits end trying to get recourse. They had to call, to visit the local Sassa and Net1 offices to lodge the complaint, constantly to follow up on the investigation, and prove that their money had been taken from them in the first place.

Initially the Black Sash struggled to get media interest in the plight of grant beneficiaries. *GroundUp* journalists recognised the crisis in the social grants systems, and profiled the stories of grant beneficiaries such as Esme Pamplin to help the public better understand the scope and impact of the problem. The stories and articles published by *GroundUp* were eventually republished in other media.

CONCLUSION

The Black Sash appointed the Public Affairs Research Institute (Pari) to undertake an evaluation of the organisation and its key programmes. The Pari evaluation concluded that the most significant of the Black Sash's achievements was the Hoog campaign:

> While many organisations were involved in the work of this programme, the Black Sash played a central role and made a significant impact on the over 17,8 million social grant

beneficiaries, particularly those affected by unauthorised deductions and abuse of social grant beneficiaries' confidential data by Net1 subsidiaries.[40]

The Black Sash's work enabled the publishing of amendments to the Social Assistance Regulations in 2016 which restricted deductions from social grant beneficiaries' bank accounts, particularly from children's and temporary grants. The 2016 regulations in part paved the way for the new Sassa/Sapo Special Disbursement Account that does not allow any debit orders or USSD platform deductions.

The evaluation found that there were a number of key achievements that could be attributed to the work of the Black Sash. These included:

- the prevention of a social grant payment crisis in 2017;
- the unlawful CPS contract was not extended any further;
- the protection of social grant beneficiaries' confidential data;
- the appointment of the Panel of Experts who supported the Constitutional Court in its oversight of Sassa; and
- the implementation of a new state-led hybrid social grant payment model in partnership with Sapo.

In its evaluation, Pari went on to say:

> Through the Hoog campaign the Black Sash has applied a unique method of activism that is grounded in understanding and evidence through case studies and the application of a mixed strategy of community mobilisation, negotiation with government and litigation as a last resort.

> This approach is an alternative to current more violent methods that are currently occurring in South Africa. It is important therefore that it is documented and the lessons learnt indicated and that it is used to teach and inform young activists.[41]

Moving ahead

This book records a shameful time in South Africa's post-apartheid democracy when the very poorest and most vulnerable in society found themselves facing the combined strength of elements within the state and the private sector that threatened the meagre social grants of those who could least afford it. The result: organisations and individuals within civil society mobilised behind the many grant recipients to secure recourse, reclaim their money, and terminate the constitutionally unlawful CPS contract.

The right to social security for vulnerable people in need is entrenched in the post-apartheid Constitution and in South Africa's international law obligations. The Constitutional Court has held that 'one of the signature achievements of our constitutional democracy is the establishment of an inclusive and effective programme of social assistance ... it has given some content to the core constitutional values of dignity, equality and freedom'.[1]

In 2019–20, almost one-third of South Africa's estimated population of 60 million people were beneficiaries of 18 million social grants.[2] These grants are indisputably crucial to poverty alleviation,[3] although they have had little effect on overall inequality in the country. South Africa is inarguably one of the most unequal societies in the world.[4] The social grant system is an important part of the government's strategy to fight the triple challenge of poverty, inequality and unemployment.[5]

The assault on South Africa's social grant system was fashioned along state capture parameters. It must be understood in terms of an attempt by the state, seemingly in partnership with a number of corporates in the financial sector, to divert government resources away from where they were most needed, ultimately enriching the already ultra-wealthy.

The importance of the work recorded in this book can be summed up under three main headings. Firstly, the book comprehensively records a time in South Africa's recent history that must never be forgotten. It traces a seven-year journey undertaken by the Black Sash, its partners and with public support, that effectively ensured that a constitutionally unlawful contract between Sassa and CPS did not endure.

Secondly, as this book unpacks the trajectory of the Hands Off Our Grants (Hoog) campaign, it shows how South Africa's civil society rose to the challenge and stood with grant beneficiaries to reclaim their social security rights entrenched in the Constitution. South Africa has a proud history of grassroots mobilisation of progressive structures that include religious groups, legal bodies, trade unions, youth, student and women's organisations, that together helped defeat the apartheid regime. What became clear in the Hoog campaign is that ground-up resistance remains necessary, and entrenched, in South African communities.

The Black Sash intervened when it became aware of the stories of unauthorised and allegedly fraudulent deductions which initially started with vulnerable senior citizens. Mobilising affected grant recipients and their communities made Hoog a grassroots campaign, driven from the bottom up, which garnered civil society and public support, as well as captured the attention of those in power. Independent media and journalists were dedicated to ensuring sustained public exposure of the exploitation of beneficiaries and the social grant payment system. Progressive lawyers and their institutions, particularly the Centre for Applied Legal Studies (Cals), threw their considerable weight behind demands for justice, and ultimately the Constitutional Court could enforce the Constitution and hold the executive to account.

Thirdly, this book places this shameful episode firmly within the context of state capture. Net1/CPS enjoyed access and influence at the highest level. Minister of Social Development Bathabile Dlamini appeared determined to gain control over Sassa's procurement processes. 'Uncooperative' officials were pushed aside or resigned and were replaced by those in 'acting' capacities whose effectivity and independence were compromised. Work streams appointed by, and directly accountable to, the minister established a parallel accountability structure that side-stepped legal decision-making processes, and at an enormous cost to the taxpayer for their 'work', the final 'value' of which has not been accounted for to date.

Each chapter of this book can be read as a step along the path of the protracted Hoog campaign, and the reader travels alongside the Black Sash and its partners as events slowly unfold. The first chapter relays the early news that began filtering into the Black Sash through advice offices and community-based organisations, particularly from the rural areas. Early reports grew in number and started coming in from all corners of the country. Rumours were verified, research conducted, and it became evident that the Black Sash and its partners were dealing with a real threat to the social welfare system that sustained a great many South Africans.

The book investigates Net1's 'first wave/second wave' strategy, which was presented at the time as an effort to secure 'financial inclusion' for the poor. While Net1 was being lauded for its efforts to draw marginalised citizens into the national banking system, it was becoming apparent to the Black Sash that social grants, often the only income of most recipients and households, were no longer safe. Uncomfortable questions had to be asked.

This book illustrates the great suffering inflicted on the poorest and most vulnerable people in South Africa. It comprehensively expands upon what is now known as the 2011 to 2017 South African social grants crisis, which was played out in households, in boardrooms, in Parliament, in the corridors of power and in various courts of law. The Hoog campaign deployed multiple strategies. With its starting point always in popular mass mobilisation, the Black Sash used advocacy, at both local and national levels, and a focused media strategy as well as producing its documentary series on various aspects of the social grants crisis, which was broadcast on national television.

With litigation as a tool of last resort, the Black Sash turned to the courts. During the Hoog campaign, the Black Sash occupied the role of *amicus curiae* or friend of the court on several occasions. At other times, it utilised the roles of both applicant and respondent, depending on how best to defend the right to social security. During the campaign, the Black Sash was sometimes required to oppose the Minister of Social Development and at other times to support the government against the powerful private companies engaged in the apparent exploitation of social grant beneficiaries. It challenged the state for its failures in the administration of the payment of social grants and it stood up to those in the private sector who were ruthlessly depleting recipients' social grants.

Finally, the social grants saga raised the issue of accountability. Deputy Chief Justice Raymond Zondo, during the Commission of Inquiry into Allegations of State Capture that he chaired between 2018 and 2021, referred to Parliament's broad failure to exercise accountability in the face of widespread government corruption and mismanagement. With regard to the social grants crisis, Parliament proved itself unable to exercise its oversight mandate and call the executive to account (see Chapter 6).

The eventual contracting of the South African Post Office (Sapo) as social grants paymaster was not without its difficulties and challenges, but the agreement secured the transition to a ring-fenced Sassa Special Disbursement (bank) Account. The significance of this cannot be overstated. This was a victory for grant recipients because it protected social grants from unauthorised and allegedly unlawful debit orders and USSD deductions. More than 70 per cent of beneficiaries now utilise the ring-fenced Sassa bank account.[6] These figures exclude those who benefit from the newly created Social Relief of Distress Grant.

The protracted court battles, including those initiated by the Black Sash and its partners, have led to legislative and regulatory changes. Furthermore, government is currently revising existing legislation to clarify the governance structure of Sassa and spell out more clearly the respective roles and responsibilities of the Sassa Chief Executive Officer, the Minister of Social Development. In 2021 Parliament promulgated the establishment of an Inspectorate reporting to the minister. Also of significance is the fact that for the first time a Cabinet minister has been held personally liable for legal costs. Its significance lies in the fact that the Constitutional Court recognised the culpability of the erstwhile Minister of Social Development in the 2017 Sassa crisis, and in her less than candid reporting to that court. The finding and court order for costs was initially contested, but during the writing of this book the minister finally complied with payment, making her the first government minister not only to be accused of culpability in the social grants crisis, but also to accept responsibility publicly for the culpability through compliance with the court order. In addition, in 2021 Ms Bathabile Dlamini was found guilty of perjury for allegedly giving false evidence in her testimony under oath to the 2018 Section 38 Constitutional Court inquiry.[7]

The significance of these outcomes can be properly appreciated by the reader who takes away from this book a sense of outrage and determination that such abuses of power must never again be condoned or allowed. Just as ordinary people gained a voice and a sense of agency by taking on those who abused their authority and demanding recourse and redress, so too can the reader understand that it is possible to hold power to account.

Opportunities to learn and act are to be found in the multiple ways in which the Hoog campaign tackled unauthorised and allegedly fraudulent and/or unlawful deductions. The lessons this book presents are the need to embrace divergent tactics that could include citizen engagements such as the Black Sash's Speak Out initiative; mobilisation through mass protest; engagement with ministers, government officials and other stakeholders; as well as litigation when required. It demonstrates the need for close observation; keeping an ear to the ground; digging for facts underlying the 'political-speak'; and engaging at all levels – from grassroots communities and civil society organisations to officials in government and business.

The emphasis throughout the Hoog campaign was on relationships between the network of small advice groups and people in their respective communities. The Black Sash was able to work with the information these stakeholders provided – by asking the right questions and developing case studies, which formed the basis of submissions and affidavits – as well as releasing this information into public spaces. Successful court cases have set important precedents that have become references for future legal arguments.

Finally, this book confirms the Black Sash's ongoing commitment to human rights, justice and dignity, carrying this legacy into its 70th decade of struggle.

Appendix 1

THE WORK OF THE PANEL OF EXPERTS

Conduct of DSD officials and Sassa employees

To give effect to the Court's order of 17 March 2017, the Panel of Experts recommended that the Court instruct National Treasury to investigate the conduct of Sassa employees and officials of the DSD in their issuing of contracts to service providers – from 2016 – to determine whether there had been any malpractice or obstruction, and whether anyone should be prosecuted in terms of Section 81, 83 or 86 of the Public Finance Management Act (No. 1 of 1999), or any other relevant law. In the end, the panel accepted that this could not be done due to time and resource constraints, and because sometimes Treasury did not have the legal authority to do so.

Sassa: governance, leadership and management

It believed that the lack of proper stewardship was a major contributing factor to the breakdown of the social assistance payment system, and the panel therefore recommended that the President, in terms of Section 97(a) of the Constitution of the Republic of South Africa, by proclamation transfer the administration of the Sassa Act and the Social Assistance Act to the Minister of Finance or the Minister of the Department of Planning, Monitoring and Evaluation (DPME) in the Presidency. This recommendation was not implemented as the President appointed a new Minister of Social Development.

Sassa's many governance issues particularly occupied the panel. It recommended that DPME set out the remedial actions necessary to ensure that there was an end to Sassa being a public entity without proper institutional governance, capacity and oversight. According to the panel, Sassa needed technically and administratively skilled management and a board of qualified expertise. The panel questioned whether Sassa was able effectively to strengthen its autonomy as well as that of its CEO under the Sassa Act. It also asked if Sassa, as a public entity, was able to perform its constitutional mandate.

DPME did investigate these governance issues and expressed an opinion to the panel, but it does not seem that its recommendations were implemented. On 16 January 2018, DPME filed a report indicating that its analysis pointed to overall weak governance systems and the need for a more detailed process to identify the root causes of Sassa's dysfunction. It also recommended revising the Sassa Act to strengthen the autonomy of the Sassa CEO, and the appointment of a permanent CEO. (A permanent CEO, Busisiwe Memela-Khambula, was appointed in May 2019.) DPME also recommended the appointment of a permanent Director General at the DSD. (The DSD still has an acting Director General.) In 2020 and 2021, the DSD initiated engagements with civil society organisations regarding changes to the Sassa Act, particularly to improve governance at the agency.[1] DSD is still preparing for changes to the Sassa Act.

Sassa was also asked to ensure that all posts were filled timeously to ensure stability across the organisation. (The instability of senior positions at Sassa had empowered Minister Dlamini to play fast and loose with accountability by appointing the parallel work streams.) In general, the DPME concurred with the obvious weaknesses identified by the panel. Sassa needed to be restructured. It needed a governance structure within the DSD with expertise that would provide effective oversight and support, undertake risk management and assist Sassa in performance management. The DPME suggested that Sassa carry out a Management Performance Assessment process, a comprehensive self-assessment process that requires national and provincial departments to review their management compliance and rate their performance on a scale of 1 to 4, with supporting evidence.

DPME indicated that it was willing to conduct a thorough investigation of the current Sassa management and the appropriateness of Sassa being a public entity without proper institutional governance, capacity and oversight. However, it is uncertain whether this investigation was ever undertaken. The DPME also offered to investigate the desirability of moving the payment function of social grants to the National Treasury, leaving the registration, verification and administration of social grants beneficiaries with Sassa or the DSD.

In the absence of a statutory mandate to do so, the panel questioned Sassa's emphasis on the importance of local economic development at cash pay points as the rationale for maintaining these.

The panel recommended that the Minster of Social Development instruct the DSD to conduct a review of the efficacy of the Sassa Act, and to table a report in Parliament on the outcome of that review. While a Social Assistance Amendment Bill was published for public comment, no official indication has been given that the Sassa Act is to be amended.

The panel recommended that Sassa change its focus on operational issues to develop a coherent strategy, master plan and risk management plan to ensure that it is able to achieve the long-term objectives of social grant payments by considering systemic risks and the opportunities offered by new innovations. The panel recommended that the DSD's Inspectorate for Social Assistance also develop a framework to monitor Sassa as an institution, and that Sassa elevate risk management to a strategic management tool for managing risk, and seize opportunities to achieve its objectives through the implementation of a systematic risk management process. The new amendments to the Social Assistance Act (promulgated in 2021) make provision for an inspectorate, to be implemented by the 2022/23 financial year.

The panel also recommended that Sassa and Sapo take the necessary steps to prevent any labour dispute from interrupting the payment of social grant services and found that the Sassa/Sapo Master Services Agreement failed to deal with certain provisions in the Sassa Act.

These lacunae may have been addressed by the time of the publication of this book, or they may be provided for in Service Level Agreements.

Protection of personal information

With regard to the protection of personal information, the panel recommended that Sassa should provide the Information Regulator with copies of any agreements between Sassa and Sapo, and between Sapo and its subcontractors, to enable the Information Regulator to assess whether these agreements provided for the protection of the personal information of beneficiaries. It indicated that it had accepted the Information Regulator's conclusion that the Sassa/Sapo agreement contained adequate safeguards for the lawful processing of personal information. It is unknown whether the safeguards have actually been implemented. In addition, it is unknown whether any documents other than the Sassa/Sapo service level agreements and sub-contractors' agreements were submitted to and vetted by the Information Regulator. At the time, not all the provisions of the Protection of Personal Information Act (No. 4 of 2013) were yet in force, and the Information Regulator was still in the process of staffing its offices.

Cash pay points

Regarding cash pay points, the panel repeatedly recommended that Sassa conduct a thorough audit. Sassa indicated to the panel that it was conducting an analysis of the number and location of cash pay points with a view to consolidating the number of payment channels and was undertaking a number of other actions that would have a positive impact on the continued and effective payment of social grants. At the time, the concern was that the service provider would try to retain cash pay points to generate income. The panel concluded that Sassa had no intention of limiting costs by restricting cash payments at pay points exclusively to people who did not live within 5 km from any ATM or point-of-sale device or facility, nor were they considering the panel's recommendation to select only one pay point that was most convenient to the beneficiaries from the options available. The panel therefore recommended that Sassa monitor the effects of decommissioning pay points to identify unintended negative consequences. In addition, Sassa should consider the question of beneficiaries who could not use a PIN to access their social grants when deciding on the closure of a pay point.

The panel further recommended that Sassa explore all potential cash payment solutions for the expected 3 066 cash pay points that would not have been decommissioned by the end of September 2018, including consideration for the provision of mobile ATM payment infrastructure by commercial banks or point-of-service devices by merchants. It is now clear that Sassa and Sapo were closing cash pay points without considering the effects of decommissioning them, and that no other alternatives were being implemented. This is contrary to the provisions of the Sassa Act, which requires service provision that respects the dignity of recipients, as not everyone – especially in certain rural areas – has easy access to ATMs or Sapo offices within 5 km of their home. The impact of the need to travel to pay points to obtain cash needs to be considered.

The panel recommended that with the pending closure of a significant number of cash pay points, it was necessary to increase the use of procurators, as alternatives to cash pay points were not likely to cater for the needs of frail and severely disabled beneficiaries. Sassa and Sapo should contact beneficiaries, at their homes, who experienced difficulties with using a PIN and, by providing the relevant information, assist them to access social grants at ATMs or at point-of-sale devices.

To alleviate the problems associated with overcrowding experienced by beneficiaries at Sapo cash pay points and ATMs, the panel recommended that Sassa and Sapo consider introducing staggering payments over a longer period. This recommendation was implemented in May 2020 – by Sassa[2] with support from the Sarb, the Banking Association of South Africa and retailers – as government tried to reduce queueing and chaos at payment channels to ensure compliance with Covid-19 protocols. Social grants are paid over three days starting with the elderly, followed by the disabled, and ending with the child support grants not linked to other grants.

Beneficiary education and communication

The panel found that beneficiary education and information was lacking and that the communication function of Sassa was poor. Sassa's and Sapo's direct communication with beneficiaries was not sufficiently targeted, nor was the content of its messages sufficiently specific to enable beneficiaries to make informed choices. Communication required a much stronger and more dedicated effort by both Sassa and Sapo.

The panel recommended that Sassa and Sapo ensure that beneficiaries were provided, in writing, the terms and conditions applicable to the Sassa-branded Sapo cards, in an official language of their choice. The panel also recommended that Sapo provide all beneficiaries who had never used a PIN or had difficulty using a PIN to access their social grants with a letter, together with a presentation in visual form, that identified the Sapo outlet that the beneficiaries should visit to access their social grants and specified the date when they should visit the Sapo outlet. The presentation should explain how social grants would be paid at Sapo outlets to beneficiaries who could not use a PIN.

The panel also found that Sassa and Sapo officials working at pay points did not always understand the problems experienced by beneficiaries and were therefore limited in the assistance they could offer.

The panel recommended that Sapo should ensure that all beneficiaries were given receipts as proof of the amount of money they had withdrawn.

With regard to complaints and dispute resolution, the panel recommended that Sassa and Sapo establish and maintain an integrated complaints and dispute resolution mechanism and procedure for the new grant payment system. During the transition phase, provision should be made for disputes to be lodged by beneficiaries up to 30 days after CPS had made its final payments.

Sapo

In one of its earliest recommendations, the panel proposed that Sassa conduct a substantive cost-benefit analysis of certain implementation options. However, when Sassa appointed Sapo, this recommendation fell away.

The panel also recommended that Sassa obtain legal assistance for drafting contracts and service level agreements. This was not done, and Sapo itself in many instances provided the texts of the agreements.

The panel recommended that Sassa obtain the services of the Government Technical Advisory Centre or an independent project management officer to assist Sassa in managing the transition. The government decided that an Inter-Ministerial Committee (IMC), assisted by officials, would guide Sassa.

The panel recommended that Sassa should develop contingency planning. This too was never followed up.

It also recommended that Sassa investigate and consider the use of new technologies or facilities (for example, e-wallets). At the time of writing there was no clear strategy on the use of technology other than within the banking environment. Experimentation and piloting of digital platforms took place during the implementation of the Covid-19 Social Relief of Distress Grant.

Later, the panel found that the cost implications of procuring cash payment services exclusively through Sapo was a matter of concern, and that the absence of a proper costing of the new operating model was, despite a reliance on the Intergovernmental Relations Framework Act (No. 13 of 2005), contrary to the provisions of Section 195(1)(b) of the Constitution.

The panel recommended that Sassa and Sapo ensure the cost-effectiveness and high levels of performance required for the uninterrupted payment of social grants. Sassa and Sapo should conclude formal service level agreements, including on costs, for the long-term role that Sapo would be playing, by agreeing on key performance areas and consequence management. The panel recommended that the Minister of Social Development and Sassa provide a comprehensive cost analysis and three-year budget that reflected expenditure to date, extraordinary expenditure, capital costs and future capital expenditure. (This has probably been done in terms of the Medium Term Expenditure Framework process.)

The panel expressed its concern that Sapo might in future hold Sassa to ransom by extracting as much revenue as possible from rendering services to Sassa unless preventative measures were provided for. The procuring of Sapo by Sassa as its sole service provider for the payment of social grants had benefits, but it was also likely to have adverse consequences for both the fiscus and the wellbeing of beneficiaries (in terms of convenience and net grant monies received) for years to come.

The panel recommended that the minister, Sassa and National Treasury should prioritise deciding on the subsidisation of electronic payments provided by banks and merchants. It recommended that Sapo should not charge beneficiaries a PIN reset fee until such time that biometrics could be used for authorisation of payments at all its outlets.

The panel recommended that Sapo and Sassa consider whether the maintenance of the alternative Integrated Grant Payment System (IGPS) separate from the other Sapo/Postbank systems made good sense from commercial, logistical and risk perspectives. Sassa should consider whether it was necessary to retain the IGPS as a separate, stand-alone system, giving detailed reasoning and indicating the consequences if not done, and what the other options were.

The panel further recommended that Sapo plan well in advance of the expiry of the current contract for the potential migration to the IGPS system, allowing sufficient time for migration of beneficiary data, protection of personal information and systems testing.

In respect of service levels, the panel recommended that Sapo ensure that signal boosters were available at all pay points, especially where connectivity problems were likely to occur, and that all equipment used for the payment of social grants was in working order prior to departing for pay points. Sapo should have contingencies in place should equipment fail in a remote rural area where it was not feasible to access replacement equipment quickly. If cash dispensing machines were used at pay points, Sapo should ensure that there was reliable connectivity.

Regarding ancillary service providers such as banks and merchants, the panel recommended that Sassa should not pursue the creation of a standardised bank account with the banking industry, but instead engage with commercial banks individually on the products that could be used to meet Sassa's requirements.

The panel recommended that Sassa and Sapo should establish formal arrangements or partnerships with banks, the Payment Association of South Africa, BankservAfrica (the payment clearing house providing interbank switching, clearing and settlement services to the South African banking sector), Sarb and other entities that could contribute to the security, enablement, cost reduction, data analysis and future innovations in the payment of social grants.

Acknowledgement
This appendix was written by Advocate Werner Krull, a former member of the Panel of Experts. The Black Sash commissioned Advocate Krull to write a summary of the recommendations made by the Panel of Experts in its reports to the Constitutional Court.

Appendix 2

NET1'S GROUP STRUCTURE AT MARCH 2014

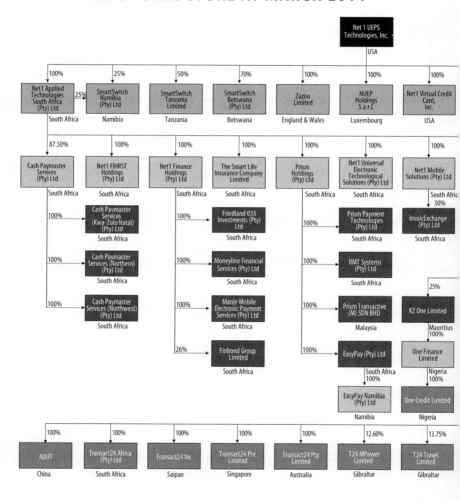

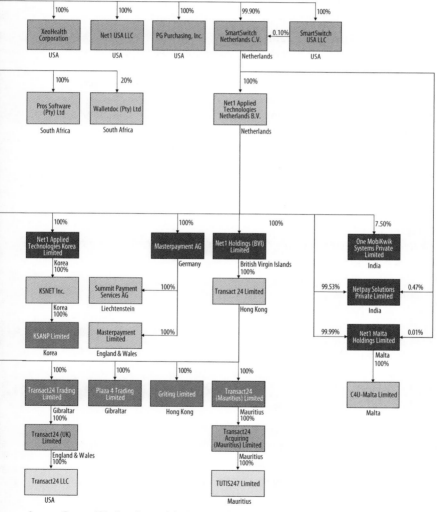

Source: GroundUp (see https://www.groundup.org.za/media/old/files/net1_group_
structure_march_2014.pdf)

Notes

Author's note

1   The significance of this distinction is made clear in this book in its consideration of the amended regulations. See the section on funeral policy deductions in Chapter 1.

Background to the Hoog campaign

1   For the consolidated report of this committee, see http://www. blacksash.org.za/images/campaigns/basicincomesupport/ TransformingThePresentProtectingtheFuture2002.pdf, accessed September 2021.

2   For the Parliamentary Monitoring Group briefing on this grant, see https://pmg.org.za/committee-meeting/2512/#:~:text=The%20 Child%20Support%20Grant%20was,very%20poor%20children%20 under%207, accessed January 2022.

3   USSD, or unstructured supplementary service data, allows users who do not have an internet connection or a smartphone to use mobile banking.

4   Foley & Swilling, 2018, 68.

Chapter 1

1   Parliamentary Monitoring Group (PMG), 6 May 2016.

2   Black Sash, 2017, 5.

3   Black Sash, 2017, 5–9.

4   Black Sash, 2017, 5–9.

5   Black Sash, 2017, 5–9.

6   Black Sash, 2017, 5–9.

7   Black Sash, 2017, 5–9.

8   Black Sash, 2017, 5–9.

9   Black Sash, 2017, 17–23.

10 Black Sash, 2017, 17–23.

11 Black Sash, 2017, 17–23.

12 Black Sash, 2017, 17–23.

13 Black Sash, 2017, 17–23.

14 Moneyline, *Terms and conditions for the use of the EasyPay Everywhere or EPE card and account*, n.d. Accessed June 2021, http://www.net1.com/ media/103819/2020-08-06-epe-terms-and-conditions.pdf.

15 Black Sash Archive, Case study compiled by the Black Sash Western Cape Regional office with beneficiary and her husband, submitted to the MTT in 2015.

16 Black Sash Archive, Case study compiled by the Black Sash Western Cape Regional office with beneficiary and her husband, submitted to the MTT in 2015.

17 Black Sash Archive, Case study compiled by the Black Sash Western Cape Regional office with beneficiary and her husband, submitted to the MTT in 2015.

18 Black Sash Archive, Case study compiled by the Black Sash Western Cape Regional office with beneficiary and her husband, submitted to the MTT in 2015.

19 Black Sash Archive, Case study compiled by the Black Sash Gauteng Regional office with beneficiary, submitted to the MTT in 2015.

20 Black Sash Archive, Case study compiled by the Black Sash Gauteng Regional office with beneficiary, submitted to the MTT in 2015.

21 Black Sash Archive, Case study compiled by the Black Sash Gauteng Regional office with beneficiary, submitted to the MTT in 2015.

22 Black Sash Archive, Case study compiled by the Black Sash Eastern Cape Regional office with LD, submitted to the MTT in 2015.

23 Black Sash Archive, Case study compiled by the Black Sash Eastern Cape Regional office with LD, submitted to the MTT in 2015.

24 Black Sash Archive, Case study compiled by the Black Sash Eastern Cape Regional office with beneficiary, submitted to the MTT in 2015.

25 Black Sash Archive, Case study compiled by the Black Sash Eastern Cape Regional office with beneficiary, submitted to the MTT in 2015.

26 Black Sash Archive, Case study compiled by the Black Sash Eastern Cape Regional office with LD, submitted to the MTT in 2015.

27 It has remained a concern for the Black Sash that grant beneficiaries are still targeted for the purchase of additional funeral cover that they arguably do not need, and for which premiums are paid by debt order deductions. This predatory conduct is not prohibited by the Social Assistance Act, and beneficiaries are free to contract in this way if they choose. That the Act permits one deduction of 10 per cent for a funeral policy does not mean that beneficiaries are required to have a funeral policy. The existence of this option appears to have been exploited by those who coerce beneficiaries into taking more policies as if this was a Sassa requirement.

28 Emerald Wealth Life changed its name to Emerald Wealth Management when 1Life stopped underwriting its funeral policies.

29 SABC 3, *Grant Grabs*, *Special Assignment*, March 2015. See https://www. blacksash.org.za/index.php/public-broadcast-documentaries, accessed August 2021.

30 Black Sash, 2017, 9–16.

31 Black Sash, 2017, 9–16.

32 Black Sash, 2017, 9–16.

33 Black Sash, 2017, 9–16.

34 Black Sash, 2017, 9–16.

35 This is an extract of an article by Barbara October commissioned by the Black Sash for this book.

Chapter 2

1 The Black Sash, in partnership with the Social Change Assistance Trust (SCAT), launched the national Community Monitoring and Advocacy Project (CMAP) to improve government service delivery to poor and marginalised communities and individuals. CMAP ran from 2009 to 2013, and had hundreds of community monitors nominated by more than 270 organisations from across South Africa, whose objective was to monitor the quality of service delivery in specified government departments and municipalities.

2 Black Sash, January 2014. The letter was supported by the Community Advice Offices of South Africa (CAOSA), the Community Law Centre at UWC, the Parliamentary Liaison Office, Section 27, the Treatment Action Campaign, the Benchmark Foundation, the Legal Resource Centre, Corruption Watch and the Centre for Law and Society.

3 Ministerial Task Team (MTT), 2014, 15.

4 MTT, 2014, 15.

5 MTT, 2014, 5. For the duration of the CPS/Sassa contract, debit orders were made remotely via Mastercard's infrastructure, which functions outside of the National Payment System operated by the South African Reserve Bank (Sarb). The Net1 cohort bypassed Sarb. This was confirmed in a presentation to the Black Sash and its partners and was stated in a submission in the Net1 case heard at the North Gauteng High Court.

6 Parliamentary Monitoring Group (PMG), 6 May 2016.

7 PMG, 6 May 2016.

8 The Speak Out initiative was aimed at giving grant beneficiaries a public platform on which to engage government officials. It was an important element of the Hoog campaign as it gave beneficiaries an opportunity to speak for themselves.

9   Black Sash Archive, Interview with LC Maart, Black Sash Director, 2014.

10 From a CPS official, who declined to be named, in conversation with the
    Black Sash Director, LC Maart, and the Black Sash Advocacy Manager,
    E Paulus, at Adelaide Speak Out meeting, 6 April 2014.

11 MTT, 2014.

12 MTT, 2014, section 3.3.8.

13 MTT, 2014, section 3.3.7.

14 MTT, 2014. In attendance at this meeting was Black Sash trustee Ms
    Mary Burton and Father Peter-John Pearson.

15 MTT, 2014, 8.

16 Dlamini, 2014.

17 Dlamini, 2014, 3.

18 A National Payment System (NPS) is a set of arrangements and
    infrastructure that enables consumers, businesses and other entities to
    effect financial transactions, including making payments to one another
    and using the accounts and payment instruments issued by financial
    institutions.

19 People's Assembly, *Infographic: Sassa beneficiaries*, 11 November 2016.
    Accessed June 2021, https://www.pa.org.za/blog/infographic-sassa-
    beneficiaries.

20 MTT, 2014, 7.

21 PMG, 1 March 2017, 11.

22 Black Sash Archive, Letter dated 16 October 2013 to Sassa CEO Virginia
    Petersen; letter dated 11 January 2014 to CEO Serge Belamant from Sassa
    CEO re Notice of Breach.

23 MTT, 2014.

24 Letter dated 16 October 2013 to Sassa CEO Virginia Petersen; letter dated
    11 January 2014 to CEO Serge Belamant from Sassa CEO re Notice of
    Breach.

25 *Grant Grabs* 3: The Green Card, 2018 Accessed July 2021. https://www.
    youtube.com/watch?v=Qa97QSi8F80.

26 PMG, 22 October 2013.

27 MTT, 2016, Untitled and unpublished final MTT report completed in
    December 2016, 12 point 23. The report was tabled for adoption at the
    January 2017 meeting, but the meeting was terminated early because
    the Black Sash had launched its case against Sassa in the Constitutional
    Court. The MTT ceased to operate after this.

28 FSB has changed to the FSCA, *FANEWS*, 06 April 2018. Accessed June
    2021, https://www.fanews.co.za/article/compliance-regulatory/2/

financial-sector-conduct-authority-fsca-was-fsb/1059/fsb-has-changed-to-the-fsca/24140.

29 Channel Life Limited and Sanlam Developing Markets Limited v South African Social Security Agency and Others, North Gauteng High Court, Pretoria, case number 79112/15 (Unreported, matter postponed without a future date).

30 Lion of Africa released a notice in February 2018 announcing its intention to close down. It cited as its reason a 'tough operating climate' and 'an onerous regulatory environment'. See https://www.fanews. co.za/article/company-news-results/1/lion-of-africa/1248/lion-of-africa-to-close-its-doors/25797, para. 5, accessed January 2022.

31 Actuarial report in respect of the deductions of funeral insurance premiums from children's social security grants, prepared by Roseanne da Silva, 4 April 2016, p.7. Accessed September 2021, http://blacksash. org.za/images/De_Silva_Acturial_Report_-_Lion_of_Africa.pdf.

32 Section 68(1) requires any person who receives, retains or reports any confidential information in terms of the Act, pertaining to a consumer or prospective consumer, to use that information only for the purpose permitted or required in terms of the Act or other applicable legislation.

33 NCR crack down on Moneyline Financial Services, *Debtfree*, 22 September 2014, para. 6. Accessed January 2022, https://debtfreedigi. co.za/ncr-end-moneyline-financial-services/.

34 The Sassa-branded Grindrod Bank account offered recipients facilities like debit orders and EFT transfers, like an ordinary cheque book account.

35 *Grant Grabs* 3: The Green Card, 2018, accessed July 2021. Accessed https://www.blacksash.org.za/index.php/public-broadcast-documentaries.

36 MTT, 2014, 17, 3.

37 Bowmans and Black Sash, n.d.

38 Implementation of the rest of the Popia took place on 1 July 2021. After the Popia commencement date or effective date (which was 1 July 2020) there was a 12-month grace period, so the Popia deadline was set at the end of the grace period.

39 Southern African Legal Information Institute, AllPay Consolidated Investment Holdings (Pty) Ltd and Others v Chief Executive Officer of the South African Social Security Agency and Others (No. 2) [2014] ZACC 12; 2014 (6) BCLR 641 (CC); 2014 (4) SA 179 (CC) (17 April 2014). Accessed June 2021, http://www.saflii.org/za/cases/ZACC/2014/12. html.

40 Southern African Legal Information Institute, South African Social Security Agency and Another v Minister of Social Development and Others (CCT48/17) [2018] ZACC 26; 2018 (10) BCLR 1291 (CC) (30 August 2018), point 10. Accessed January 2021, http://www.saflii.org/za/cases/ZACC/2018/26.html.

41 Bowmans and Black Sash, n.d.

42 Southern African Legal Information Institute, Zalisa and Others v South African Social Security Agency and Others (82073/2018) [2019] ZAGPPHC 4 (29 January 2019). Accessed June 2021, http://www.saflii.org/za/cases/ZAGPPHC/2019/4.html.

43 When applying for a social grant, would-be recipients must complete Annexure C of their Sassa application forms, if they wish to give Sassa permission to pay their funds into a personal bank account such as the Grindrod EPE account.

44 Black Sash, 26 January 2014, 9.

45 MTT 2014, 3.

46 *Grant Grabs* 3: The Green Card.

47 *Grant Grabs* 3: The Green Card.

48 MTT, 2014, 8.

49 CPS won't re-bid for Sassa's social grant tender – Net1, *Politicsweb*, 18 May 2015. Accessed June 2021, https://www.politicsweb.co.za/politics/cps-wont-rebid-for-sassas-social-grant-tender--net.

50 On 5 November 2015, Sassa filed a report in the Constitutional Court, stating that it would not award a new contract, but intended to take over the payment function of social grants from 1 April 2017, when the suspension of invalidity would lapse. Constitutional Court of South Africa, 2018, SASSA and another v Minister of Social Development and others CCT 48/17: Media summary. Accessed 20 January 2022, https://collections.concourt.org.za/bitstream/handle/20.500.12144/34605/Pre-hearing%20summary.pdf?sequence=55&isAllowed=y.

51 Thamm, M, SASSA social grants distribution doomsday and behind the scenes move to save 17-million grants, *Daily Maverick*, 14 November 2016. Accessed January 2022, https://www.dailymaverick.co.za/article/2016-11-14-sassa-social-grants-distribution-doomsday-and-behind-the-scenes-move-to-save-17-million-grants/.

52 The Black Sash later obtained, through the Constitutional Court, a copy of the proposed arrangement between CPS and Sassa to extend the contract period and increase the price. While the CPS contract was extended initially for one year, the intervention by the Black Sash ensured that the price remained the same as that in the 2012 agreement between Sassa and CPS (see Chapter 3).

Chapter 3

1   People's Assembly, *Infographic: Sassa beneficiaries*, 11 November 2016. Accessed June 2021, https://www.pa.org.za/blog/infographic-sassa-beneficiaries.

2   Black Sash Trust v Minister of Social Development and Others CCT 48/17 (17 March 2017) at fn 1, para. 36.

3   The Court made provision for CPS to approach Treasury to renegotiate the financial terms of the contract. Treasury was obliged to report its recommendations to the Court for approval. This was exceptional, and the extension of the contract has bearing for private companies stepping into the role of the state in the outsourcing of the state's constitutional obligations. Treasury did not support CPS's motivations for increased payments.

4   Black Sash Trust v Minister of Social Development (2017) (3) SA 335 (CC).

5   See Judge Ngoepe's report to the Constitutional Court, https://www.judiciary.org.za/images/news/2018/Report.pdf, accessed January 2022.

6   McKune C, Serge Belamant, Sassa and the 'war-chest' of poor people, *amaBhungane*, 16 March 2017, accessed September 2017, http://amabhungane.co.za/article/2017-03-16-serge-belamant-sassa-and-the-war-chest-of-poor-people; Torkelson E, Deductions from social grants: How it all works, *GroundUp*, 3 March 2017, accessed September 2017, https://www.groundup.org.za/article/deductions-social-grants-how-it-works/; Dlamini B, Social grant beneficiaries being preyed upon, *Politicsweb*, 13 September 2014, accessed September 2017, http://www.politicsweb.co.za/news-and-analysis/social-grant-beneficiaries-being-preyed-upon—bath.

7   Net1 Applied Technologies South Africa and Others v Chief Executive Officer of the South African Social Security Agency and Others; Finbond Mutual Bank v Chief Executive Officer of the South African Social Security Agency and Others; Smart Life Insurance Company Limited v Chief Executive Officer of the South African Social Security Agency and Others (43557/16; 46024/16; 46278/16; 47447/16) [2017] ZAGPPHC 150 (9 May 2017) para. 12. Accessed September 2017, http://www.saflii.org/za/cases/ZAGPPHC/2017/150.html.

8   Delany A & Jehoma S, Implementation of social grants: Improving delivery and increasing access, *South African Child Gauge* 2016, 60. Accessed September 2017, http://www.ci.uct.ac.za/sites/default/files/image_tool/images/367/publication/2016/implementation-of-social-grants.pdf. Following an outcry by civil society, the Minister of Social Development

established a Ministerial Task Team in 2014 to prevent further deductions (see Chapter 2). Dlamini B, 2014.

9   The head of micro-insurance at South Africa's Financial Services Board, Jacky Huma, is quoted as saying 'There's a big demand for it because of the cultural behaviour that we need to have these big, dignified funerals'. Nyambura-Mwaura H & Blair E, Coffin cover: Africa's booming funerals business, *Reuters*, 14 August 2013, para. 10. Accessed 19 September 2017, http://www.reuters.com/article/africa-funerals-insurance/coffin-cover-africas-booming-funerals-business-idUSL5N0EU29120130814.

10   The FinScope survey estimates that 19 million adults have funeral policies. Van Rensburg D, State targets death payouts, *City Press*, 13 November 2016. Accessed September 2017, http://www.fin24.com/Money/Insurance/state-targets-death-payouts-20161111.

11   Channel Life Limited and Sanlam Developing Markets limited v South African Social Security Agency and Others, North Gauteng High Court, Pretoria, case number 79112/15 Unreported, matter postponed without a future date on 10 May 2016.

12   Social Assistance Act (13 of 2004) Section 20(4) and Regulation 26A.

13   Amendment: Regulations Relating to the Application for and Payment of Social Assistance and the Requirements or Conditions in Respect of Eligibility for Social Assistance in GN611 GG 39978 of 6 May 2016.

14   The Applicant's Founding Affidavit, Lion of Africa Life Assurance Company Ltd v South African Social Security Agency and Minister of Social Development of the Republic of South Africa (8 December 2015) at 26. Accessed January 2022, https://collections.concourt.org.za/bitstream/handle/20.500.12144/3867/Founding%20Affidavit%20Pretoria%20High%20Court-25135.pdf?sequence=14&isAllowed=y.

15   The Applicant's Founding Affidavit (8 December 2015) at 23, 28.

16   Channel Life Limited v Minister of Social Development and South African Social Security Agency and Others (NGHC case number 36212/2011) at para. 6. The Black Sash was not involved in this Channel Life matter, which the dated back to 2011.

17   This was held in Coughlan NO v RAF (2015) (1) SA 1 (CC) at para. 55.

18   Social Assistance Act Section 20(4).

19   While the Constitutional Court declined to admit the new evidence filed for the first time on appeal, and by a friend of the court, for consideration in the hearing, the evidence remains in the application as part of the court record in the public domain. While Lion of Africa has denied these findings in the media, there is no counter study.

20 Lion of Africa subsequently went into liquidation and ceased to operate
    in 2018, citing amongst other reasons, a 'lack of profitability' and 'tough
    operating climate in its chosen markets combined with an onerous
    regulatory environment'. See https://www.fanews.co.za/article/
    company-news-results/1/lion-of-africa/1248/lion-of-africa-to-close-its-
    doors/25797, para. 5, accessed January 2022.

21 The four challenges were brought by:
    Net1 Applied Technologies South Africa, Moneyline Financial
    Services and Manje Mobile Electronic Payment Services v the Chief
    Executive Officer of the South African Social Security Agency, the
    South African Social Security Agency, Minister of Social Development
    of the Republic of South Africa, the South African Reserve Bank, the
    Payment Association of South Africa and Grindrod Bank Limited NGHC
    43557/16;
    Finbond Mutual Bank v the Chief Executive Officer of the South
    African Social Security Agency, the South African Social Security Agency,
    Minister of Social Development of the Republic of South Africa, the
    South African Reserve Bank, the Payment Association of South Africa
    and Grindrod Bank Limited 46024/16;
    Smart Life Insurance Company v the Chief Executive Officer of the
    South African Social Security Agency, the South African Social Security
    Agency, Minister of Social Development of the Republic of South Africa,
    the South African Reserve Bank, the Payment Association of South
    Africa, the Financial Services Board and the Registrar of Long-Term
    Insurance NGHC 46278/16; and Information Technology Consultants
    v the Chief Executive Officer of the South African Social Security
    Agency, the South African Social Security Agency, Minister of Social
    Development of the Republic of South Africa, the South African Reserve
    Bank, the Payment Association of South Africa, Grindrod Bank Limited
    and Mercantile Bank Limited NGHC 47447/16.

22 The case citation is 43557/16; 46024/16; 46278/16; 47447/16) [2017]
    ZAGPPHC 150, and judgment was delivered in the Pretoria High Court
    on 9 May 2017.

23 Minister's written argument para. 21–23.

24 Net1 Applied Technologies South Africa and Others v Chief Executive
    Officer of the South African Social Security Agency and Others; Finbond
    Mutual Bank v Chief Executive Officer of the South African Social
    Security Agency and Others; Smart Life Insurance Company Limited
    v Chief Executive Officer of the South African Social Security Agency
    and Others (43557/16; 46024/16; 46278/16; 47447/16) [2017] ZAGPPHC

150 (9 May 2017). Accessed September 2017, http://www.saflii.org/za/cases/ZAGPPHC/2017/150.html.

25 Minister of Health and Another N.O. v New Clicks South Africa (Pty) Ltd and Others (2006) (2) SA 311 (CC).

26 See Appendix for details of the work of the Panel of Experts.

27 CPS subsequently went into liquidation, see https://www.businesslive.co.za/bd/national/2020-09-30-cash-paymaster-services-agrees-to-go-into-liquidation/.

Chapter 4

1 World Bank, 2018.

2 Net1, n.d.

3 Melzer I, The dark side of financial inclusion: Financial services companies in South Africa are monetizing financial illiteracy, *Next Billion*, n.d. Accessed June 2021, https://nextbillion.net/the-dark-side-of-financial-inclusion/.

4 Damodaran, 2013.

5 The Promotion of Administrative Justice Act intends to give effect to the right to administrative action that is lawful, reasonable and procedurally fair and to the right to written reasons for administrative action as contemplated in section 33 of the Constitution of the Republic of South Africa.

6 Vally, 2016.

7 In 2014, StatsSA reported that 81.9 per cent of households had access to at least one cell phone, while 12.9 per cent of households had access to both a landline and a cell phone. Only 0.2 per cent of households had only a landline. Statistics South Africa, 2015.

8 World Biographical Encyclopedia, *Serge Christian Pierre Belamant*, n.d. Accessed June 2021, https://prabook.com/web/serge.belamant/339415.

9 World Biographical Encyclopedia, *Serge Christian Pierre Belamant*.

10 These provinces were KwaZulu-Natal, North West Province, Northern Cape and Eastern Cape.

11 World Biographical Encyclopedia, *Serge Christian Pierre Belamant*.

12 Net1, 2006.

13 Net1, 2009.

14 2009–2018 Net1 UEPS Technology Annual Reports.

15 2009–2018 Net1 UEPS Technology Annual Reports.

16 Net1, 2009.

17 Not to be confused with the EasyPay Everywhere bank account and card initiated in 2015.

18 A financial switch is electronic payment software for driving ATM terminals, transaction switching, card management and interfacing to the National Financial Switch and financial switches of other banks.

19 EasyPay processed 580.7 million transactions with a total value of R131.2 billion during the 2009 fiscal year. Net1, 2009.

20 'The smart card provides the holder with access to all of the UEPS functionality, which includes the ability to have the smart card funded with pension or welfare payments, make retail purchases, enjoy the convenience of pre-paid facilities and qualify for a range of affordable financial services, including insurance and short-term loans.' Net1, 2009, 11.

21 Torkelson, 2020.

22 Hull & James, 2012.

23 Net1, 2009, 8.

24 See https://ir.net1.com/static-files/23408c8a-7780-4605-a128-2d0a73051c78. The figure of 10 million has been rounded off, taking into account reports from a number of documents from Sassa, the DSD, the MTT first report, and media articles.

25 Unstructured supplementary service data (USSD), sometimes referred to as 'quick codes' or 'feature codes', is a communications protocol where the user types in a code on their phone to access a list of services.

26 Vally, 2016.

27 Vally, 2016.

28 Sassa was ordered by the Constitutional Court in the *AllPay* 2 matter to initiate a new tender process (see Chapter 3).

29 Crotty A, Net1 speaks of plans for rural 'bank', *Sunday Times*, 24 May 2015. Accessed May 2021, https://www.timeslive.co.za/sunday-times/business/2015-05-24-net1-speaks-of-plans-for-rural-bank/.

30 Crotty A, Net1 speaks of plans for rural 'bank', para. 1.

31 Net1, 2018, para. 4.

32 Net1, 2018, para. 4.

33 In 2015, Corruption Watch had approached the North Gauteng High Court citing irregular expenditure incurred for the re-registration of beneficiaries. The organisation's argument was that the re-registration process was already catered for in the original contract between Sassa and CPS and it did not make sense for an extra payment to be made to CPS. Sassa contested the legal action when it was instituted, but later withdrew its opposition to the review application after two years. This left CPS on its own. Sassa CEO, Thokozani Magwaza, conceded to Scopa that the transaction, entered into by his predecessor, Virginia Pietersen and CPS, had presented many problems for Sassa.

34 Net1, 2020.

35 Net1, 2020. 9.

36 Mahlaka R, CPS: The R500m headache for loss-making former social grants paymaster, *Business Maverick*, 16 February 2020. Accessed June 2021, https://www.dailymaverick.co.za/article/2020-02-16-cps-the-r500m-headache-for-loss-making-former-social-grants-paymaster/.

37 Net1, 2020.

38 Net1, 2020.

39 McKune C, How Net1 flouts the financial rules. *Mail & Guardian*, 3 April 2017. Accessed June 2021, https://mg.co.za/article/2017-04-03-how-net-1-flaunts-the-financial-rules/.

40 The Black Sash thanks Craig McKune and *amaBhungane* for permission to use this article. For the original article, see https://amabhungane.org/stories/the-minister-the-middleman-the-mansion-and-the-new-corporate-kid/, accessed January 2022.

41 World Bank, 2018.

42 World Bank, 2018.

43 World Bank, 2018.

44 Black Sash, January 2014.

45 Rose R, Firm denies exploiting the poorest of poor, *Times Live*, 27 April 2014, para. 4, 5.

46 Rose, Firm denies exploiting the poorest of poor, para. 18.

47 Crotty A, n.d., Banking the unbanked. On paper it looked like a brilliant idea – the quintessential free-market response to a major socio-economic challenge. Unpublished article commissioned by the Black Sash.

48 Dower, 2017.

49 Lapping, 2017.

Chapter 5

1 Foley & Swilling, 2018.

2 AFP, State Capture named SA word of the year, *Daily Maverick*, 16 October.

3 Public Protector, 2016.

4 Public Affairs Research Institute (Pari), 2014.

5 The State Capacity Research Project (SCRP) is convened by Prof. Mark Swilling of the Centre for Complex Systems in Transition, Stellenbosch University. The members of the SCRP comprise Prof Haroon Bhorat from the Development Policy Research Unit at the University of Cape Town; Prof Ivor Chipkin from the Public Affairs Research Institute, Wits University; Prof Mzukisi Qobo, part of the South African Research Chair Initiative – African Diplomacy and Foreign Policy, University

of Johannesburg; Mr Lumkile Mondi, Department of Economics, Wits University; Dr Camaren Peter, Centre for Complex Systems in Transition, Stellenbosch University; and Vicki Robinson, independent journalist.

6   AllPay Consolidated Investment Holdings (Pty) Ltd and Others v Chief Executive Officer of the South African Social Security Agency and Others (CCT 48/13) (2015) ZACC 7; 2015 (6) BCLR 653 (CC) 24 March 2015. Accessed June 2021, http://www.saflii.org/za/cases/ZACC/2015/7.html.

7   Bhorat, et al. 2017.

8   Bhorat, et al. 2017.

9   Mbeki's speech at ANC conference: Part 1, *IOL*, 16 December 2007. Accessed January 2022, www.iol.co.za/news/politics/mbekis-speech-at-anc-conference-part-1-382829.

10 Bhorat, et al., 2017.

11 Public Affairs Research Institute (Pari), 2014.

12 Pari 2020, 5.

13 Foley & Swilling, 2018.

14 Foley & Swilling, 2018.

15 Foley & Swilling, 2018.

16 Foley & Swilling, 2018.

17 Foley & Swilling, 2018.

18 Foley & Swilling, 2018.

19 Foley & Swilling, 2018, 13.

20 Foley & Swilling, 2018, 13.

21 Adjudication Committee, 2008.

22 Adjudication Committee, 2008.

23 Foley & Swilling, 2018, 14.

24 Foley & Swilling, 2018, 14.

25 Foley & Swilling, 2018, 13.

26 Arendse, 2009.

27 Foley & Swilling, 2018, 15.

28 Foley & Swilling, 2018, 15.

29 Foley & Swilling, 2018, 16.

30 Sapa, Social security head rolls, *Sunday Times,* 23 April 2010. Accessed May 2021, www.timeslive.co.za/sunday-times/business/2010-04-23-social-security-head-rolls.

31 In 2012, Mr Coceko Pakade was appointed acting DG, and for a brief time Mr Wiseman Magasela also filled this role. By May 2013, Mr Pakade had been appointed DG of the DSD.

32 Foley & Swilling, 2018, 16.

33 McKune, C, 'Name your price' bribe offer for R7 billion tender, *Mail & Guardian*, 24 February 2012. Accessed May 2021, https://mg.co.za/article/2012-02-24-name-your-price-bribe-offer-for-r7billion-rand-tender/.

34 Adjudication Committee, 2008.

35 Arendse, 2009.

36 Foley & Swilling, 2018, 15.

37 Foley & Swilling, 2018, 53.

38 Foley & Swilling, 2018, 53.

39 Foley & Swilling, 2018, 53.

40 Pillay V, Zuma replaces seven ministers in reshuffle, *Mail & Guardian*, 31 October 2010. Accessed May 2021, https://mg.co.za/article/2010-10-31-zuma-replaces-seven-ministers-in-cabinet-reshuffle/.

41 Foley & Swilling, 2018, 13.

42 Dlamini, 2011.

43 Foley & Swilling, 2018, 18.

44 Foley & Swilling, 2018, 19.

45 McKune C, Serge Belamant, Sassa, and the 'useful Blacks', *Daily Maverick*, 14 December 2016. Accessed June 2021, https://www.dailymaverick.co.za/article/2016-12-14-amabhungane-serge-belamant-sassa-and-the-useful-blacks/.

46 Foley & Swilling, 2018, 209.

47 Foley & Swilling, 2018, 22.

48 McKune, Serge Belamant, Sassa, and the 'useful Blacks'.

49 Foley & Swilling, 2018, 22.

50 Adjudication Committee, 2008.

51 In 2015, Corruption Watch asked the Gauteng High Court to review and set aside the exorbitant payment from Sassa to CPS, contending that it went beyond the scope of the contractual arrangement. In 2018 the North Gauteng High Court ordered CPS to pay back the additional R316 million it had irregularly received for the 'additional' registration of social grant beneficiaries. The Supreme Court of Appeal upheld this judgment in 2018.

52 Foley & Swilling, 2018, 44.

53 McKune C, How Sassa paid R316-million to a contractor based on a 'lie', *Mail & Guardian*, 30 September 2016. Accessed May 2016, https://mg.co.za/article/2016-09-30-00-how-sassa-paid-r316-million-to-a-contractor-based-on-a-lie/.

54 Corruption Watch (NPC) (RF) v Chief Executive Officer of the South African Social Services and Others (21904/2015) [2018] ZAGPPHC 7 (23 March 2018).

55 Cash Paymaster Services (Pty) Ltd v Chief Executive Officer of the SASSA and Others (1029/2018) [2019] ZASCA 131 (30 September 2019).

56 Foley & Swilling, 2018, 54.

57 This evidence was an affidavit by a Mr Kay. He related a clandestine meeting with Mr Tsalamandris, an employee of Sassa who had provided administrative assistance when the tenders were evaluated, at a restaurant a year before. In preparation for the meeting Mr Kay purchased a device with which he recorded their conversation. See https://www.politicsweb.co.za/opinion/allpay-vs-sassa-and-cash-paymaster-services-the-sc.

58 McKune C & Sole S, Tape implicates Zuma lawyer in 'farcical' tender, *Mail & Guardian*, 23 March 2013. Accessed May 2021, https://mg.co.za/article/2013-03-22-00-tape-implicates-zuma-lawyer-in-farcical-tender/.

59 Foley & Swilling, 2018, 53.

60 McKune C, Zuma's lawyer and the mega tender, *Mail & Guardian*, 9 March 2012. Accessed May 2021, https://mg.co.za/article/2012-03-09-zumas-man-and-the-mega-tender.

61 McKune, Zuma's lawyer and the mega tender.

62 Foley & Swilling, 2018, 53.

63 AllPay vs Sassa and CPS [2015] ZACC 7 (24 March 2015) – Judgment (*AllPay* 2).

64 Dlamini, 5 March 2017.

65 Quoted in Constitutional Court judgment Black Sash Trust v Minister of Social Development and Others (Freedom Under Law NPC Intervening) (CCT48/17) [2017] ZACC 20; 2017 (9) BCLR 1089 (CC) (15 June 2017), at para. 20. Accessed January 2022, http://www.saflii.org/za/cases/ZACC/2017/20.html#_ftn18.

66 Foley & Swilling, 2018.

67 Foley & Swilling, 2018, 24.

68 The term 'kitchen cabinet' refers to an inner circle of unofficial advisers to the head of a government.

69 Foley & Swilling, 2018, 24.

70 Thamm M, Anatomy of a crisis: How Sassa's plan to take grants in-house was dead in the water, *Daily Maverick*, 14 November 2018. Accessed June 2021, https://www.dailymaverick.co.za/article/2018-11-14-anatomy-of-a-crisis-how-sassas-plan-to-take-grants-in-house-was-dead-in-the-water/.

71 Thamm, Anatomy of a crisis.

72 McKune, Tape implicates Zuma lawyer in 'farcical' tender.

73 Foley & Swilling, 2018, 33.

74 Black Sash Trust v Minister of Social Development and Others [2017] ZACC 20 (15 June 2017) – Dangor Affidavit 10 April 2017.

75 Black Sash Trust v Minister of Social Development and Others [2017] ZACC 20 (15 June 2017) – Judgment 2.

76 Thamm, Anatomy of a crisis.

77 Foley & Swilling, 2018, 38.

78 Foley & Swilling, 2018, 38.

79 McKune C, Bathabile Dlamini's game of chicken, *Mail & Guardian*, 25 February 2017. Accessed May 2021, https://mg.co.za/article/2017-02-25-bathabile-dlaminis-game-of-chicken/.

80 Foley & Swilling, 2018, 38.

81 Bhorat et al., 2016.

82 Foley & Swilling, 2018.

83 Ms Dlamini's special advisor prior to his appointment as Director General.

84 Thamm M, SassaGate reloaded: Expert panel and AG warn of serious risk in future social grant payments, *Daily Maverick*, 18 October 2017. Accessed May 2021, https://www.dailymaverick.co.za/article/2017-10-18-sassagate-reloaded-expert-panel-and-ag-warn-of-serious-risk-in-future-social-grant-payments/.

85 Sapo CEO confirms signed Sassa agreement, *eNCA*, 20 July 2017. Accessed May 2021, https://www.enca.com/south-africa/sapo-ceo-confirms-signed-sassa-agreement.

86 Ensor L, Bathabile Dlamini names Pearl Bhengu acting Sassa head, *Business Day*, 19 July 2017. Accessed May 2021, https://www.businesslive.co.za/bd/national/2017-07-19-sassa-names-pearl-bhengu-acting-head. Copyright Arena Holdings (Pty) Ltd. All rights reserved.

87 Thamm, SassaGate reloaded: Expert panel.

88 Even though it had been announced in March that President Zuma would undertake this role.

89 Foley & Swilling, 2018.

90 Herman P, Sassa should not have disqualified Post Office: Treasury letter, *Mail & Guardian*, 8 November 2017, para. 5. Accessed January 2022, https://mg.co.za/article/2017-11-08-sassa-should-not-have-disqualified-post-office-treasury-letter/.

91 Herman, Sassa should not have disqualified Post Office.

92 Herman P, Sapo finally gets the nod to prove grants scheme capacity, *Mail & Guardian*, 21 November 2017. Accessed May 2021, https://mg.co.za/article/2017-11-21-sapo-finally-gets-the-nod-to-prove-grants-scheme-capacity/.

93 Foley & Swilling, 2018, 15.
94 Herman P, Sassa: Clock ticking for post office to deliver, says Scopa, *News24,*
    11 December 2017. Accessed June 2021, https://www.news24.com/
    SouthAfrica/News/sassa-clock-ticking-for-post-office-to-deliver-says-
    scopa-20171211.
95 Foley & Swilling, 2018, 60.
96 Constitutional Court of South Africa. 2018. Black Sash Trust v Minister of
    Social Development and Others CCT 48/17 (23 March 2018) – Order 3.
97 Saba A, Bathabile Dlamini slapped with court costs, possible perjury
    probe, *Mail & Guardian,* 27 September 2018. Accessed May 2021, https://
    mg.co.za/article/2018-09-27-bathabile-dlamini-slapped-with-court-
    costs-possible-perjury-probe.
98 Black Sash Trust v Minister of Social Development and Others ZACC 36
    (27 September 2018) – Costs Order Dlamini.
99 News24, Bathabile Dlamini pays back the money, settles personal costs
    order over Sassa debacle, *Polity,* 13 May 2021, para. 14. Accessed May
    2021, https://www.polity.org.za/article/bathabile-dlamini-pays-back-
    the-money-settles-personal-costs-order-over-sassa-debacle-2021-05-13.
100 Thamm M, SassaGate: As dark clouds gather, Bathabile Dlamini fires
    special adviser Sipho Shezi, *Daily Maverick,* 11 April 2017. Accessed May
    2021, https://www.dailymaverick.co.za/article/2017-04-11-sassagate-
    as-dark-clouds-gather-bathabile-dlamini-fires-special-adviser-sipho-
    shezi.
101 Rajgopaul D, Ithala board appoints new IDFC chief, *IOL,* 1 November
    2018. Accessed May 2021, https://www.iol.co.za/business-report/
    careers/ithala-board-appoints-new-idfc-chief-17732722.
102 Pijoos I, More than 1.8m grant beneficiaries migrated to new Sassa card,
    Mail & Guardian, 12 July 2018. Accessed May 2021, https://mg.co.za/
    article/2018-07-12-more-than-18m-grant-beneficiaries-migrated-to-new-
    sassa-card.
103 Thamm M, SassaGate: Life after CPS and Net1: Sassa charts new course
    for social grant payments, *Daily Maverick,* 4 June 2018. Accessed May
    2021, https://www.dailymaverick.co.za/article/2018-06-04-life-after-
    cps-and-net1-sassa-charts-new-course-for-social-grant-payments.
104 Black Sash Trust v Minister of Social Development and Others: Sixth
    report to the Constitutional Court by Auditor-General and Panel of
    Experts.
105 Thamm M, High Court ruling on Sassa grants sees Net1 US market
    value plunge. *Daily Maverick,* 1 February 2019. Accessed May 2021,
    https://www.dailymaverick.co.za/article/2019-02-01-high-court-ruling-
    on-sassa-grants-sees-net1-us-market-value-plunge/.

106 Department of Social Development, Social Assistance Act: Regulations: Method of Payment, 21(1)(a), 34. Accessed May 2021, https://www.gov. za/sites/default/files/gcis_document/202101/44099rg11227gon39.pdf.

107 Foley, 2018.

108 Foley & Swilling, 2018, 30.

109 Foley & Swilling, 2018, 30.

110 Parliamentary Monitoring Group, 23 November 2016.

111 October A, R1.2m lost after Dlamini pulls plug on event to respond to Zuma directive, *City Press*, 23 November 2016. Accessed May 2021, https://www.news24.com/citypress/news/r11m-lost-after-dlamini-pulls-plug-on-event-to-respond-to-zuma-directive-20161123. The 'Mikondzo' project was an attempt to address social delivery backlogs. The minister failed to show up at the event as she was 'deployed' by the president. Scant details were provided on the nature of the deployment.

112 Brauteseth T, Hawks must investigate former Sassa CEO – DA, *Politicsweb*, 23 November 2016. Accessed May 2021, https://www. politicsweb.co.za/documents/hawks-must-investigate-former-sassa-ceo-da.

113 Agency staff, Sassa roasted over R1,1bn in irregular spend, *Tech Central*, 23 November 2016. Accessed May 2021, https://techcentral.co.za/sassa-roasted-over-r11bn-in-irregular-spend/70297/.

114 Thamm, Anatomy of a crisis.

115 Thamm M, Sassa grant switchover: Minister Dlamini fumbles her way through Scopa, displays no clear grasp of issues, *Daily Maverick*, 24 November 2016. Accessed May 2021, https://www.dailymaverick. co.za/article/2016-11-24-sassa-grant-switchover-minister-dlamini-fumbles-her-way-through-scopa-displays-no-clear-grasp-of-issues/.

116 Parliament of the Province of the Western Cape, Committee Reports, 6 September 2016. Accessed June 2021, https://www.wcpp.gov.za/ sites/default/files/Atc%2064-2016%206%20Sept.%202016%20reports__ Com.dev_.eng_.pdf.

117 Black Sash Trust v Minister of Social Development and Others: Tenth report to the Constitutional Court by Auditor-General and Panel of Experts.

118 Foley & Swilling, 2018.

Chapter 6

1   The Portfolio Committee on Social Development conducts oversight over the DSD and its associated entities, including Sassa and the National Development Agency (NDA).

2   The Standing Committee on Public Accounts (Scopa) acts as Parliament's
    watchdog over the way taxpayers' money is spent by the executive.
    Every year the Auditor General tables reports on audits and financial
    management of government departments and state institutions.
    Ministers and senior executives of departments and institutions are
    regularly called in by Scopa to report and account for expenditure. The
    committee can recommend that the National Assembly takes corrective
    action when necessary.

3   Parliamentary Monitoring Group (PMG), 1 July 2010, question 2632.

4   PMG, 1 July 2010, question 2632.

5   PMG, 30 June 2012.

6   PMG, 30 June 2012, question 631.

7   PMG, 15 March 2013.

8   Ensor, L, Legal challenge to grant distributor over deductions, *Business
    Live*, 10 June 2013. Accessed September 2021, https://www.businesslive.
    co.za/archive/2013-06-10-legal-challenge-to-grant-distributor-over-
    deductions2/. Copyright Arena Holdings (Pty) Ltd. All rights reserved.

9   PMG, 22 October 2013.

10 PMG, 22 October 2013.

11 PMG, 22 October 2013.

12 PMG, 22 October 2013.

13 PMG, 22 October 2013.

14 PMG, 15 October 2014.

15 PMG, 15 October 2014.

16 PMG, 15 October 2014.

17 PMG, 1 December 2014, question 1897.

18 PMG, 1 December 2014, question 1897.

19 PMG, 22 October 2014.

20 PMG, 1 December 2014, question 2286.

21 PMG, 1 December 2014, question 2286.

22 PMG, 25 March 2015.

23 PMG, 3 June 2015.

24 PMG, 12 November 2015.

25 PMG, 12 November 2015.

26 PMG, n.d., *Illegal Deductions from Social Grants*.

27 PMG, n.d., *Illegal Deductions from Social Grants*.

28 PMG, 31 August 2016.

29 PMG, 31 August 2016.

30 PMG, 19 October 2016.

31 PMG, 23 November 2016.

32 PMG, 23 November 2016.
33 Mr Magwaza would later submit to the Constitutional Court without permission from Minister Dlamini to avoid being held accountable for non-compliance and expenditure emanating under the leadership of previous CEOs.
34 PMG, 23 November 2016.
35 PMG, 30 November 2016.
36 PMG, 30 November 2016, para. 1.
37 PMG, 30 November 2016.
38 PMG, 30 November 2016.
39 PMG, 30 November 2016.
40 PMG, 30 November 2016.
41 PMG, 1 February 2017.
42 PMG, 1 February 2017.
43 PMG, 1 February 2017.
44 PMG, 1 February 2017.
45 PMG, 1 February 2017.
46 PMG, 1 February 2017, para. 50.
47 PMG, 1 February 2017, para. 50.
48 PMG, 1 February 2017, para. 51.
49 PMG, 1 February 2017, para. 59.
50 PMG, 1 February 2017, para. 55.
51 PMG, 1 February 2017.
52 PMG, 1 February 2017.
53 PMG, 22 February 2017.
54 PMG, 30 November 2016.
55 PMG, 30 November 2016.
56 PMG, 1 February 2017.
57 PMG, 22 February 2017.
58 PMG, 28 February 2017.
59 PMG, 28 February 2017.
60 PMG, 28 February 2017.
61 PMG, 28 February 2017.
62 PMG, 28 February 2017, para. 148.
63 PMG, 7 March 2017.
64 PMG, 7 March 2017.
65 PMG, 8 March 2017.
66 PMG, 8 March 2017.
67 PMG, 15 March 2017.
68 PMG, 15 March 2017.

69 PMG, 15 March 2017.

70 Child K, Only one day left to ensure social grants are paid, CPS boss warns, *Times Live*, 14 March 2017. Accessed June 2021, https://www. timeslive.co.za/news/south-africa/2017-03-14-breaking-only-one-day-left-to-ensure-social-grants-are-paid-cps-boss-warns/.

71 Pather R, CPS director Serge Belamant: We work for profit, *Mail & Guardian*, 15 Mar 2017.

72 PMG, 10 May 2017.

73 PMG, 10 May 2017.

74 PMG, 10 May 2017.

75 PMG, 10 May 2017.

76 PMG, 10 May 2017.

77 PMG, 16 May 2017, recording: minutes 1:21:15–1:23:30.

78 PMG, 10 May 2017.

79 PMG, 10 May 2017.

80 PMG, 10 May 2017.

81 PMG, 10 May 2017.

82 PMG, 10 May 2017.

83 PMG, 10 May 2017.

84 PMG, 31 May 2017, see Sassa presentation.

85 PMG, 31 May 2017.

86 PMG, 31 May 2017.

87 PMG, 31 May 2017.

88 PMG, 14 June 2017, para. 19.

89 PMG, 14 June 2017.

90 PMG, 21 June 2017, see presentation.

91 PMG, 21 June 2017.

92 PMG, 5 September 2017.

93 PMG, 5 September 2017.

94 PMG, 5 September 2017, para. 4.

95 PMG, 5 September 2017, para. 4.

96 PMG, 5 September 2017.

97 PMG, 6 September 2017.

98 PMG, 6 September 2017.

99 PMG, 6 September 2017.

100 PMG, 6 September 2017.

101 PMG, 6 September 2017.

102 PMG, 6 September 2017.

103 Warning issued: another grants crisis looming, *eNCA*, 16 October 2017. Accessed June 2021, https://www.enca.com/south-africa/warning-issued-another-grants-crisis-looming.

104 *eNCA*, Warning issued, para. 6, 7.

105 Section 56 of the Constitution empowers the committee to summon anyone to appear before it. Section 14 of the Powers, Privileges and Immunities of Parliaments and Provincial Legislatures Act (2004) provided for committees to issue a summons to concerned parties. Section 17 of the same Act declared that noncompliance with the summons could result in imprisonment for 12 months or a fine. The procedure was for the chairperson to write to the Secretary to Parliament instructing her to follow Section 14 to issue a summons.

106 PMG, 18 October 2017.

107 *eNCA*, Warning issued.

108 PMG, 18 October 2017, para. 24.

109 PMG, 18 October 2017, para. 29.

110 PMG, 18 October 2017.

111 PMG, 18 October 2017.

112 PMG, 18 October 2017.

113 PMG, 24 October 2017.

114 PMG, 24 October 2017.

115 PMG, 24 October 2017.

116 PMG, 24 October 2017.

117 PMG, 24 October 2017.

118 Dlamini B, 30 October 2017.

119 DA: Bridget Masango says dodging Dlamini's announcement about SAPO very suspicious, *Polity*, 30 October 2017. Accessed June 2021, https://www.polity.org.za/article/da-bridget-masango-says-dodging-dlaminis-announcement-about-sapo-very-suspicious-2017-10-30.

120 *Polity*, DA: Bridget Masango, para. 5.

121 *Polity*, DA: Bridget Masango, para. 6.

122 *Polity*, DA: Bridget Masango, para. 8.

123 PMG, 31 October 2017, para. 11.

124 PMG, 31 October 2017, para. 3.

125 PMG, 31 October 2017.

126 PMG, 31 October 2017.

127 PMG, 1 November 2017.

128 PMG, 1 November 2017.

129 PMG, 1 November 2017.

130 PMG, 8 November 2017.

131 PMG, 21 November 2017.

132 PMG, 21 November 2017.

133 PMG, 10 December 2017, para. 12.

134 PMG, 12 December 2017.
135 PMG, 12 December 2017.

Chapter 7

1 Black Sash, 2018, 5.
2 With considerably diminished responsibilities compared to those of CPS.
3 Heard P, Black Sash steps up 'Hands off our grants' campaign, *GroundUp*, 15 October 2015. Accessed July 2021, https://www.groundup.org.za/article/black-sash-steps-hands-our-grants-campaign_3403/.
4 Black Sash, 2015.
5 Gontsana M, Black Sash gathers support for social grants campaign: 'Hands Off Our Grants' event in St George's Cathedral, *GroundUp*, 12 October 2016. Accessed June 2021, https://www.groundup.org.za/article/black-sash-gathers-support-social-grants-campaign/.
6 South African Government News Agency, 2016.
7 The Regulations of Gatherings Act 205 of 1993 requires organisers of gatherings of 16 or more people to 'give notice' to the relevant authorities in advance (to allow for a process to discuss arrangements and/or conditions of the proposed protest), failing which a protest may be prohibited. Special 'permission' is required for protests within 100 m of Parliament, the union buildings and at courts.
8 What if your funder's business contradicts your social impact mandate?, *Nation Builder*, 24 January 2020). Accessed June 2021, https://proudnationbuilder.co.za/what-if-your-funders-business-contradicts-your-social-impact-mandate/.
9 Dower R, 2017.
10 Crotty A, Stocks spike on R3bn Sassa contract, *Business Day*, 2 March 2017. Accessed June 2021, https://www.businesslive.co.za/bd/companies/2017-03-02-stock-spikes-on-r3bn-sassa-contract/. Copyright Arena Holdings (Pty) Ltd. All rights reserved.
11 Crotty, Stock spikes on R3bn Sassa contract.
12 Crotty A, Not even a prick of conscience? *Business Day*, 9 March 2017, para. 6. Accessed June 2021, https://www.businesslive.co.za/fm/opinion/boardroom-tails/2017-03-09-ann-crotty-not-even-a-prick-of-conscience/. Copyright Arena Holdings (Pty) Ltd. All rights reserved.
13 Crotty, Not even a prick of conscience?, para. 6, 7.
14 Crotty A, Allan Gray should put its ear to the ground, *Business Day*, 10 March 2017, para. 1. Accessed June 2021, https://www.businesslive.co.za/bd/national/2017-03-10-ann-crotty-allan-gray-should-put-its-ear-to-the-ground/. Copyright Arena Holdings (Pty) Ltd. All rights reserved.

15 Editorial: Should you invest in Net1? *Business Day,* 10 March 2017. Accessed June 2021, https://www.businesslive.co.za/bd/opinion/ editorials/2017-03-10-editorial-should-you-invest-in-net1/. Copyright Arena Holdings (Pty) Ltd. All rights reserved.

16 Wierzycka M, Sassa saga: How CPS cross-sells microloans, insurance and services to poor grant recipients, *Daily Maverick,* 7 March 2017, para. 8. Accessed June 2021, https://www.dailymaverick.co.za/ opinionista/2017-03-07-sassa-saga-how-cps-cross-sells-microloans-insurance-and-services-to-poor-grant-recipients/.

17 Nortje B, Net1's role in grants fiasco puts spotlight on social responsibility, *Business Day,* 16 March 2017, para. 5. Accessed June 2021, https://www.businesslive.co.za/bd/opinion/columnists/2017-03-16-bronwyn-nortje-net1s-role-in-grants-fiasco-puts-spotlight-on-social-responsibility/. Copyright Arena Holdings (Pty) Ltd. All rights reserved. Copyright Arena Holdings (Pty) Ltd. All rights reserved.

18 Elster A & Fraser D, Opinion: Shareholders can no longer exist in accountability Gray area, *Business Day,* 29 March 2017, para. 20–25. Accessed June 2021, https://www.businesslive.co.za/bd/opinion/2017-03-29-shareholders-can-no-longer-exist-in-accountability-gray-area/.

19 Crotty A, Allan Gray considers removal of Net1 board, *Business Day,* 17 March 2017. Accessed June 2021, https://www.businesslive.co.za/ bd/companies/financial-services/2017-03-17-exclusive-allan-gray-consideres-removal-of-net1-board/. Copyright Arena Holdings (Pty) Ltd. All rights reserved.

20 Agency staff, Allan Gray sounds warning on Net1, *Tech Central,* 20 April 2017. Accessed June 2021, https://techcentral.co.za/allan-gray-sounds-warning-on-net1/73324/.

21 Crotty, Allan Gray considers removal of Net1 board, para. 7.

22 Agency staff, Allan Gray sounds warning on Net1.

23 Maregele B, Allan Gray commits to putting pressure on Net1, *GroundUp,* 19 May 2017, para. 4, 5. Accessed June 2021, https://www.groundup. org.za/article/allan-gray-commits-putting-pressure-net1/.

24 Maregele B, Social grants company appoints 'independent ombudsman', *GroundUp,* 6 June 2017, para. 3. Accessed June 2021, https://www. groundup.org.za/article/social-grants-company-appoints-independent-ombudsman/.

25 Maregele, Social grants company appoints 'independent ombudsman'.

26 News24Wire, How Net1 will make money after social grant contract ends, *BusinessTech,* 21 August 2017. Accessed June 2021, https:// businesstech.co.za/news/technology/193418/how-net1-will-make-money-after-social-grant-contract-ends/.

27 Third report to the Constitutional Court by the Auditor-General and the
    Panel of Experts in the matter of Black Sash Trust v Minister of Social
    Development and others: Case CCT 48/17, 29 January 2018. Accessed
    June 2021, https://www.blacksash.org.za/images/concourtfiles/
    HOOGConCourtPapers2017/PanelofExperts/3rd_report_panelofexperts.
    pdf.

28 Barbara October (né Maregele) was commissioned by the Black Sash to
    write about her experience as a journalist reporting for *GroundUp* on the
    social grants crisis during the Hoog Campaign.

29 Crotty A, Net1 CEO Serge Belamant to take early retirement, *Business
    Day*, 25 May 2017. Accessed June 2021, https://www.businesslive.
    co.za/bd/companies/financial-services/2017-05-25-serge-belamant-to-
    take-early-retirement/. Copyright Arena Holdings (Pty) Ltd. All rights
    reserved.

30 Moyo A, Net1 appoints ombudsman for dispute resolution, *ITWeb*,
    6 June 2017, para. 5. Accessed June 2021, https://www.itweb.co.za/
    content/XGxwQDq125vlPVoZ.

31 Lapping, Naude & Koornhof, 2017.

32 Abrahams was former Executive Producer of SABC's flagship current
    affairs show, *Special Assignment*.

33 SABC 3, *Grant Grabs, Special Assignment*, March 2015. All four videos
    in the Black Sash investigative documentary series, *Grant Grabs*, are
    available on the Black Sash website. Accessed June 2021, https://www.
    blacksash.org.za/index.php/public-broadcast-documentaries.

34 Third report to the Constitutional Court by the Auditor-General and the
    Panel of Experts in the matter of Black Sash Trust v Minister of Social
    Development and others: Case CCT 48/17, 29 January 2018.

35 Ensor L, Grant beneficiaries given 'reckless' loans by Net1 unit, must be
    helped, *Business Day*, 25 November 2016. Accessed June 2021, https://
    www.businesslive.co.za/bd/national/2016-11-25-grant-beneficiaries-
    given-reckless-loans-by-net1-unit-must-be-helped/. Copyright Arena
    Holdings (Pty) Ltd. All rights reserved.

36 The Community Media Trust is a not-for-profit company that specialises
    in communication in the fields of health and human rights. CMT
    produces all forms of media. See https://www.cmt.org.za/.

37 The Centre for Social Science Research is an interdisciplinary research
    centre at the University of Cape Town dedicated to conducting and
    building capacity for systematic, policy-relevant social science research
    in South Africa, the region and across Africa. See http://www.cssr.uct.
    ac.za/.

38 Kelly G & *GroundUp* staff, Everything you need to know about social
    grants, 7 April 2017. Accessed June 2021, https://www.groundup.org.
    za/article/everything-you-need-know-about-social-grants_820/.
39 Maregele B, 'Now I can't afford groceries': Grant recipient after illegal
    debt deductions, *GroundUp*, 19 May 2014. Accessed June 2021, https://
    www.groundup.org.za/article/e2809cnow-i-cane28099t-afford-
    groceriese2809d-grant-recipient-after-illegal-debt-deductions_1793/.
40 Black Sash, 2018, 5.
41 Black Sash, 2018, 7.

Moving ahead

1 Black Sash Trust v Minister of Social Development and Others CCT
   48/17 (17 March 2017) at para 1.
2 Department of Social Development, 2022, departmental database,
   SCOPEN. The number of beneficiaries increased by at least 10 million
   after 2020, with the introduction of the Social Relief of Distress Grant.
3 Leibbrandt et al., n.d., 38.
4 World Bank, 2017.
5 Black Sash Trust v Minister of Social Development and Others CCT
   48/17 (17 March 2017) at para 1.
6 Sassa, *Progress Update on Sassa Transition & Payment of Social Grants:
   Presentation to Portfolio Committee on Social Development*, March 2019,
   slides 8 & 9. Approximately 71% (7 877 224) of the beneficiaries are paid
   through Postbank. The number of beneficiaries paid through the Post
   Office has increased by 515 114 from December 2018.
7 Bathabile Dlamini loses bid to have perjury charges dropped, *News24*,
   17 December 2021. Accessed January 2022, https://www.news24.com/
   news24/southafrica/news/bathabile-dlamini-loses-bid-to-have-perjury-
   charges-dropped-20211217.

Appendices

1 Meetings attended by Black Sash and other civil society organisations in
   2020 and 2021.
2 Grant Payments Staggered, *The Witness*, 1 May 2020

References

Adjudication Committee (2008) *Narrative Report of the Adjudication Committee for Tender: SASSA 19/06/BS*. Pretoria: South African Social Security Agency

Arendse N (2009) Statement of Norman Arendse. *GroundUp*. Accessed May 2021, https://www.groundup.org.za/media/uploads/documents/StatementNorman%20Arendse.pdf

Bhorat H, Buthelezi M, Chipkin I, Duma S, Mondi L, Peter C, Qobo M, Swilling M & Friedenstein H. (2016) *Betrayal of the promise: How South Africa is being stolen*. State Capacity Research Project. Accessed May 2021, https://www0.sun.ac.za/cst/wp-content/uploads/2017/09/Betrayal-of-the-Promise.pdf

Black Sash (2014, January) *Holding social development and SASSA to account: Black Sash stop SASSA-CPS debits campaign*, media release. Accessed January 2022, https://www.blacksash.org.za/index.php/media-and-publications/media-statements/42-holding-social-development-and-sassa-to-account-black-sash-stop-sassa-cps-debits-campaign

Black Sash (2014, 26 January) *Unauthorised, undocumented and unlawful debit deductions campaign*, presentation to Minister Bathabile Dlamani. Accessed September 2021, http://blacksash.org.za/images/Black_Sash_Presentation_Minister_Bathabile_Dlamini_26January2014.pdf

Black Sash (2015) *Media release: Appointment of new SASSA social grant service provider* (14 October). Accessed June 2021, https://www.blacksash.org.za/index.php/media-and-publications/media-statements/46-media-release-appointment-of-new-sassa-social-grant-service-provider

Black Sash (2017) *Black Sash selected recourse case studies* (12 December). Black Sash Archive

Black Sash (2018) PARI evaluation of Black Sash. In *Annual Report 2018*. Accessed June 2021, https://www.blacksash.org.za/images/publications/Annualreports/WEB_B_Sash_An_report_2018_Final.pdf

Bowmans and Black Sash (n.d.) *The protection of personal information of social grant beneficiaries*. Accessed June 2021, http://www.blacksash.org.za/images/docs/BowmansBlackSashPOPI.pdf

Damodaran A (2013) Financial Inclusion: Issues and Challenges. *AKGEC International Journal of Technology* 4(2). Accessed June 2021, https://www.researchgate.net/publication/309194840_Financial_Inclusion_Issues_and_Challenges

Da Silva, R and Associates (2016) *Actuarial Report in respect of the deductions of funeral insurance premiums from children's social security grants* (4 April). Accessed September 2021, http://blacksash.org.za/images/De_Silva_Acturial_Report_-_Lion_of_Africa.pdf

Delany A & Jehoma S (2016) Implementation of social grants: Improving delivery and increasing access. *South African Child Gauge.* Accessed September 2017, http://www.ci.uct.ac.za/sites/default/files/image_tool/images/367/publication/2016/implementation-of-social-grants.pdf

Department of Social Development (2022) SOCPEN, departmental database of daily statistics

Dlamini B (2011, 21 April) *Minister Dlamini welcomes the appointment of new CEO for SASSA,* media statement. Accessed June 2021, https://www.gov.za/minister-dlamini-welcomes-appointment-new-ceo-sassa

Dlamini B (2014, 11 September) *Media briefing by the Minister of Social Development, Ms Bathabile Dlamini, MP, on the occasion of the media briefing on unauthorised deductions.* Department of Social Development. Accessed June 2021, http://blacksash.org.za/images/Minister_Dlamini_-_Media_statement_11_September_2014_after_MTT_1st_report.pdf

Dlamini B (2017, 5 March) *Minister of Social Development media briefing.* Pretoria: Department of Social Development

Dlamini B (2017, 30 October) *Media briefing on payment of social grants.* Accessed June 2021, https://www.gov.za/speeches/minister-bathabile-dlamini-media-briefing-payment-social-grants-30-oct-2017-0000

Dower R (2017) Clarifying our position on Net1, *Allan Gray* (9 March). Accessed June 2021, https://www.allangray.co.za/latest-insights/esg/clarifying-our-position-on-net1/

Foley R (2018) *How one word can change the game: A case study of state capture and the South African Social Security Agency.* Paper presented at Black Sash Social Security Seminar 2018: Facing A World Without Full Employment. Accessed January 2022, http://blacksash.org.za/images/Report/State_Capture_of_SASSA_Presentation_Social_Security_Seminar_2018.pdf

Foley R & Swilling M (2018) *How one word can change the game: Case study of state capture and the South African Social Security Agency.* State Capacity Research Project. Accessed May 2021, https://www0.sun.ac.za/cst/wp-content/uploads/2018/07/SASSA-State-Capture-_2018-07_-A4-report-for-web-standard.pdf

Hull E & James D (2012) Introduction: Popular economies in South Africa. *Africa,* 82(1): 4 2012

Lapping A (2017) Net1: Do the right thing, *Allan Gray* 17 March. Accessed January 2022, https://www.allangray.co.za/latest-insights/esg/net1-do-the-right-thing/

Lapping A, Naude R & Koornhof P (2017) Allan Gray stewardship report: Calendar year 2017. *Allan Gray*. Accessed in June 2021, https://www.allangray.co.za/globalassets/other-documents/stewardship-report/stewardship-report-2017.pdf

Leibbrandt M, Woolard I, McEwen H & Koep C (n.d.) *Employment and inequality outcomes in South Africa*. Southern Africa Labour and Development Research Unit (SALDRU) and School of Economics, University of Cape Town, 38, para. 4.5. Accessed January 2022, http://www.oecd.org/els/emp/45282868.pdf

Ministerial Task Team (MTT) (2014) *Report to the Minster of Social Development, Minister Bathabile Dlamini: Re: Unlawful and/or immoral debit deductions from the SASSA bank accounts of grant beneficiaries* (first report). Department of Social Development (27 August). Accessed September 2021, http://blacksash.org.za/images/Ministerial_Task_Team_FirstReport_August2014.pdf

MTT (2015) *Second Work in Progress Report to the Minister of Social Development, Minister Bathabile Dlamini for the Period September 2014 to December 2015*. Department of Social Development (December). Accessed September 2021, http://blacksash.org.za/images/Ministerial_Task_Team_SecondReport_December2015.pdf

MTT (2016) Untitled and unpublished final MTT report completed in December 2016

Net1 (n.d.) *About*. Accessed May 2021, http://www.net1.com/about/overview/

Net1 (2006) Presentation at 34th Annual JPMorgan Technology Conference (24 May). Accessed June 2021, https://ir.net1.com/static-files/adbc8120-139f-4325-b38f-cf678d878de3

Net1 (2009) *Annual Report 2009*. Accessed June 2021, https://ir.net1.com/static-files/2902ec73-d8be-4e44-a0b5-801c082da1b8

Net1 (2018) *Annual Report 2018*. Accessed January 2022, https://ir.net1.com/static-files/4ae5e8f1-96ad-434b-92c9-fc28d5a022e4

Net1 (2020) *Annual Report 2020*. Accessed June 2021, https://ir.net1.com/static-files/cd276308-256a-44e6-b99e-ae7ecdab605c

Parliamentary Monitoring Group (PMG) (n.d.) *Illegal deductions from social grants*. Accessed June 2021, https://pmg.org.za/page/Illegal%20Deductions%20from%20Social%20Grants

PMG (2010, 1 July) *Questions & Replies: Social Development*. Accessed June 2021, https://pmg.org.za/question_reply/217/

PMG (2012, 30 June) *Questions & Replies: Social Development*. Accessed June 2021, https://pmg.org.za/question_reply/386/

PMG (2013, 15 March) *Questions & Replies: Social Development.* Accessed June 2021, https://pmg.org.za/question_reply/445/

PMG (2013, 22 October) *South African Social Security Agency on its 2012/13 Annual Report.* Committee on Social Development. Accessed January 2022, https://pmg.org.za/committee-meeting/16598/

PMG (2014, 15 October) *Minister on Department of Social Development & SASSA 2013/14 Annual Reports; AGSA on their audit outcomes.* Accessed June 2021, https://pmg.org.za/committee-meeting/17634/

PMG (2014, 22 October) *The Budgetary Review and Recommendation Report (BRRR) of the Portfolio Committee on Social Development, on the performance of the Department of Social Development and its entities for the 2013/14 financial year.* Accessed June 2021, https://pmg.org.za/tabled-committee-report/2155/

PMG (2014, 1 December) *Questions & Replies: Social Development.* Accessed June 2021, https://pmg.org.za/question_reply/521/

PMG (2015, 25 March) *Questions & Replies: Social Development.* Accessed June 2021, https://pmg.org.za/question_reply/552/

PMG (2015, 3 June) *Department of Social Development & SASSA on their 3rd quarter 2014/15 performance, in presence of Minister.* Accessed June 2021, https://pmg.org.za/committee-meeting/21019/

PMG (2015, 12 November) *Question NW3780 to the Minister of Social Development.* Accessed September 2021, https://pmg.org.za/committee-question/1600/

PMG (2016, 6 May) *Unauthorised grant deductions: Briefing & replies to media by Minister of Social Development.* Accessed September 2021, https://pmg.org.za/briefing/22484/

PMG (2016, 31 August) *Department of Social Development on its 4 Quarter 2015/16 performance, in presence of Deputy Minister.* Accessed June 2021, https://pmg.org.za/committee-meeting/23171/

PMG (2016, 19 October) *Social Development Budget Review and Recommendations Report.* Accessed June 2021, https://pmg.org.za/committee-meeting/23454/

PMG (2016, 23 November) *SASSA, with Minister: Hearing on irregular, fruitless and wasteful expenditure.* Accessed June 2021, https://pmg.org.za/committee-meeting/23728/

PMG (2016, 30 November) *Grant payment insourcing: SASSA progress report,with Minister.* Accessed June 2021, https://pmg.org.za/committeemeeting/23795/

PMG (2017, 1 February) *SASSA on ensuring April 2017 social grant payments.* Accessed June 2021, https://pmg.org.za/committee-meeting/23903/

PMG (2017, 22 February) *Minister & SASSA on readiness to implement Constitutional Court ruling.* Accessed June 2021, https://pmg.org.za/committee-meeting/24008/

PMG (2017, 28 February) *SASSA: Hearing on Cash Paymaster Services (CPS) contract.* Accessed June 2021, https://pmg.org.za/committee-meeting/24045/

PMG (2017, 1 March) *Social grant payment system: SARB on their role, position & readiness; SASSA weekly report.* Portfolio Committee on Social Development. Accessed January 2022, https://pmg.org.za/committee-meeting/24075/

PMG (2017, 7 March) *Minister of Social Development briefing on CPS contract.* Accessed June 2021, https://pmg.org.za/committee-meeting/24087/

PMG (2017, 8 March) *SASSA's weekly report.* Accessed June 2021, https://pmg.org.za/committee-meeting/24111/

PMG (2017, 15 March) *SASSA's weekly report.* Accessed June 2021, https://pmg.org.za/committee-meeting/24162/

PMG (2017, 10 May) *SASSA and Minister on Constitutional Court order & Pretoria High Court ruling.* Accessed June 2021, https://pmg.org.za/committee-meeting/24335/

PMG (2017, 16 May) *SASSA court decision implementation; SASSA irregular, fruitless and wasteful expenditure: Hearing.* Accessed June 2021, recording: https://soundcloud.com/pmgza/sassa-and-minister-on

PMG (2017, 31 May) *SASSA engagement with South African Post Office (SAPO) on payment of grants; with Minister* (SASSA presentation). Accessed June 2021, https://pmg.org.za/committee-meeting/24518/

PMG (2017, 14 June) *Department of Social Development progress report.* Accessed June 2021, https://pmg.org.za/committee-meeting/24609/

PMG (2017, 21 June) *SASSA weekly progress report; with Minister.* Accessed June 2021, https://pmg.org.za/committee-meeting/24666/

PMG (2017, 5 September) *SASSA and Post Office on social grant payments contract.* Accessed June 2021, https://pmg.org.za/committee-meeting/24966/

PMG (2017, 6 September) *SASSA progress report, with Minister.* Accessed June 2021, https://pmg.org.za/committee-meeting/24958/

PMG (2017, 18 October) *SASSA progress report: Briefing postponed.* Accessed June 2021, https://pmg.org.za/committee-meeting/25263/

PMG (2017, 24 October) *SASSA progress in procurement of alternative payment services: Hearing.* Accessed June 2021, https://pmg.org.za/committee-meeting/25323/

PMG (2017, 31 October) *SASSA progress with SAPO: Hearing with Ministers.* Accessed June 2021, https://pmg.org.za/committee-meeting/25348/

PMG (2017, 1 November) *SASSA and SAPO: Progress in overcoming deadlock on social grant contract.* Accessed June 2021, https://pmg.org.za/committee-meeting/25408/

PMG (2017, 8 November) *Inter-Ministerial Committee briefing on SASSA and SAPO impasse, with Ministers present.* Accessed June 2021, https://pmg.org.za/committee-meeting/25450/

PMG (2017, 21 November) *IMC on resolution of SASSA/SAPO impasse, with Minister in the Presidency.* Accessed June 2021, https://pmg.org.za/committee-meeting/25530

PMG (2017, 10 December) *Comprehensive Social Security Report: Statement by Minister Jeff Radebe, briefing.* Accessed June 2021, https://pmg.org.za/briefing/25681/

PMG (2017, 12 December) *Review of Parliament 2017.* Accessed June 2021, https://pmg.org.za/blog/Review%20of%20Parliament%202017

Public Affairs Research Institute (PARI) (2014) *The contract state: Outsourcing & decentralisation in contemporary South Africa.* Accessed May 2021, https://Pari.org.za/contract-state/

Pari (2020) *Draft Public Procurement Bill [B-2020] Submission of Public Comments* (3 July). Accessed March 2021, https://47zhcvti0ul2ftip9rxo9fj9-wpengine.netdna-ssl.com/wp-content/uploads/2020/07/Pari_20200630_DraftProcurementBill_Submission.pdf

Public Protector (2016) *State of capture.* Pretoria. Report no. 6 of 2016/17. Accessed May 2021, http://www.pprotect.org/sites/default/files/legislation_report/State_Capture_14October2016.pdf

South African Government News Agency (2016) *SASSA stops unlawful social grant deductions* (6 May). Accessed June 2021, https://www.sanews.gov.za/south-africa/sassa-stops-unlawful-social-grant-deductions

Statistics South Africa (2015) *General household survey 2014* P0318. Pretoria: StatsSA

Torkelson E (2020) Collateral damages: Cash transfer and debt transfer in South Africa. *World Development* 126, February, 104711. Accessed June 2021, http://www.erinmtorkelson.com/uploads/1/1/2/0/112020995/1-s2.0-s0305750x19303596-main.pdf

Vally N (2016) *South African social assistance and the 2012 privatised National Payment System: An examination of insecurities and technopolitics in social grant administration and payment.* PhD Thesis, University of the Witwatersrand

World Bank (2017) *The World Bank in South Africa* (3 May). Accessed July 2021, http://www.worldbank.org/en/country/southafrica

World Bank (2018) *Financial inclusion: Financial inclusion is a key enabler to reducing poverty and boosting prosperity.* Accessed May 2021, https://www.worldbank.org/en/topic/financialinclusion/overview

Index

Note: Acronyms have been placed as if they were written out.

South Africa has one of the largest social security systems, which has been lauded by the Constitutional Court as an important achievement of the post-apartheid government. The livelihoods of millions of poor people, particularly in rural and peri-urban areas, have come to depend on it. The distribution of social grants continues to contribute significantly towards alleviating poverty and inequality. However, during the Zuma era, the social security system came under brazen attack, enabled by the alleged complicity of those in political power.

Hands Off Our Grants is more than a grim tale of state capture. The book details how the Black Sash's Hands Off Our Grants (Hoog) campaign, supported by civil society organisations, mobilised behind beneficiaries to reclaim their constitutional rights to social security. It is a story of grit, dedication and collective victory in achieving social justice for those affected by irregular, fraudulent and unlawful deductions from social grants.

It is also an important reminder that accomplishing a fair and just society needs citizens who are prepared to take a stand together.

ISBN 978-1-928246-50-3

9 781928 246503

www.bestred.co.za

BEST RED